Private Conscience and Public Law

The American Experience

RICHARD J. REGAN, S.J.

New York

Fordham University Press

1972

LC 72–77602
ISBN 0–8232–0945–8

Printed in the United States of America

To MICHAEL, ANNE, and CAROLE

Contents

Preface ix

1 Private Conscience and Public Interest 1

2 Conscience and National Security (*i*) 21
Conscription and Pacifism
Conscription and Selective Conscientious Objection
The Armed Services and Conscientious Objection
Miscellaneous

3 Conscience and National Security (*ii*) 57
Conscientious Objection and Naturalized Citizenship
Conscientious Objection and War Protests
Conscientious Objection and State Penalties

4 Conscience and Public Order 81
Prevention of Violence
Civil Disobedience
Use of Public Facilities
Prevention of Fraud
Taxes on Incidents of Religious Proselytism
Miscellaneous

5 Conscience and Public Welfare 115
Protection of Life
Eugenics and Population Control
Control of Drugs
Rest and Recreation
Miscellaneous

6 Conscience, Family, and Education 149
Marriage
Child Welfare
Education: Parochial Schools and Civic Virtue
Education: Public Schools and Patriotic Exercises
Education: Public Schools and Religious Exercises

7 Conclusion 185

Appendix 207
Western Traditions of Conscience

Index 235
Table of Cases
General Index

TABLES
1. Moral Claims and Public Law 14
2. Cases and Votes 201

Preface

This book was prompted by the protests against the Vietnamese war and domestic racial inequities. I was dissatisfied with the state of the argument because many dissenters seemed to assume the self-justification of their appeals to conscience, and because many opponents seemed to discount the value accorded to conscience in our history and law. It was from this starting point that I undertook a comparative study of conflicts between private conscience and public law in the American constitutional system.

The perspective of this book is a narrow one insofar as it is restricted to claims of specifically religious or moral conscience in conflict with public law, but events of the last decade have amply shown its analytical and practical importance. Moreover, considerably more historical dust will have to settle before the larger political and social significance of the current dissent can be well evaluated.

In the Appendix, I have indicated in summary fashion various Western traditions which have influenced the formation and function of conscience in human life. But since I am concerned with the conflicts between conscience, however formed, and law, I have attempted to classify claims of conscience only in terms of the degrees of perceived moral obligation. Similarly, I have made no general attempt to assess the strength of public interests opposed to claims of private conscience but rather have accepted the assessments made by the United States Supreme Court as final—at least for the present—in our constitutional system. Thus Chapter 1 indicates the conceptual framework of this study; Chapters 2 through 6 survey the conflicts recorded in American legal history; and Chapter 7 summarizes the results.

I am indebted to Rev. Francis P. Canavan, S.J., for his patience in serving as a sounding-board for my ideas, and to the people of St. Joseph's parish, Rawlins, Wyoming for their hospitality during the preparatory stages of the manuscript.

RICHARD J. REGAN, S.J.

Fordham University

1

Private Conscience and Public Interest

ALTHOUGH THE APPENDIX INDICATES the wide diversity of Western philosophical and theological traditions with respect to the structure and role of conscience in human affairs, it will not be necessary for the purposes of this study to weigh their merits. It will be sufficient to classify the degrees of moral obligation perceived by individuals and to relate these degrees to the prescriptions or prohibitions of public law with which they conflict. The perspective of this study is one of moral duty in conflict with public law. Claims of moral right, therefore, are relevant only insofar as they are related to perceptions of moral duty. From this perspective, complaints against the justice of public laws unrelated to perceptions of moral duty are irrelevant.

First of all, there are moral imperatives which are recognized as prohibitions ("thou shalt not"), for example, "don't salute the flag," "don't work on the Sabbath," or "don't fight in Vietnam." This class of negative moral imperatives should not necessarily be identified with a code of ethical absolutes. Some, perhaps most, negative moral imperatives are based on codes of ethical absolutes, as is the case with Jehovah's Witnesses, who feel morally obliged to refrain from saluting the flag, and with Orthodox Jews, who feel morally obliged to refrain from working on the Sabbath. But other negative moral imperatives refer only to specific situations, as is the case with selective conscientious objectors to the war in Vietnam.

The peculiar characteristic of the negative moral imperative, when considered to be of sufficient importance, is that the individual cannot responsibly perform the prohibited acts without conscious loss of moral integrity, of respect for himself as a personal agent. Of course, to the extent that the individual does not consider himself bound in particular circumstances by a negative moral imperative which he generally recognizes—in which case there is no operative moral prohibition at all—he will not feel any loss of moral integrity. Or to the extent that the psychologically adult individual lacks the necessary freedom to consider an act properly his own, he will also not feel any loss of moral integrity. Yet where the individual does consider a serious moral prohibition applicable and himself a free agent, he cannot perform the act prohibited without a consciousness of serious moral fault because applicable negative moral imperatives are absolutely specific.

Secondly, there are moral imperatives which are recognized as mandates of action ("thou shalt"), for example, "handle snakes as a demonstration of faith," "practice polygamy," or "preach the gospel." These affirmative moral imperatives are divisible in turn into two classes according to their relative degree of specificity. One class, as in the case of those Christians who handle snakes to demonstrate faith according to their interpretation of Mk 16:18 and in that of the Mormons who practiced polygamy in response to their interpretation of divine revelation, is based on relatively specific prescriptions. Circumstances may not be favorable to the execution of these prescriptions for one reason or another—the unavailability of snakes or the ineligibility of spouses—and the psychologically adult individual would not feel under such conditions that he has in any way compromised his religious or moral integrity by his inability to carry out the prescriptions. But if circumstances are favorable, and if the individual perceives the prescription to be of sufficient importance, then he is likely to feel at least a sense of moral incompleteness, if not moral fault, for failing to carry out the prescriptions.

The other class of affirmative moral imperatives, as in the example of Jehovah's Witnesses' preaching the gospel on street corners or from door to door, is based on general prescriptions. The time, place, and means of implementing the prescriptions are determined by the individual himself, and if specific modes of implementation are unavailable to him, alternate modes remain available: assemblies, parades, telephones, the mails. Accordingly, the individual prevented by law or other circumstances from using particular means to fulfill a general religious or moral duty is not likely to feel any sense of moral failure or fault for that reason alone, however great he may perceive the injustice of a legal prohibition.

This typology of moral obligation, I submit, is both introspectively verifiable and logically consistent, and conforms to the psychological evidence of a greater sense of guilt for violation of what an individual perceives as negative moral imperatives than for failure to implement what he perceives as positive duties.[1] But since it is purely formal and does not take into consideration varieties of subject matter, the question arises whether it is sufficient. Critics of American policies on race and war in particular might argue that such a typology reflects an individualistic bias and does not accurately represent man's highest moral obligation to involve himself in the quest for social justice and world peace. The point may be well taken to the extent that it criticizes preoccupation of moral consciousness with the individual rather than with society and with abstinence from doing wrong rather than with activity to overcome it. But the argument is properly addressed to the formation of conscience, not to the quality of its end-product.

One who condemns the Vietnamese war as immoral, for example, can distinguish between his moral obligation not to fight in that war and his moral obligation to engage in a specific mode of protest against the war. The conscientious objector to the war cannot participate in it without a sense of serious moral fault, though he can refrain from a particular act of protest without such a sense. If he does nothing to protest the war over a long enough period of time, of course, the conscientious objector may feel a profound sense of moral failure, but he will not feel this sense with respect to any particular nonparticipation or inactivity unless he perceives the particular act as a relatively specific duty. Precisely insofar as the individual perceives the war as gravely unjust and at the same time is unable to alter the government's course of action or persuade the mass of his fellow-citizens, at least in the short run, by ordinary means of political advocacy, he will be led to perceive various degrees of coercion (nonviolent to violent) as a morally obligatory pattern of action. What might otherwise be perceived as only a general moral duty to oppose the war may thus be transformed into the perception of a relatively specific moral duty to oppose the war by coercive activity. Such a claim of moral obligation is similar to the classical justification of resort to revolution, although the contemporary claim is usually directed against a particular government policy (the war), not the legitimacy of the government itself. Thus the suggested typology of conscience can take account of the moral consciousness professed by anti-war and other activists, but it serves to classify the end-product of perceived moral obligation rather than to evaluate the issue itself or its mode of perception.

As I indicated at the beginning of this chapter, it is possible to study the conflicts between individual conscience and public law without making any attempt to assay the merits of different traditions and systems of morality. Thus we can prescind from questions about the norm of morality: (1) whether it ought to be instinctive (anticipation-oriented) or rational (consequence-oriented); (2) whether it ought to be theologically oriented, cosmologically oriented, or anthropologically oriented; (3) whether it ought to be teleological (oriented toward human perfectibility) or utilitarian (oriented toward usefulness for the individual and/or society); (4) whether it ought to be eudaimonistically oriented (toward a state of human happiness) or duty-oriented; (5) whether it can arrive at absolute principles or must be satisfied with the application of general principles to particular cases; (6) whether it ought to focus on individual acts or habitual behavior; and (7) whether it ought to be legalistically or prophetically oriented. Indeed, it is impossible for courts to adjudicate these questions in a pluralistic democracy, and the First Amendment to the federal Constitution specifically excludes religious and moral beliefs from the sphere of government competence. It is necessary, therefore, to study conflicts between individual conscience and public law without attempting to determine whether the individual conscience is correct or incorrect in its judgment, although it is impossible to make such a study without assessing the countervailing public interest(s) at stake.

One issue which will arise in some cases is whether an individual claimant to exemption from a public law is sincere. The sincerity of conscience can be challenged on two grounds: one, that the individual is deceiving himself; the other, that he is attempting to deceive others, especially the government. Whatever the psychological and moral problems connected with the former type of deception, it is the latter which poses the main legal problem, a problem amenable to legal reasoning. To assert a moral duty to follow one's conscience and especially to insist on the moral duty of others to respect that conscience implies a recognition of a moral order transcending the individual, and the United States Supreme Court in the *Seeger* and *Welsh* cases has made such a recognition a requirement for claimants to qualify for exemption from military service as conscientious objectors.[2] But how can administrative and judicial officers determine whether an individual claimant truly represents his moral beliefs and consciousness?

In some cases, there will be a strong presumption of sincerity because the individual has nothing to gain materially by his claim of conscience (the claim of Jehovah's Witnesses against saluting the flag), or because he was raised in a well-recognized tradition identified with the views he claims (the claim of Quakers against participation in war), or because he is willing to accept equivalent risks if his claim is upheld (conscientious objectors who are willing to accept noncombatant assignments in war zones) or to go to jail if his claim is denied (conscientious objectors like Seeger and Welsh). Moreover, an individual's history and demeanor may tend to confirm or disprove the sincerity of his claim. These presumptions are only presumptions and therefore rebuttable, but they and similar principles do provide some evidentiary guidelines.

In some cases, attempts to distinguish sincere from insincere claims of conscience may not be worth much effort because there is acknowledged to be not even a moderate countervailing public interest at stake (the public interest in the loss of revenue from a flat license fee on door-to-door itinerant peddlers of religious tracts).[3] But in other cases, it may be important to make such a distinction because moderate to high public interests are considered to be at stake (the public interest in the loss of revenue from fraudulent claims to tax-exemption as religious organizations or the public interest in the loss of military manpower from fraudulent claims to exemption as conscientious objectors). Since administrative boards and courts regularly weigh issues of fraud in many types of cases, there should be no overwhelming reason why they cannot also assess the sincerity of claims of conscience to exemption from the operation of public laws. This is undoubtedly a sensitive area, but sensitivity ought not to prevent use of the normal rules of evidence and inference.

This consideration of conscience has centered on its role for the individual, but the interest of the individual in his own moral integrity also serves the interest of society. Plato and Aristotle, for example, identified the development of moral virtue in citizens as the highest function of politics and the practice of citizenship as the highest function of morals. The former thesis was essentially Socrates' defense against the charges of undermining belief in the gods and of corrupting the youth of Athens, namely, that his inquiries were aimed at the discovery of wisdom, that genuine wisdom constituted moral virtue, and that the acquisition of moral virtue would make for good citizens. Medieval theologians similarly maintained the supremacy of the moral purposes of human society, but since they believed that men had a destiny which transcended their lives in an earthly city and that the Church was the supreme teacher of the way to salvation in another world, they could not accept political life as the highest goal of moral virtue.

Confronted by the politically divisive effects of the Reformation, Hobbes held that public law, for all practical purposes, was the supreme interpreter of private morality. Where Socrates and Aquinas thought it a function of public law to promote the individual's quest for virtue and a function of private virtue to support the goals of political life, Hobbes sought to make private virtue dependent on, rather than subsidiary to, public law. Locke, on the other hand, attempted to solve the political problem posed by the Reformation's proliferation of religious doctrines by positing a constitutional limitation on the competence of government in matters of religion, although he well recognized that this would not remove conflicts between governments and individuals about what actions are morally good or bad for citizens.

At least as a practical matter, Locke stood for the principle that the public interest in the peace and unity of pluralistic societies would be best served by wide deference to individual perceptions of religious and moral duties. This principle does not depend on the validity of the Greek and medieval concept of an objective moral order and the relation of political goals to it, but only on the empirical evidence that most individuals recognize moral imperatives as subjectively important to them for religious or humanistic reasons, and that these imperatives diverge widely. Moreover, society as a whole shares an interest in the freedom of individuals to act according to their religious or moral conscience because the freedom of all is intimately linked to the freedom of each. Furthermore, individuals who habitually behave according to their perception of religious or moral duties may be more likely to internalize their legal duties as citizens than individuals who habitually act contrary to their consciousness of such duties. As Chief Judge Charles Wyzanski said in a decision favorable to the draft-exempt status of a selective conscientious objector to the Vietnamese war, "the true secret of legal might lies in the habits of conscientious men disciplining themselves to obey the law they respect without the necessity of judicial and administrative orders." [4]

Thus conscience may be said to have a value not only for the individual but also for society—whether that value is grounded on normative or empirical considerations. But if individual conscience itself is one public interest, other public interests may run counter to it. In this context, a "public" interest may be described, without prejudice to further philosophical analysis, as one which is recognized by public law to affect many or most citizens. These interests have been traditionally classified according to subject matter: national security against foreign enemies, domestic order, public health, welfare, morals. In the broadest sense, every declaration of a public interest by law rests on a perception of societal value or values by public authorities. From this perspective, conflicts between private conscience and public law represent not simply conflicts between morality on the one hand and law on the other but also conflicts between the perception of moral value by individuals and the perception of moral value by society. Such conflicts are thus, in part, between competing moral claims.

There are other viewpoints on the relation of private morality to public law. Latter-day disciples of Hobbes, for example, would argue that whatever is illegal is immoral, i.e., that law governs morality. This analysis in effect denies the reality or relevance of one element of the conflictual situation, namely, a moral consciousness on the part of the individual in any way autonomous from that of society. Since, however, many or most individuals do not regard public law as the source of all moral obligations, and since the First Amendment of the United States Constitution specifically disavows such a position, the Hobbesian analysis will not be very helpful in resolving conflicts between individual conscience and public law. Individuals do perceive moral obligations which apparently conflict with law, and the Constitution does take this into account—at least as a general policy.

A second analysis of the relation of morality to law is offered by the legal positivists. According to their analysis, what is illegal is simply illegal, and law creates its own duty by the imposition of penalties. Thus the individual who challenges the morality of a law is entitled to no different treatment than any other individual who disobeys the law. Like the Hobbesian analysis, legal positivism is subject to the objections that individuals do in fact judge whether public laws conform to moral norms, and that the First Amendment gives legal recognition to individual perceptions of duties higher than those owed to the government. The positivist analysis discounts both the empirical evidence that individuals do weigh the morality of public laws, and that there is potentially a legal status under the Constitution for the moral claims of individuals. Moreover, legal positivists do not satisfactorily refute the argument that laws themselves are essentially based on the perception of moral value or values by public authorities.

Both the Hobbesian and positivist analyses are frequently linked to an argument based on the "consent" implicit in democratic government. The Hobbesian democrat would argue that the individual, by giving his consent to majority rule, implicitly accepts the morality of society's laws as applied to himself; the positivist democrat would argue that the individual, by giving his consent to majority rule, implicitly accepts the legitimacy of society's laws as applied to himself. Yet this type of argument does not really meet the objections advanced against these analyses. Indeed, the argument for conformity to democratically made law under all circumstances not only is deadening to moral sensitivity but may also reflect a bias in favor of the status quo.

Since the First Amendment guarantees freedom of religious—and, by implication, moral—exercise, conflicts between individual conscience and public law involve competing legal and moral claims. It is the professional task of philosophers and theologians to assess the latter, of lawyers and political scientists to assess the former. Such an assessment is the main purpose of this study.

Accordingly, it will be necessary to integrate the degrees

of moral obligation perceived by individuals into a legal frame of reference, that is, to relate them to the prescriptions of public law with which they conflict. First, a law may command under threat of imprisonment what the conscience of an individual forbids absolutely (as is the case when the federal government requires selective conscientious objectors to the Vietnamese war to serve there). Or a law may command under threat of severe economic penalties what the conscience of an individual forbids absolutely (as was the case when a state governmental agency required a Sabbatarian to accept work on Saturday in order to be eligible for unemployment compensation[5]). Or a law may command under threat of severe political penalties what the conscience of an individual forbids absolutely (as was the case when the federal government denied naturalized citizenship to conscientious objectors to military service[6]). Since public laws in these cases directly and severely coerce individuals to act contrary to religious or moral duties perceived as important and absolutely obligatory, these claims of individual conscience ought to be ranked high.

Secondly, a public law may forbid under threat of severe penalties activities which the conscience of an individual perceives as a right instrumental to an absolute duty imposed by a negative moral imperative (as is the case when state and local laws prohibit Sabbatarians from engaging in business on Sundays[7]). Similarly, a law may promote activities of citizens on a voluntary basis which the conscience of an individual perceives as social pressure to act contrary to an absolute duty imposed by a negative moral imperative—pressure from which the individual claims a right to be free (as was the case when state governments required holding voluntary religious exercises in public schools, and nonbelievers objected [8]). Since individuals in both these situations concede that the public laws at stake conflict only indirectly with religious or moral duties perceived by them as absolute, and since the laws conflict less severely with their duties than direct coercion, these claims of individual conscience ought to be rated moderate rather than high.

A third class of conflicts between public laws and individual consciences occurs whenever laws forbid what the consciences of individuals command. Thus a law may forbid, typically under threat of imprisonment, acts or activities which the conscience of an individual perceives as a specific religious or moral duty (as was the case when the federal government applied prohibitions against polygamy to Mormons[9]). Since, however, individuals perceive even such specific religious or moral duties as obligatory only if circumstances are favorable to their performance, that is, as relative to that extent, these claims of individual conscience ought to be rated as moderate rather than high.

A fourth class of conflicts between public laws and individual consciences appears whenever laws forbid what the consciences of individuals command as means of implementing general religious or moral duties. Thus a law may forbid, again typically under threat of imprisonment, acts or activities which the conscience of an individual perceives as a right to implement a general religious or moral duty (as was the case when a local government forbade itinerant evangelists to canvass private residences without invitation from the occupants[10]). Since individuals perceive such duties as morally obligatory only in general rather than in specific terms and choose the time, place, and means of implementing them, these claims of individual conscience based on relative and general duties ought to be rated low in relation to the preceding classes of claims.

If respect for the moral dilemma of an individual forced to choose between obedience to his conscience and obedience to a law is an important value at stake in such conflicts, then the most pressing legal claim of conscience ought to be that based on a negative moral imperative which the individual perceives as so important that he cannot perform a contrary act commanded by law without a fundamental loss of personal integrity, and the lowest legal claim of conscience ought to be that based on a positive but general moral imperative which allows the individual discretion concerning its implementation. Between the two extremes are claims of conscience which assert rights substantially related to obligations imposed by negative moral imperatives and those based on relatively specific positive moral imperatives. The following table represents the status of these classes of moral claims in conflict with public law (page 14).

One important variable not directly represented in the first table is the quality of the penalty with which an individual is threatened if he does not conform to the law. It is evident enough that an individual will be influenced by law to act against his moral judgment to the extent that he fears the coercive power of the law. Most laws immediately or ultimately threaten imprisonment for nonconformity, and most individuals are likely to regard that penalty as most severe. Other laws threaten financial loss in various degrees of severity, at least in the short run, e.g., the cost of private schooling to the Jehovah's Witnesses whose children refused to salute the flag and were subsequently expelled from public school, or the cost of licenses to itinerant evangelist peddlers of religious literature. Other laws threaten political penalties, e.g., denial of citizenship to conscientious objectors to military service. Still other laws threaten social penalties, e.g., the social pressure on those with conscientious objections to participation in otherwise voluntary public-school religious exercises sponsored by state or local authorities. (Social pressure on the dissenter is by definition indirect because it is the result of other citizens' activities rather than of any categorical command of government.)

TABLE 1

PRESCRIPTION OF PUBLIC LAW	CONFLICTING MORAL IMPERATIVE PERCEIVED BY INDIVIDUAL	PERCEIVED DEGREE OF MORAL OBLIGATION	RANK
Command, e.g., "salute the flag" [a]	Prohibition, e.g., "don't salute the flag"	Absolute duty	High
Prohibition, e.g., "don't work on Sunday" [b]	Prohibition, e.g., "don't work on Saturday"	Right instrumental to absolute duty, e.g., right to work on Sunday because of duty not to work on Saturday	Moderate
Prohibition, e.g., "don't practice polygamy" [c]	Command, e.g., "practice polygamy"	Specific but relative duty	Moderate
Prohibition, e.g., "don't canvass private residences unless invited"	Command, e.g., "preach the gospel"	Right to specific mode of implementing a general and relative duty	Low

[a] This command may impose on conscientious objectors the penalty of the financial cost of private schooling for their children or the penalty of imprisonment if they are unable or unwilling to assume such costs.[11]

[b] A case similar to this is one in which public law prescribes a voluntary program of religious exercises in public schools, and parents object to the exercises because of the indirect, socially coercive effects on their nonparticipating children. Such parents claim a right not to have their children socially pressured into conformity by the publicly sponsored religious exercises of other children, a right instrumental to what they perceive as an absolute duty for their children not to participate.

[c] There may also be a conflict between public policy and the claim of a conscientious objector to a right instrumental to a specific religious or moral duty. Thus patrons of church-related schools, if they perceive the religious orientation of even their children's secular education as a specific duty imposed by church law, may claim a right to financial aid which public laws do not provide.

Despite these undoubtedly different kinds of coercion and the different degrees of coercion perceived by individuals, penalties threatened by law for nonconformity can be considered at least as serious enough to lead many objectors to litigate a claim of conscience. From this perspective, all legal coercion threatened against conscientious objectors may qualify as "serious" to the extent that individuals raise legal claims of conscience against it, although such a generalization abstracts from the widely divergent degrees of severity which individuals may perceive to be at stake.

Public interests against claims of individual conscience may be classified according to subject matter, but they also may be rated higher or lower according to the perception of legislators and judges. (When judges recognize no constitutionally valid public interest, they rate that interest as null from the legal viewpoint, and this is evidently the lowest possible rating.) Insofar as conflicts between individual consciences and public laws reach courts for adjudication, it is the perception of public interests by judges rather than by legislators which is important, although judges' perception of their role in the political system as one of "restraint" in relation to that of the legislature may make an expression of their evaluation of the public interests at stake unnecessary or superfluous. Moreover, insofar as conflicts between individual consciences and public laws are finally adjudicated by the United States Supreme Court, and insofar as justices of that Court have taken an increasingly "activist" role since 1938 in cases involving civil liberties, it is their perception of public interests which is important and even critical for understanding their concurrence or dissent in the Court's decisions. Since the Court divided in many of the cases to be considered in succeeding chapters, and in some cases sharply, there may be at least two quite different evaluations of the public interests at stake by the justices—one by the majority, the other by the minority.

When individuals challenge the validity of public laws, the public interests generally alleged in support of the laws are at stake. When individuals claim exemption or immunity in the name of conscience from public laws otherwise admitted as valid, however, the public interests opposed to a grant of exceptions to those individuals are at stake rather than the general purposes of the laws. Exceptions for conscientious objectors, of course, may threaten the general purposes of a law, but this need not be the case. If other citizens are not significantly affected by individual nonperformance of legally mandated acts, for example, then exceptions for conscientious objectors may be compatible with the general public interests served by a law. Mandated acts may not impose burdens on individuals which other citizens would be forced to bear in the event of their exemptions, or the number of potential conscientious objectors may be relatively small. But exceptions for conscientious objectors are likely to be incompatible with the general purposes of legal prohibitions against acts regarded as contrary to moderately high public interests.

Exceptions for conscientious objectors who use coercive acts against the government in order to change its policies are likely to be incompatible not only with the purpose of the particular law violated but also with the existence of the legal system itself. The government does sanction (and regulate) some nonphysical forms of coercion, strikes, for example, but these are directed against private individuals rather than the government. The First Amendment guarantees rights of speech, press, and assembly to protest government policies, and the exercise of these rights may indirectly pressure the government to change its course of action because they threaten defeat of the administration in a future election. Individuals may also legally challenge the validity of particular laws by direct action and subsequent court test where no other way is available to obtain a ruling, e.g., sit-ins against the segregation laws of Southern states.

But no court is likely to recognize an exception for conscientious objectors who challenge governmental policies by direct violation of laws held by that court to be valid—laws which objectors themselves may admit to be valid—and at the same time to maintain the legitimacy of the existing political system. As individuals may claim a moral right or duty to revolt against the government—but by definition they have no legal right to do so unless the government has substantially violated constitutional limitations on its powers—so individuals may be able to claim only a moral rather than a legal right or duty to coerce the government by violation of its laws. Of course, widespread violation of public laws to redress social grievances both indicates a breakdown in the political system and constitutes a challenge to political institutions to greater responsiveness.

If public interests are judged to outweigh the conflicting claims of individual conscience, however, courts can take into consideration the motivation of law-violators when penalties are imposed on them. This is true even in the case of those individuals whose moral consciousness leads them to violate admittedly valid laws in order to attack government policies. The punishment can be designed to fit the crime, and those who violate laws in the name of conscience are not ordinary criminals. Thus not only can public interests be weighed against exemptions for conscientious objectors to laws; public interests in the severity of penalties as well can be weighed against the good motivations of those objectors whose claims of immunity are denied. In short, legislators and especially judges may conclude that the more severe the penalties imposed on conscientious objectors, the higher should be the public interests served by those specific penalties.

At one extreme of conflicting claims of private conscience and public law, judges are most likely to vote against low claims of conscience by individuals when they rate high the public interests at stake. Indeed, whenever judges rate high the public interests at stake, they are unlikely to vote in favor of any claim of conscience by an individual. Since the purpose of public law is to protect public interests in addition to those of the individual conscience, individual claimants of conscience will have to do more than convince judges of the threat posed against their moral integrity by obedience to public laws if they wish to vindicate their claims; they will also have to convince judges that no serious public interests are opposed to their claims of immunity before they can expect a sympathetic hearing.

At the other extreme, when judges rate low the public interests at stake, they are more likely to vote in favor of high claims of conscience by individuals. They may even support moderate or low claims of conscience by individuals if they perceive only low public interests opposed to the claims. As some public interests may be perceived as too important to sacrifice for the moral integrity of individuals, so other public interests may be perceived as too unimportant to weigh against any claim of conscience. This expectation will be modified to the extent that judges accept a limited role for themselves in the review of legislative judgments or take a Hobbesian view of private conscience.

Between the two extremes are those cases in which judges rate only moderately high the public interests at stake. To the extent that they limit their role in relation to the other powers of government or lack sympathy for immunizing conscientious objectors to public laws, of course, judges will vote in favor of the public interests against claims of conscience. But even those judges who conceive a more active role for themselves and have broad sympathy for conscientious dissenters are likely to vote in favor of the government when they perceive at least moderately high public interests at stake adverse to the dissenters. Moreover, when judges disagree, one judge is less likely to rate public interests unambiguously high and another judge to rate the same interests unambiguously low than one judge is to rate public interests moderately high and another judge to rate them unambiguously high or low. Accordingly, courts may be expected to divide more often and more closely when at least some judges rate public interests only moderately high.

If judges vote in favor of individual claimants of conscience, they are more likely to do so on the ground that there are no constitutionally valid countervailing public interests at stake than they are to carve out an exception specifically for conscientious objectors. Thus they are likely to rest decisions favorable to individual claimants on such constitutional prohibitions as those against a religious establishment or abridgment of freedom of speech if they can. This preference is to be expected because exceptions for conscientious objectors are less amenable to judicial standards in the absence of legislative specifications. Similarly, judges are more likely to favor individual claims of conscience to the extent that they are claims to rights of speech rather than of action.

NOTES

1. Cf. Edmund Bergler, *The Battle of Conscience* (Washington: Washington Institute of Medicine, 1948), pp. 7–13. The author-psychiatrist distinguishes positive ideals and negative imperatives of conscience and then describes their interrelations.

2. *U.S. v. Seeger,* 380 U.S. 163 (1965) and *Welsh v. U.S.,* 398 U.S. 333 (1970).

3. See *Jones v. Opelika,* 316 U.S. 584 (1942) and *Murdock v. Pennsylvania,* 319 U.S. 105 (1943).

4. *Sisson v. U.S.,* 297 F. Supp. 902, 911 (1969).

5. See *Sherbert v. Verner,* 374 U.S. 398 (1963).

6. See *U.S. v. Schwimmer,* 279 U.S. 644 (1929) and *U.S. v. Macintosh,* 283 U.S. 605 (1931).

7. See *Braunfeld v. Brown,* 366 U.S. 599 (1961).

8. See *Engel v. Vitale,* 370 U.S. 421 (1962) and *Abington v. Schempp,* 374 U.S. 203 (1963).

9. See *Reynolds v. U.S.,* 98 U.S. 145 (1878) and *Davis v. Beason,* 133 U.S. 333 (1890).

10. See *Martin v. Struthers,* 319 U.S. 141 (1943).

11. Cf. *Minersville School District v. Gobitis,* 310 U.S. 586 (1940) and *West Virginia State Board of Education v. Barnette,* 319 U.S. 624 (1943).

2

Conscience and National Security (i)

CONSCRIPTION AND PACIFISM

THE FIRST CONSCIENTIOUS OBJECTORS to military service in America were members of religious sects opposed to war as a matter of principle. Chief among these were the Quakers, the Mennonites, and the Brethren; there also were smaller pacifist sects like the Shakers. Gradually, they won recognition from colonial legislatures and exemption from militia duty. During Indian uprisings, the French and Indian War, and the American Revolution, pacifists were legally required, but rarely forced, to pay special taxes or to hire substitutes.[1] By the time of the Civil War, there existed state practices of exempting conscientious objectors to war on religious grounds, provided that they pay set fees or hire substitutes.[2] Some pacifists objected to the fees both as taxes on conduct dictated by conscience and as equivalent to personal participation in the waging of war.[3] Some also objected on the latter ground to the hiring of substitutes and even to the payment of general taxes earmarked for military expenses.[4]

The Civil War brought the first action by the federal government to conscript men into the United States Army. The Federal Conscription Act of 1863 made all men between the ages of twenty and forty-five liable to military service if called by the President, but it allowed for the payment of $300 in lieu of service or for the hiring of a substitute.[5] As a result of energetic petitions by the pacifist churches, Congress in 1864 granted exemption from combatant military service to "members of religious denominations who . . . are conscientiously opposed to the bearing of arms, and who are prohibited from doing so by the rules and articles of faith and practice of said religious denominations." [6] Those qualifying for the exemption, however, were to be drafted into military service as noncombatants and assigned to duty in hospitals or to care for freedmen. (As an alternative, they could avoid military service entirely by paying $300 for the benefit of sick and wounded soldiers.) But even the accommodations of the Draft Act of 1864 were unacceptable to those conscientious objectors who considered any cooperation with armed forces a betrayal of their principles, and they accordingly refused to serve in military hospitals. When Northern officials found that neither alternate service nor payment for a substitute was acceptable to absolute pacifists, they arranged to "parole" them for the duration of the war.[7]

Conscription was not needed again until World War I. The Selective Service Act of 1917 granted exemptions from combatant military service to conscientious objectors affiliated with a "well-recognized religious sect or organization [then] organized and existing . . . whose . . . creed or principles forbid its members to participate in war in any form. . . ." [8] The act required all such persons to be inducted into the armed services but allowed them to serve in noncombatant capacities declared by the President. In the *Selective Service Cases,* the provision of this act for conscientious objectors was upheld without argument against constitutional attack as an establishment of religion,[9] and conscription in general was upheld against constitutional attack as a form of involuntary servitude prohibited by the Thirteenth Amendment.

Those claiming exemption as conscientious objectors during World War I included members not only of the older pacifist religions like the Quakers and Mennonites but also of pacifist sects newer to American life like the Molokans, Dukhobors, Seventh-Day Adventists, and Jehovah's Witnesses. Some pacifist churches advised their eligible members to register and accept noncombatant military service, but many pacifists took exception to this policy which would place them under military jurisdiction. On March 16, 1918, Congress authorized the Secretary of War to grant "furloughs" without pay to enlisted conscientious objectors who would then work on farms or in Red Cross units under civilian control; military directives, however, were not issued to this effect until June and July, 1918.[10] Besides these objectors, there were groups whose objection to war was not religiously motivated: socialists, radicals, and many secular humanists opposed to war on purely philosophical and political grounds. The Adjutant General of the Army in a directive of December 10, 1917, declared that " 'personal scruples against war' should be considered to constitute 'conscientious objection,' and such persons should be treated in the same manner as other "conscientious objectors.' " [11]

In the Selective Training and Service Act of 1940, Congress broadened the exemption afforded conscientious objectors in 1917. This act exempted from combatant military service anyone who, "by reason of religious training and belief, is conscientiously opposed to participation in war in any form." [12] Thus Congress determined that mere "religious training and belief" rather than formal membership in a recognized pacifist church was required for qualification for conscientious-objector exemption.

The act also provided that any person qualifying for an exemption from combatant military service because of conscientious objection was liable to induction into the armed forces for assignment to noncombatant military service as defined by the President. But if an individual was also found to be conscientiously opposed to such noncombatant military service, he was liable to assignment to "work of national importance under civilian direction." [13] Conscientious objectors to noncombatant service under military authorities were accordingly assigned to perform "work of national importance" in Civilian Public Service camps, and they were supervised by members of such pacifist churches as the Quakers, Mennonites, and Brethren.[14] In the event, these camps furthered the work of the Civilian Conservation Corps inaugurated by the New Deal during the "Great Depression." Some conscientious objectors to noncombatant as well as combatant military service freely sought work in mental hospitals or social agencies, and others were volunteers for medical experimentation. Conscientious objectors participating in the Civilian Public Service program were not paid, and they received none of the fringe benefits granted soldiers on active service; they either supported themselves or were supported by their families or churches.

Jehovah's Witnesses were a class apart as conscientious objectors during World War II. They were generally refused classification as conscientious objectors to "participation in war in any form" because they believed in the use of force in defense of "Kingdom interests" and in the waging of "theocratic" wars commanded by Jehovah. They also claimed exemption as ministers because every member was held by his church to be a minister of the gospel, but these claims were likewise generally denied. After the outbreak of hostilities in Korea in 1950, the question of exemption for Jehovah's Witnesses arose anew, and the United States Supreme Court in 1955 upheld the claim of one of their members to such exemption (*Sicurella v. United States*).[15]

Sicurella, a Jehovah's Witness, registered with his local draft board in 1948. Although he worked forty-four hours a week at a Railway Express office, he was first classified as qualified for exemption as an ordained minister. After the outbreak of the Korean conflict, he was reclassified as eligible for general service. He then filed a claim as a conscientious objector. When his claim was disallowed and he failed to report for induction into the armed services, he was convicted of violating the Universal Military Training and Service Act of 1948, and the conviction was affirmed by a federal court of appeals.[16] The Supreme Court overturned the conviction and accepted Sicurella's claim to exemption as a conscientious objector.

The issue was whether, in view of his acceptance of the use of force to defend "Kingdom interests" and his willingness to fight in "theocratic" wars commanded by Jehovah, Sicurella could qualify for exemption as a conscientious objector to "participation in war in any form." Justice Clark, speaking for the majority, thought that Sicurella could and did. Acknowledging certain inconsistencies and obscurities in the petitioner's claim, Clark pointed out that Sicurella was admittedly sincere, that the force accepted by him to defend "Kingdom interests" involved no arms or "carnal" weapons, that "theocratic" wars were unlikely, and that, in any case, such wars were not the shooting wars Congress had in mind.[17] Justices Reed and Minton dissented on the grounds that the petitioner admitted that he would use force to defend "Kingdom interests" and participate in "theocratic" wars in some carnal form.[18]

In 1946, the federal Court of Appeals for the Ninth Circuit held that the phrase "religious training and belief" did not refer to ethical, humanitarian, or political grounds.[19] A decision of the Second Circuit Court of Appeals, however, had held in 1943 that a general humanitarian opposition to war was essentially religious in character.[20] Then in 1948 Congress amended the language of the 1940 statute to declare in section 6 that "religious training and belief" was to be defined as "an individual's belief in a relation to a Supreme Being involving duties superior to those arising from any human relation, but . . . not [including] essentially political, sociological, or philosophical views or a merely personal moral code."[21] Thus exemption for humanistically motivated conscientious objection to war seems to be excluded by the act of 1948.

In 1965 the Supreme Court unanimously held that the test of belief in relation to a Supreme Being is not whether a given belief in God is orthodox but whether it "occupies a place in the life of its possessor parallel to that filled by the orthodox belief in God . . ." (*United States v. Seeger*).[22] Although one claimant to exemption as a conscientious objector, Daniel Andrew Seeger, admitted his skepticism about the existence of God, he acknowledged a "belief in and devotion to goodness and virtue for their own sakes, and a religious faith in a purely ethical creed."[23] A second claimant, Arno S. Jakobson, acknowledged belief in a Supreme Reality to which man was partly akin, and he called his opposition to war "religious" in the sense that religion is the "sum and essence of one's basic attitudes to the fundamental problems of human existence."[24] The third claimant, Forest Britt Peter, to describe the grounds of his opposition to war, accepted a definition of religion as "consciousness of some power manifest in nature which helps man in the ordering of his life in harmony with its demands."[25]

The Supreme Court found that all three claims to exemption as conscientious objectors were based, not on a "merely personal moral code," but on "the broader concept of a power or being, or faith, 'to which all else is subordinate or upon which all else is ultimately dependent.'"[26] This construction of the statutory language "religious training or belief . . . in relation to a Supreme Being" was undoubtedly broad and historically tenuous, but the alternative, as concurring Justice Douglas pointed out, would have been to raise a constitutional question whether the statutory exemption preferred some religious beliefs over others and invidiously discriminated between different forms of religious expression.[27] At any rate, the Court did insist that a claim to exemption as a conscientious objector had to be based on ethical grounds which transcend the individual's own desires for himself.

Five years after *Seeger,* in a 5–3 vote, the Supreme Court applied the rationale of that decision to cover a conscientious objector who denied even more explicitly that his views on war were religious in the traditional sense (*Welsh v. United States*).[28] (Justice Blackmun took his seat on June 9, 1970, but did not participate in the decision.) Elliot Welsh 2d was convicted in a federal district court of refusing to submit to induction into the armed forces and was sentenced to three years' imprisonment. The Court of Appeals affirmed the conviction,[29] but the Supreme Court reversed it "because of its fundamental inconsistency with *United States v. Seeger*." [30]

Justice Black, joined by Justices Brennan, Douglas, and Marshall, interpreted *Seeger* to apply to any individual who "deeply and sincerely holds beliefs which are purely ethical or moral in source and content but which nonetheless impose upon him a duty of conscience to refrain from participating in any war at any time." [31] Although Welsh struck out the word "religious" on his conscientious-objector application and later characterized his beliefs as formed by reading in the fields of sociology and history, Black argued that the claimant's description of his beliefs as nonreligious was inconclusive and even unreliable because few registrants are aware of the broad scope of the word "religious" as used in section 6(j) of the Universal Military Training and Service Act of 1948.

Nor did Black think that section 6(j)'s "exclusion of

those persons with 'essentially political, sociological, or philosophical views or a merely personal moral code' should be read to exclude those who hold strong beliefs about our domestic and foreign affairs or even those whose conscientious objection to participation in all wars is founded to a substantial extent upon considerations of public policy." [32] According to Black, only two groups were excluded from the statutory exemption for conscientious objectors to war: (1) those whose beliefs are not deeply held; and (2) those whose beliefs do not rest at all on moral or religious principles but solely on considerations of policy or expediency. Thus Black held section 6(j) to exempt "all those whose conscience, spurred by deeply held moral, ethical, or religious beliefs, would give them no rest or peace if they allowed themselves to become a part of an instrument of war." [33]

Justice Harlan concurred in the result but not in Black's statutory construction.[34] In fact, Harlan recanted his participation in the *Seeger* opinion and noted that Black had made explicit the "total elimination of the statutorily required religious content for conscientious objector exemptions." [35] But Harlan accepted Black's test on the exemption of conscientious objectors in order to salvage congressional policy from what he conceived to be the constitutional infirmity of a religious establishment. Although Harlan thought that Congress could deny exemptions to all conscientious objectors, he argued that Congress could not grant exemptions to theistic conscientious objectors and at the same time deny them to nontheistic conscientious objectors. Thus the Court, in his view, had the choice of voiding exemptions for conscientious objectors altogether or extending them to nontheists by judicial act. In the light of the longstanding congressional policy of exempting religious conscientious objectors, Harlan chose the second course and so joined the majority in the disposition of the case.

Justice White, with Chief Justice Burger and Justice Stewart, dissented.[36] First, White argued that, whatever the constitutionality of granting exemptions only to theistic conscientious objectors, Welsh himself had no standing to contest the policy and no excuse for refusing to report for induction. Second, White found no violation of the establishment clause in the selective grant of exemptions. Congress may have had in mind the purely practical consideration that religious conscientious objectors are unsuitable for military service. Third, Congress may have granted the exemptions to safeguard the freedom of religious exercise in the same way in which some states grant exemptions from Sunday laws to Sabbatarians. White was accordingly unwilling to strike down the statutory exemption of religious conscientious objectors "because it does not also reach those to whom the free exercise clause offers no protection whatsoever." [37]

Section 6(j) of the Universal Military Training and Service Act of 1948 distinguished between the recognition of "duties superior to those arising from any human relation" and the recognition of duties on the basis of "essentially political, sociological, or philosophical views or a merely personal moral code." As a result of the *Seeger* and *Welsh* decisions in which the phrase "religious training and belief" was construed to apply to humanistic moral codes, a question arises about the continuing legal character and force of the statutory distinction. How can moral judgments about war be isolated from human relations, political analysis, philosophical views, or personal moral codes? Apparently, the essence of the distinction after the two decisions is whether a claimant to classification as a conscientious objector recognizes a moral force or order which transcends himself as an individual. Thus a conscientious objector to war for human, political, philosophical, or personal moral reasons may qualify for an exemption under the statute if his objection is grounded on cosmic considerations irreducible to personal whim or expediency. This may be the same thing as saying that a conscientious objector to war may qualify for exemption if his objection to war is universal and sincere.

Although there was no question of the sincerity of Seeger and Welsh, the decisions in their cases admittedly complicate the administrative difficulties of determining the sincerity of applicants for the status of conscientious objectors. According to Selective Service figures as of April 30, 1970, there were 37,834 men in the conscientious-objector categories (1-O and 1-A-O) before the *Welsh* decision, a total 24 per cent above the number the year before and 101 per cent above that of 1966.[38] A partial answer to some of the genuine difficulties which lie ahead in implementing the *Welsh* decision will be found in the options for substitute service which are already provided for those freed from the obligation of military duty.

Immediately after the *Welsh* decision, Selective Service Director Curtis Tarr issued guidelines to local draft boards indicating that applicants for the status of conscientious objector must have taken into account the "thoughts of wise men," based their objections to war on "some system of belief" beyond their own wishes in the matter, and arrived at their beliefs after "some kind of rigorous training." [39] These guidelines, of course, would seriously discriminate against conscientious objectors with little formal education. Tarr also insisted that the Court's decision was not retroactive, but this interpretation is not likely to survive legal testing.

At any rate, the court majorities in the *Seeger* and *Welsh* cases were not overwhelmed by the administrative difficulties likely to result from their decisions. And they stopped just short of holding the public interest against exemption of ethically motivated conscientious objectors to war an unconstitutional establishment of religion when objectors to war motivated by traditionally religious beliefs are exempted. Thus, in the face of undoubtedly high claims of moral conscience, the Court majorities apparently rated low the public interests adverse to those claims.

One year later, the Court added a footnote to the *Welsh* decision in the well-publicized case of former heavyweight champion Cassius Clay (Mohammed Ali). Although a hearing officer of the Department of Justice had concluded that Clay, a Black Muslim, was sincere in representing his conscientious objections to war, the Department recommended to the Selective Service Appeals Board that Clay be denied exemption as a conscientious objector. The Board followed the recommendation of the Department without advancing any reasons, and Clay was convicted of refusing induction into the armed forces. Clay appealed his conviction to the Supreme Court, and the government there conceded that he was both religiously motivated and sincere but denied that he was opposed to all war. (Like Jehovah's Witnesses, Black Muslims are apparently willing to fight in "holy" wars in behalf of their religion.) In a *per curiam* opinion, the Court unanimously overturned the conviction.[40] Because the Selective Service Appeals Board had not given a reason for its denial of conscientious-objector status to Clay, the Court argued that it was impossible to determine whether the Board had followed the *Welsh* ruling. Thus Clay might have been illegally denied exemption as a conscientious objector, and could not be prosecuted for refusing his order of induction.

But the relatively generous provisions of present Selective Service regulations for pacifists, as interpreted by the Court, have limitations. Pacifists are required to register with local draft boards, and those exempted from military duty are required to perform alternate civilian service. At least one pacifist, Richard Boardman, objected to the latter requirement.

Boardman, an adviser to draft registrants with the American Friends Service Committee, was ordered by his local board to report for work at the Massachusetts General Hospital as alternate civilian service for his exemption from military duty. He was convicted of failing so to report, and the Court of Appeals for the First Circuit affirmed his conviction.[41] Boardman argued that a system of conscription is unjust and that he could not morally cooperate with such a system. But the Court of Appeals did not think that Congress was required to grant total exemptions for conscientious objectors even if the free-exercise clause of the First Amendment guaranteed a right to some exemption. The court thought that the provision for alternate civilian service promoted two objectives: (1) it avoided unfairness to those who are conscripted and the resulting impairment of the morale of the armed services; (2) it mitigated the necessity of ferreting out fraudulent applicants for exempt status as conscientious objectors. The Supreme Court declined without dissent to grant certiorari.[42]

Pacifist conscientious objectors to war claim that they should not be forced by threat of imprisonment to act against their moral convictions. Their claims are based on negative moral prescriptions of conscience perceived as absolute duties and are accordingly of the highest order. The objection of conscience may extend only to combatant military service, to all military service, or to various forms of cooperation with war activities. Quakers, for example, complained during the Civil War of the commutation and substitution provisions of the Federal Conscription Act of 1863, and Boardman objected to alternate civilian service as cooperation with a Selective Service System which he regarded as unjust.

The further an individual presses his conscientious objection to war beyond combat service, the more doubts may be cast on the sincerity of his representations. Assuming that the individual is sincere, however, we must concede that he is the only judge of how extensively he perceives his moral principles to apply. If he sincerely objects to various forms of cooperation with war activities, he raises the highest claim of conscience—namely, a claim not to be forced to do something which he regards as seriously wrong. For him the claim is the same as his objection to combat duty. But, of course, the further an individual presses his conscientious objection to war in the matter of associated activities, the more substantial may be the public interests opposed to his claim.

Congress has rated low the public interest in the draft eligibility of pacifists opposed to war for religious reasons, and the Supreme Court has extended that rating to cover the draft eligibility of Jehovah's Witnesses who like Sicurella are willing to fight in "theocratic" wars, and of humanist conscientious objectors to war like Seeger and Welsh. But by declining to review the *Boardman* decision, the Court has apparently rated moderately high the public interest in the alternate civilian service of pacifists qualified for exemption from military duty as conscientious objectors. At least the court of appeals in that case contended expressly that alternate civilian service was important for the morale of the armed services and for control of fraudulent applications. Indeed, as long as a draft is considered necessary for national defense, there is little likelihood of eliminating the requirement either of registration or of alternate civilian service.

CONSCRIPTION AND SELECTIVE CONSCIENTIOUS OBJECTION

The issue of exemptions for selective conscientious objectors was raised by controversy over the Vietnamese war to a high level of popular discussion and legal adjudication. One objector to that war, David Mitchell, was convicted in 1966 of failing to report for induction into the armed forces and was sentenced to five years in prison. He initially registered with his local draft board but later refused to cooperate with the board in any way. He acknowledged receipt of a notice to report for induction on January 11, 1965, but did not report as ordered. Mitchell made no claim as a conscientious objector to all war, but sought to produce evidence to show that the war in Vietnam was being waged in violation of various treaties to which the United States was a signatory, and that the Selective Service System was an instrument of that combat. The trial judge ruled against the admission of all such evidence as immaterial, and the Court of Appeals for the Second Circuit upheld the ruling of the trial judge because, "as a matter of law, the congressional power 'to raise and support armies' and 'to provide and maintain a navy' is a matter quite distinct from the use which the Executive makes of those who have been found qualified and who have been inducted into the Armed Forces." [43]

Mitchell appealed to the Supreme Court, but it declined to review his conviction.[44] Justice Douglas, however, thought that the petitioner had raised serious substantive questions and that review should have been granted.[45] According to Douglas, the case presented the following questions: (1) whether the Treaty of London of August 8, 1945, which declared that the "waging of a war of aggression" was a "crime against peace" imposing "individual responsibility," was a treaty within the meaning of Article VI of the United States Constitution; (2) whether the question as to the waging of an aggressive war was, in the context of Mitchell's prosecution, a justiciable question; (3) whether the Vietnamese conflict was a "war" in the sense of the treaty; (4) whether the petitioner had standing to raise the question; and (5) whether, if he had standing, the Treaty of London might be offered as a defense in his case or in amelioration of the punishment.

Mitchell was a selective conscientious objector to the Vietnamese war, but he presented his case exclusively in terms of international law. (Had Mitchell been permitted to submit evidence on the legal questions he sought to raise, however, the war-crimes trial of government leaders effectively resulting would have extensively involved issues of moral judgment.) The Supreme Court declined to review his conviction, presumably for one or more of the following reasons: (1) Mitchell lacked standing to sue because there was no evidence that he would be sent to Vietnam; (2) the war in Vietnam was a "political question," i.e., Article I committed to Congress the power to raise armies, and Article II constituted the President Commander-in-Chief in the disposition of the armed forces; (3) the Treaty of London was inapplicable because it was concerned only with the prosecution of European Axis war criminals; (4) the Treaty of London was, in any case, superseded by the subsequent Selective Service Act; and (5) the Nuremberg trials were not precedents for trying conscripted privates as war criminals.

Another conscientious objector to the Vietnamese war, Steven Spiro, was convicted in a federal district court of refusing to accept induction into the armed services of the United States. The district court judge, trying the case without a jury, found Spiro's 1-A-O classification for noncombatant military service proper, and that due-process requirements had been satisfied by the local and review draft boards. On appeal of his conviction, Spiro argued that his rights to religious freedom and equal protection of the laws were violated because he, a Catholic willing to fight in a "just" war, was denied 1-O classification and exemption as a conscientious objector, when Jehovah's Witnesses willing to fight in "theocratic" wars were granted such a classification.

The Court of Appeals for the Third Circuit upheld Spiro's conviction.[46] Since the draft boards and the district court had found that Spiro did not meet the statutory test to qualify as a conscientious objector, the appellate court limited its review to the procedural fairness and adequacy of factual support for the boards' findings. On the first point, the court found no prejudice to the appellant's case even if the local board had not followed one or more of the applicable Selective Service regulations. On the second point, the court held that the boards' findings did have factual support, and that it lacked jurisdiction to "delve into the legal and theological implications of appellant's beliefs." [47] The Supreme Court, over the dissents of Justices Black and Douglas, denied certiorari.[48]

In a letter to his Selective Service Board of Appeals, Spiro explained that he thought it "inconceivable that a just war will ever happen—since there has never been one . . . and I hardly expect that Men [*sic*] will suddenly change." [49] Thus Spiro's objection to war would seem to have been nearly as total as Sicurella's. Perhaps this is, in part, why Justice Black would have granted certiorari with respect to Spiro although he voted against the more evidently selective conscientious objector Gillette three years later. The majority of the Court, however, may have recognized that the near-pacifist Spiro could become the stalking-horse of selective "just" warriors to a degree impossible for Sicurella to match in behalf of prospective "theocratic" warriors.

Still another conscientious objector to the Vietnamese war, John Heffron Sisson, failed to submit to induction and was accordingly convicted by a jury of violating the Military Selective Service Act of 1967. Sisson contended from the outset that the statute under which he was convicted deprived him of his constitutional rights under the First and Fifth Amendments. He claimed exemption as a conscientious objector on ethical rather than traditionally religious grounds, and there was no doubt of his sincerity. After his conviction, Chief Judge Wyzanski of the United States District Court of Massachusetts arrested the judgment, holding that Sisson could not be subject to military orders, unreviewable in a civilian court, which might require him to kill in Vietnam.[50] Although Wyzanski had previously ruled that it was not open to Sisson to offer as a statutory excuse the argument that he regarded the Vietnamese war as immoral, he upheld Sisson's constitutional claims after the conclusion of the trial.

(The United States Supreme Court granted review of the *Sisson* case on government appeal, but a majority of five justices subsequently dismissed the appeal—and thus effectively ruled for Sisson—on the technical jurisdictional ground that Wyzanski's action constituted an unappealable directed verdict rather than an arrest of judgment.[51] An unlikely coalition of Chief Justice Burger, Justice Douglas, and Justice White dissented.[52] Newly appointed Justice Blackmun took no part in the consideration or decision of the case.)

Wyzanski assumed *arguendo* that Congress had the power to draft men in time of peace and that conscientious objectors could be conscripted even for combatant military service. The question for him was whether Sisson could be compelled to submit to nonreviewable military orders to render combat service in Vietnam. This was not, in his view, an "area of constitutional absolutism" but rather an "area in which competing claims must be explored, examined, and marshalled with reference to the Constitution as a whole." [53] Wyzanski admitted that competing claims of public interest and private conscience could not be "mathematically graded," but he did not anticipate "insuperable difficulties in distinguishing orders of magnitude." [54] When the sincerely conscientious man believes that he will act wrongly if he kills, "his claim obviously has great magnitude," a magnitude "not appreciably lessened if his belief relates . . . to a particular war or to a particular type of war." [55]

Although Wyzanski agreed with the government that Sisson did not meet the congressional definition of religion in the 1967 act, he observed that "it is not the ancestry but the authenticity of the sense of duty which creates constitutional legitimacy."[56] Some might fear that recognition of individual conscience would make it easy for individuals to perpetrate fraud on the public, but Wyzanski thought it "often harder to detect a fraudulent adherent to a religious creed than to recognize a sincere moral protestant": "we all can discern Thoreau's integrity more quickly than we might detect some churchman's hypocrisy."[57]

Wyzanski conceded that there would be a public interest of great magnitude in the conscription of manpower for common defense if the nation were "fighting for its very existence," but he denied that "a campaign fought with limited forces for limited objectives with no likelihood of a battlefield within this country and without a declaration of war is . . . a claim of comparable magnitude."[58] Nor was there "any suggestion" of a present national need for combat service from Sisson as distinguished from other forms of service, and this was said to be reflected "in the nation's lack of calls for sacrifice by civilians in any serious way."[59] Since the magnitude of Sisson's moral interest against combatant military service outweighed the magnitude of the country's need for him to be so employed, the religious-exercise clause of the First Amendment and the due-process clause of the Fifth were held to prohibit application of the 1967 draft law to require combatant service in Vietnam of one like Sisson conscientiously opposed to it. Wyzanski did not consider the magnitude of the public interests in equitable administration of the draft and in obedience to law as also opposed to recognition of Sisson's claim to exemption, and he weakened his analysis to that extent.

Wyzanski acknowledged limits to the right of conscientious objectors to exemption from military service, and he admitted that Sisson perhaps could be drafted for noncombatant service in Vietnam or elsewhere. But he argued that

> It would be a poor court indeed that could not discern the small constitutional magnitude of the interest that a person has in avoiding all helpful service whatsoever or in avoiding all general taxes whatsoever. His objection, of course, may be sincere. But some sincere objections have greater constitutional magnitude than others.[60]

This means that Wyzanski did not fully accommodate the conscientious objections of Sisson to all service in the armed forces while the United States waged war in Vietnam. Instead of attempting to distinguish the magnitude of claims of conscience against different degrees of military or other public service in the course of the Vietnamese war, however, Wyzanski could have more convincingly distinguished the magnitude of public interests opposed to recognition of different degrees of such conscientious objection to the war.

Wyzanski also rested his decision on a narrower ground—namely, that statutory exemption for conscientious objectors to war for religious reasons without any provision for conscientious objectors not formally religious preferred traditionally religious beliefs over nonbelief and thus constituted a prohibited establishment of religion.[61] Even if this last argument is conceded, however, it is difficult to see how it could apply to Sisson. All the argument would seem to prove is that conscientious objectors to war for purely ethical reasons should have the same eligibility for exemption as conscientious objectors to war for religious reasons. But the latter are entitled to exemption by statute only if they are opposed to *all* war, which Sisson was not. Moreover, the *Seeger* and *Welsh* decisions would qualify Sisson for exemption as a conscientious objector to war on religious grounds within the statutory provisions of the 1967 draft act if he was otherwise eligible.

On the same day on which it disposed of the *Sisson* case on technical grounds—and probably because of that evasive decision—the Supreme Court granted certiorari in the case of another conscientious objector to military service during the Vietnamese war.[62] Guy Gillette, who based his objection to the war on humanistic rather than traditionally religious grounds, was convicted of failing to report for induction at the end of 1967, and the Court of Appeals for the Second Circuit affirmed his conviction.[63]

Unlike Wyzanski in *Sisson,* that court was willing to assume that Gillette's views on war were religious within the meaning of the Military Selective Service Act of 1967. But the court denied that he qualified for exemption as a conscientious objector because he was not opposed to "participation in war in any form." Moreover, the court denied him standing, as it had denied Mitchell standing, to challenge his induction on the basis of conscientious objection to service in Vietnam. According to the court, "the mere potentiality, arising upon his induction, that Gillette would have to violate his conscientious objection to service in Vietnam is not sufficient to outweigh the application of congressional power [to raise armies] to him."[64] (Wyzanski, on the other hand, had argued in an earlier ruling in the *Sisson* case that a prospective inductee had standing to object to induction on the basis of his conscientious objections to service in Vietnam since draft calls at the time of induction notices in 1968 were "so closely connected" with military demands in Vietnam "as to be unmistakably interdependent," and since the prospective inductee, once inducted, did not appear to have standing to raise a constitutional issue about his transfer to Vietnam in any civilian or military court.[65])

On March 8, 1971, over the sole dissent of Justice Douglas, the Supreme Court ruled against Gillette.[66] The sweep of the majority opinion and the margin of the vote left little room for doubt about the current constitutional status of selective conscientious objectors. Justice Marshall, speaking for the majority, admitted by silence the petitioner's standing to challenge his induction on the basis of conscientious objection to service in Vietnam but agreed with the circuit court that the petitioner did not qualify for the statutory exemption as a conscientious objector to "participation in war in any form." Thus the Court was confronted with the petitioner's constitutional claim to exemption based on the religious guarantees of the First Amendment.

On the establishment-of-religion issue, Marshall found valid, secular purposes which were not related to the favoring of any religious organization or sect in the granting of exemptions to pacifists: such exemptions might reflect the congressional view that pacifists make poor soldiers, or a congressional concern for "the hard choice that conscription would impose on conscientious objectors to war as well as respect for the value of conscientious action and for the principle of supremacy of conscience." [67]

Marshall also found valid, religiously neutral reasons for limiting the exemption to conscientious objectors to all war. He cited the difficulty of distinguishing morally motivated from purely political objection to a particular war (the government had argued that objection to a particular war is necessarily political, that is, that the judgment against it must be based on the same factors which the government itself had considered and authoritatively evaluated when it decided to wage war), the mutability of moral judgment on a particular war because of the large number of variables involved (the purposes of the war, the legality of the war, the means employed in the war, the character of the foe, the character of allies, the place of the war, and the destruction necessary to achieve the goals of the war), the difficulty of determining sincerity, the advantages which might accrue to the more articulate, the better educated, and the better counseled, the advantages which might accrue to adherents of traditional religions (e.g., Catholic "just" warriors), and the danger of greater governmental involvement in determining a person's character, beliefs, and religious affiliation. Though Marshall thought that selective conscientious objection, however political and particular, "still might be rooted in religion and conscience,"[68] he recognized the further risk to which the government argument pointed—namely, that exemption for selective conscientious objectors might open the doors to a general theory of selective disobedience to law.

For these reasons Marshall concluded that selective conscientious objectors are not unconstitutionally denied freedom of religious exercise by denial of exemption from military service: "The incidental burdens felt by persons in petitioner's position are strictly justified by substantial governmental interests that relate directly to the very impacts questioned."[69] And "more broadly," Marshall added almost in passing, "there is the government's interest in procuring the manpower necessary for military purposes pursuant to the constitutional grant of power to Congress to raise and support armies."[70]

Justice Black concurred in the judgment of the Court but only in the reasoning of the majority opinion restrictively interpreting the statutory exemption to pacifists.[71] Justice Douglas was the sole dissenter.[72] Stressing the moral plight of all conscientious objectors to war, Douglas found the denial of exemption to selective conscientious objectors an invidious discrimination violative of Fifth Amendment guarantees of due process of law.

Marshall's analysis of the religious-establishment issue was straightforward and conformed to previous court decisions, especially *Schempp*.[73] He argued well that the reasons Congress offered for denying exemption to selective conscientious objectors were substantial and did not evince religious discrimination. Indeed, even Douglas did not base his dissent specifically on this issue. But Marshall's analysis of the religious-exercise issue was inadequate because he did not consider whether "substantial" governmental interests against a grant of exemptions to selective conscientious objectors are to be identified with the "compelling" public interests canonized in *Sherbert.*[74] Nor did Justice Brennan, who was the author of the *Sherbert* opinion, nor Black, who has always insisted on evidence of the highest public interests to justify governmental restrictions on dissenters, nor Douglas, who dissented. If the government is required to show "substantial" or "compelling" public interests specifically against a grant of exemptions to selective conscientious objectors, then the government should likewise be required to prove that alternate civilian service, perhaps for a longer period than military service, would be unlikely to obviate administrative difficulties or would continue to invite selective disobedience to law or would be otherwise inadequate. This neither the government nor the Court did explicitly.

In declining to review the convictions of Mitchell and Spiro, the Court sought to avoid the constitutional question of exemption for selective conscientious objectors, partially at least in deference to the principle of separate powers. Judge Wyzanski forced the Supreme Court's hand when he declared that Sisson had a constitutional right to exemption from combatant military service. Although the Court disposed of *Sisson* on technical grounds, it agreed to review *Gillette*. Gillette lost decisively, when the Court rated at least moderately high the public interests at stake against his claim to exemption.[75] Selective conscientious objectors represent the highest claims of conscience—namely, an absolute duty not to do what the law commands in the serious matter of killing. Despite the strength of these moral claims, the Court majority ruled against them because it rated high the opposing public interests. This illustrates the obvious principle that no claims of conscience, however high, are likely to be recognized as constitutional rights when judges rate high the public interests opposed to them.

Similarly, selective conscientious objectors to the Vietnamese war seeking exemption from the draft have failed to persuade the public and Congress that vindication of their claims would be compatible with equitable administration of the draft system. Yet selective conscientious objectors may be able to convince the public and Congress to accept their claims to exemption from the draft in the postwar period when fewer men are called to service. Their combatant service may not have been needed in 1968, as Wyzanski argued, but their exemption while others fought proved politically unpalatable to the American public. In any case, selective conscientious objectors are more likely to vindicate their claims to exemption from the draft if an acceptable alternate service to the public, possibly for a longer period than military service, can be devised. The whole problem of conscientious objectors, of course, would be eliminated if the armed forces of the United States were to become entirely voluntary—although other problems might thereby result.

THE ARMED SERVICES AND CONSCIENTIOUS OBJECTION

The armed services currently permit personnel to apply for discharge or noncombatant duty on the basis of their conscientious objections to war. In 1969, 943 Army, 313 Navy, and 159 Air Force personnel requested discharge as pacifists. By contrast, 101 Army, 83 Navy, and 59 Air Force personnel made similar requests in 1965 before large-scale American involvement in Vietnam. Of the requests in 1969, the Army granted 21 per cent, the Navy 44 per cent, and the Air Force 34 per cent. The Army also granted 64 per cent of the requests for assignment to noncombatant duty from servicemen who claimed to be pacifists.[76]

But servicemen who would challenge decisions of military authorities have no direct legal recourse in civilian courts. Military authorities derive their jurisdiction from Congress' broad power under Article I, section 8 of the Constitution to make all laws "necessary and proper" for the "government and regulation of the land and naval forces" of the United States, and civilian courts have generally adhered to the doctrine of separate legislative and judicial powers in matters of military regulations. Nor have servicemen ever successfully gained a hearing for challenges to their disposition by the President as Commander-in-Chief, because civilian courts have adhered strictly to the doctrine of separate executive and judicial powers on matters of military employment. Because military courts have not been considered courts in "law or equity" in the sense of Article III of the Constitution, civilian courts have never directly reviewed the proceedings or decisions of military tribunals. Civilian courts have, however, reviewed such proceedings and decisions collaterally by means of the writ of habeas corpus in cases in which the scope of inquiry has been limited to questions of the jurisdiction of the military tribunal over the subject matter and person on trial and of the legal authority for the sentence imposed.[77] Many servicemen have attempted to challenge their assignment to Vietnam in civilian courts on legal and moral grounds, but only one (Negre) obtained a full review on the merits.

An Army private, Robert Luftig, brought suit in the District Court of the District of Columbia in 1966 to enjoin the Secretary of Defense from sending him to Vietnam. He did not challenge his induction nor did he seek release from the Army. Rather, he contended that the military activities in Vietnam were unconstitutional and illegal, and that the Army consequently had no legal authority to assign him there. The district court dismissed the suit because of what it conceived to be the "political question" involved and because the United States had not consented to the suit.[78] The Court of Appeals for the District affirmed (*Luftig v. United States*),[79] and the Supreme Court without dissent declined to grant certiorari.[80]

In another case, three Army privates, Dennis Mora, James Johnson, and David Samas, sought through their federal suit in district court to enjoin the Secretary of Defense and the Secretary of the Army from assigning them to combat duty in Vietnam and requested a declaratory judgment that the war in Vietnam was illegal. The petitioners were drafted into the Army late in 1965, and they were ordered six months later to a West Coast replacement center for shipment to Vietnam. At this point, they instituted their suit, not as pacifists but as selective conscientious objectors to what they held to be an illegal and immoral conflict. The district court dismissed the suit for want of jurisdiction, and the Court of Appeals for the District of Columbia affirmed the decision (*Mora* et al. *v. McNamara*).[81] The petitioners sought review by the United States Supreme Court, but that review was denied over the dissents of Justices Douglas and Stewart.[82] (Justice Marshall, who had been Solicitor General in the preparatory stages of the case before the Court and who had now replaced Justice Clark, took no part in the decision.) The three petitioners were court-martialed and sentenced to three (Mora) or five (Johnson and Samas) years' imprisonment at hard labor for disobeying military orders.[83]

Justice Stewart, dissenting, raised the following questions: (1) Was the United States military activity in Vietnam a "war" within the meaning of Article I, section 8 of the Constitution? (2) If so, was the Chief Executive constitutionally empowered to order the petitioners to participate in that military activity in the absence of a declaration of war by Congress? (3) Did the treaty obligations of the United States give a legal basis for the President's commitment of military forces to Vietnam? (4) Did United

States military operations in Vietnam fall within the terms of the "Tonkin Bay" joint resolution of August 10, 1964? and (5) If so, was the resolution a constitutionally impermissible delegation of all or part of Congress' power to declare war?[84] Whether the Court would ultimately reach these questions, Justice Stewart admitted, would depend upon resolving "serious preliminary issues of justiciability," i.e., issues concerning the competence of the Court to decide the questions.[85] But he did not think that the Court could "make these problems go away simply by refusing to hear the case of three obscure Army privates." [86] Douglas also thought that the petitioners should be told at least whether their case was within judicial cognizance.[87]

Since Justice Douglas had dissented in *Mitchell,* his dissent in *Mora* does not call for any special explanation; but since Justice Stewart had not dissented in *Mitchell,* his dissent in *Mora* does prompt us to ask why he did so in this case. On the available record, there is no way of answering that question, unless Stewart grew more uneasy with the course of the Vietnamese war as calendar year 1967 progressed.

An Army doctor, Captain Howard Levy, was convicted by a military court in 1967 of refusing to obey an order to train Special Forces medical troops bound for Vietnam, of stirring disloyalty among troops, and of making intemperate statements to enlisted personnel.[88] He was dishonorably discharged, sentenced to three years in prison, and ordered to forfeit all pay. Levy sought to stay his military trial in civilian federal courts, but was twice rebuffed.[89] After his conviction, Levy petitioned for a writ of habeas corpus in a federal district court pending his appeal in the military courts, but the petition was denied. The Court of Appeals affirmed,[90] and the Supreme Court over the dissent of Justice Douglas denied certiorari.[91] (Justice Marshall, who had been Solicitor General in the preparatory stages of the case, did not participate.) The United States

Court of Military Appeals affirmed Levy's conviction,[92] and Levy, having exhausted all military remedies, petitioned anew in a federal district court for a writ of habeas corpus. On August 2, 1969, Justice Douglas intervened to grant him a temporary release on bail in order to preserve his claim before he completed his sentence.[93] The full Court supported Douglas' action, again without the participation of Justice Marshall,[94] but no further Supreme Court consideration of the Levy case ensued.

In 1968, Captain Dale Noyd, an instructor at the Air Force Academy, was dishonorably discharged, sentenced to one year in prison at hard labor, and ordered to forfeit all pay for refusing to accept an assignment to a training center for pilots bound for Vietnam.[95] Noyd had offered to resign from the Air Force or to accept noncombatant duty as alternatives to his combat-connected assignment, but the offer was rejected. Before his conviction, Noyd had tried unsuccessfully in civilian federal courts to obtain his discharge or a noncombat-connected assignment.[96] After conviction, Noyd petitioned, again unsuccessfully, for a writ of habeas corpus in a federal district court pending his appeal in the military courts.[97] The denial of his petition was affirmed by the Court of Appeals because he had not exhausted the available remedy of habeas corpus from the United States Court of Military Appeals.[98] In a separate action, Justice Douglas granted Noyd a temporary release from prison in order to preserve the latter's claim before he completed his sentence.[99] The United States Supreme Court affirmed the denial of habeas corpus by the district court, although it preserved Noyd's right to petition for his release from the military court.[100] Justice White would have revoked the initial grant of certiorari because Noyd's sentence had only two days to run,[101] and Justice Marshall did not participate in the decision. No further Court consideration of the Noyd case ensued.

The one conscientious objector to the Vietnamese war in

military service who gained a full review on the merits was Louis Negre. Although Negre would accept service elsewhere, he objected to any duty in Vietnam. He was inducted into the Army in 1967 and ordered to Vietnam in 1968. He then sought separation from the Army as a conscientious objector, but was judged not to qualify principally because his objection did not extend to all war. After exhausting his administrative military remedies, Negre petitioned for a writ of habeas corpus in a federal district court. The district court judge denied his petition, and the Court of Appeals for the Ninth Circuit affirmed.[102] In the wake of the indecisive result in *Sisson,* the Supreme Court granted certiorari together with *Gillette.*[103]

The Gillette and Negre cases were decided in the same opinion, and the decision in the latter case was the same as in the former; a majority of eight justices voted against Negre over the sole dissent of Justice Douglas.[104] Negre's military status played no prominent part in the Court's opinion because, if Gillette had no constitutional right to exemption from the draft as a selective conscientious objector, then *a fortiori* a military subject like Negre had no constitutional right to refuse assignments as such an objector. In fact, Negre was no longer on active duty at the time of the decision because he had been discharged under honorable conditions.[105]

Luftig, Mora and his companions, Levy, and Noyd never received a hearing before the Court on the merits of their legal and moral objections to serve in the Vietnamese war. Negre did receive a hearing but lost decisively. The moral claims of military men against service in conflicts deemed immoral are as high as those of selective conscientious objectors who refuse induction into the armed forces. But the public interests opposed to recognition of the former claims are even higher than the public interests opposed to recognition of the latter claims, because of the demands of military discipline.

MISCELLANEOUS

The Selective Service Act of 1917 exempted ordained ministers and students for the ministry from service and training under the act. This exemption was upheld by the Supreme Court without argument against the objection that it constituted an establishment of religion.[106] Subsequent selective service acts have maintained the exemption, and there have been no further legal challenges to it. But divinity students opposed to the Vietnamese war have occasioned incidental issues which led to disposition by the Court.

One such divinity student, James Oestereich, returned his registration certificate to his local draft board for the sole purpose of expressing his dissent from American participation in the Vietnamese war. His local board then declared him delinquent for failure to have the certificate in his possession and for failure to notify the board of his local status. He lost his administrative appeal and was ordered to report for induction. The student brought suit to enjoin his induction, but the suit was dismissed by the district court.[107] The dismissal of the suit was affirmed by the Court of Appeals.[108] The Supreme Court reversed and ruled for Oestereich on the merits.[109] Justice Douglas, speaking for five justices, held that the conduct of the local board was "basically lawless," [110] and that pre-induction judicial review was not precluded in cases of this type by the Military Selective Service Act of 1967. Justice Harlan concurred separately.[111] Justice Stewart, with Justices Brennan and White, dissented on the basis of a specific provision of the 1967 draft law which he construed strictly.[112] (In a companion case of the same day, the court summarily reversed the decision of a district court judge enjoining the induction of a prospective draftee, Charles Gabriel, who claimed exemption as a conscientious objector [*Clark v. Gabriel*].[113] The evidence supporting the draftee's claim was ambiguous, and the Court was accordingly unwilling to interfere with the administrative process in the case. Only Justice Black would have noted probable jurisdiction.[114])

Another divinity student, Vincent McGee, was so thoroughly opposed to the Vietnamese war that he did not formally apply for a ministerial exemption and took no steps to appear before the local board or to appeal its decision against his claim to exemption as a conscientious objector. Classified 1-A and ordered to induction, he refused to report. He was convicted and sentenced to two years in prison, and the Court of Appeals affirmed.[115] Over the sole dissent of Justice Douglas, the Supreme Court likewise affirmed the conviction (*McGee v. United States*).[116] Speaking for the Court, Justice Marshall held that McGee could not claim a ministerial exemption as a defense in his trial for draft evasion since he had "completely sidestepped the administrative process," [117] and that he could not claim a conscientious-objector exemption as a defense since he had not invoked the administrative processes available to contest the local board's ruling. Justice Douglas argued in dissent that the local board had never properly considered McGee's claim to exemption as a conscientious objector and therefore had erroneously rejected his claim.[118]

William Ehlert, after receipt of his induction notice, for the first time sought exemption from the draft as a conscientious objector. When he failed to report for induction, he was convicted of draft evasion. The Court of Appeals affirmed his conviction,[119] as did the Supreme Court (*Ehlert v. United States*).[120] Justice Stewart, speaking for a majority of six justices, thought that armed services procedures gave Ehlert sufficient opportunity to vindicate his claim as a conscientious objector. Dissenting Justices Brennan, Douglas, and Marshall thought that Ehlert was entitled to civilian review of his claim, especially in view of the ambiguity of the applicable selective service regulation.[121]

In an action not directly related to the claims of conscientious objectors to the Vietnamese war, the Commonwealth of Massachusetts brought an original suit in the United States Supreme Court to declare American military participation in Vietnam unconstitutional and to enjoin the Secretary of Defense from further orders to increase the level of troops in Indochina, and, if there were no congressional action within ninety days, to enjoin him from further orders of Massachusetts citizens to action in Indochina. The Court, however, without opinion denied Massachusetts leave to file the bill of complaint (*Commonwealth of Massachusetts v. Laird*).[122] Dissenting Justice Douglas thought that Massachusetts had standing to raise the issue of the war's legality, that the issue was justiciable, and that the Court should decide the issue of its merits after full argument.[123] Dissenting Justices Harlan and Stewart would have set the motion for argument only on the questions of standing and justiciability.[124]

NOTES

1. Lillian Schlissel, ed., *Conscience in America: A Documentary History of Conscientious Objection in America, 1757–1967* (New York: Dutton, 1968), p. 18. As subsequent notes will make apparent, I have relied on Schlissel's work for the history of conscientious objection in America up to the end of World War II.

2. *Ibid.*, pp. 56–57, 262.

3. See, e.g., the 1795 letter of an anonymous Quaker and the report of a meeting with Secretary of State Seward in 1865, included *ibid.*, pp. 49–54 and 100–101, respectively.

4. See, e.g., the statement of the Quaker John Woolman, *ibid.*, pp. 34–38.

5. *Ibid.*, p. 88.

6. 13 Stat. 9; Schlissel, *Conscience in America*, p. 98.

7. *Ibid.*, p. 89.

8. 40 Stat. 76, 78; Schlissel, *Conscience in America*, pp. 133, 262 (Clark in *Seeger*).

9. *Selective Service Cases,* 245 U.S. 366, 389–90 (1918).
10. Schlissel, *Conscience in America,* p. 129.
11. *Ibid.,* p. 130.
12. 54 Stat. 889; Schlissel, *Conscience in America,* p. 214.
13. *Ibid.*
14. *Ibid.,* p. 215.
15. *Sicurella v. U.S.,* 348 U.S. 385 (1955).
16. *Sicurella v. U.S.,* 213 F.2d 911 (1954).
17. *Sicurella v. U.S.,* 348 U.S. 385, 388–91 (1955).
18. *Ibid.,* pp. 392 and 393, respectively.
19. *U.S. v. Berman,* 156 F.2d 377 (1946).
20. *U.S. v. Kauten,* 133 F.2d 703 (1943).
21. 50 U.S.C.A. App. #456 (j); Schlissel, *Conscience in America,* pp. 255, 263.
22. *U.S. v. Seeger,* 380 U.S. 163, 166 (1965); cf. 216 F.Supp. 516 (1963) and 326 F.2d 846 (1964).
23. *U.S. v. Seeger,* 380 U.S. 163, 166 (1965).
24. *Ibid.,* p. 168; cf. *U.S. v. Jakobson,* 325 F.2d 409 (1963).
25. *Seeger,* p. 169; cf. *Peter v. U.S.,* 324 F.2d 173 (1963).
26. *Seeger,* p. 174; cf. *Webster's New International Dictionary* (2d ed.).
27. *Seeger,* p. 188.
28. *Welsh v. U.S.,* 398 U.S. 333 (1970).
29. *Welsh v. U.S.,* 404 F.2d 1078 (1968).
30. *Welsh v. U.S.,* 398 U.S. 333, 335 (1970).
31. *Ibid.,* p. 340.
32. *Ibid.,* p. 342.
33. *Ibid.,* p. 344.
34. *Ibid.*
35. *Ibid.,* p. 345.
36. *Ibid.,* p. 367.
37. *Ibid.,* p. 374.
38. *The Los Angeles Times,* May 25, 1970, p. 6.
39. *The New York Times,* June 17, 1970, p. 1.
40. *Clay v. U.S.,* 403 U.S. 698 (1971); Justices Douglas and Harlan concurred separately (pp. 705 and 710, respectively), and Justice Marshall did not participate.
41. *U.S. v. Boardman,* 419 F.2d 110 (1969).
42. *Boardman v. U.S.,* 397 U.S. 991 (1970). The Court had denied certiorari to two earlier pacifist petitioners convicted of refusing to report for civilian work in lieu of military service (*Holmes v. U.S.,* 391 U.S. 936 [1968] and *Hart v. U.S.,* 391 U.S. 956 [1968]; cf. 387 F.2d 781 [1967] and 382 F.2d 1020 [1967], respectively). Justice Douglas dissented in both cases, but only on the constitutional question of a peacetime draft. Justice Stewart submitted a memorandum in *Holmes* indicating his willingness to hear the case, had military service in armed

conflict overseas been involved; see his dissent in *Mora* et al. *v. McNamara,* pp. 46–47.

43. *U.S. v. Mitchell,* 369 F.2d 323 (1966), quoted in Schlissel, *Conscience in America,* p. 293.

44. *Mitchell v. U.S.,* 386 U.S. 972 (1967).

45. *Ibid.;* see Schlissel, *Conscience in America,* pp. 294–295.

46. *U.S. v. Spiro,* 384 F.2d 159 (1967).

47. *Ibid.,* p. 161.

48. *Spiro v. U.S.,* 390 U.S. 956 (1968).

49. "Petition for Writ of Certiorari to the U.S. Court of Appeals for the Third Circuit," *U.S. Supreme Court Briefs and Records,* Spiro v. U.S., 390 U.S. 956, Appendix, p. 33a.

50. *U.S. v. Sisson,* 297 F.Supp. 902 (1969).

51. *U.S. v. Sisson,* 399 U.S. 267 (1970).

52. *Ibid.,* pp. 308–349.

53. *U.S. v. Sisson,* 297 F.Supp. 902, 908 (1969).

54. *Ibid.*

55. *Ibid.*

56. *Ibid.,* p. 909.

57. *Ibid.*

58. *Ibid.,* pp. 908–909.

59. *Ibid.,* p. 909.

60. *Ibid.,* p. 910.

61. *Ibid.,* p. 911.

62. *Gillette v. U.S.,* 399 U.S. 925 (1970).

63. *U.S. v. Gillette,* 420 F.2d 298 (1970).

64. *Ibid.,* p. 300.

65. *U.S. v. Sisson,* 294 F.Supp. 511, 512 (1968).

66. *Gillette v. U.S.,* 401 U.S. 437 (1971).

67. *Ibid.,* p. 453.

68. *Ibid.,* p. 458.

69. *Ibid.,* p. 462.

70. *Ibid.*

71. *Ibid.,* p. 463.

72. *Ibid.*

73. Cf. *Abington School District v. Schempp,* 374 U.S. 203 (1963) and Chap. 6, n. 33, p. 183.

74. Cf. *Sherbert v. Verner,* 374 U.S. 398, 406 (1963) and Chap. 4, pp. 105–107.

75. One month after *Gillette,* the Court vacated the judgment of the Northern District Court of California in favor of another selective conscientious objector and remanded the case "for reconsideration in light of *Gillette v. U.S.* and *Negre v. Larsen.*" Justice Douglas dissented. *U.S. v. McFadden,* 401 U.S. 1006 (1971); cf. 309 F.Supp. 502 (1970).

76. *The New York Times,* March 22, 1970, p. 25.

77. In recent years, the writ of habeas corpus has been used

to review the fundamental fairness of the trial itself. See, e.g., *Burns v. Wilson,* 346 U.S. 137 (1953).

78. *Luftig v. McNamara,* 252 F. Supp. 819 (1966).

79. *Luftig v. McNamara,* 373 F.2d 664 (1967).

80. *Luftig v. McNamara,* 387 U.S. 945 (1967).

81. *Mora* et al. *v. McNamara,* 387 F.2d 862 (1967).

82. *Mora* et al. *v. McNamara,* 389 U. S. 934 (1967).

83. *The New York Times,* September 8, 1966, p. 1, and September 10, 1966, p. 4.

84. *Mora* et al. *v. McNamara,* 389 U.S. 934 (1967).

85. *Ibid.,* p. 935.

86. *Ibid.*

87. *Ibid.*

88. *The New York Times,* June 3, 1967, p. 1.

89. *Levy v. Corcoran,* 389 F.2d 929 (1967); cert. denied, 389 U.S. 960 (1967). *Levy v. Corcoran,* 387 U.S. 915 (1967).

90. *Levy v. Resor,* 384 F.2d 689 (1967).

91. *Levy v. Resor,* 389 U.S. 1049 (1968).

92. *The New York Times,* January 7, 1969, p. 46.

93. *Levy v. Parker,* 396 U.S. 1204 (1969).

94. *Levy v. Parker,* 396 U.S. 804 (1969).

95. *The New York Times,* March 9, 1968, p. 1.

96. *Noyd v. McNamara,* 267 F.Supp. 701 (1967); 378 F.2d 538 (1967); cert. denied (Justice Douglas dissenting and Justice Marshall not participating), 389 U.S. 1022 (1967).

97. *Noyd v. Bond,* 285 F.Supp. 785 (1968).

98. *Noyd v. Bond,* 402 F.2d 441 (1969).

99. *Noyd v. Bond,* 89 S.Ct. 478 (1968).

100. *Noyd v. Bond,* 395 U.S. 683 (1969).

101. *Ibid.,* p. 699.

102. *Negre v. Larsen,* 418 F.2d 908 (1969).

103. *Negre v. Larsen,* 399 U.S. 925 (1970).

104. *Negre v. Larsen,* 401 U.S. 437 (1971).

105. *Ibid.,* p. 440, n. 2.

106. *Selective Service Cases,* 245 U.S. 366, 389–90 (1918).

107. *Oestereich v. Selective Service Board No. 11,* 280 F.Supp. 78 (1968).

108. *Oestereich v. Selective Service Board No. 11,* 390 F.2d 100 (1968).

109. *Oestereich v. Selective Service Board No. 11,* 393 U.S. 233 (1968). See also *Gutknecht v. U.S.,* 396 U.S. 295 (1970) and *Breen v. Selective Service Board No. 16,* 396 U.S. 460 (1970).

110. *Ibid.,* p. 237.

111. *Ibid.,* p. 239.

112. *Ibid.,* p. 245.

113. *Clark v. Gabriel,* 393 U.S. 256 (1968); cf. 287 F.Supp. 369 (1968).

114. *Clark v. Gabriel,* 393 U.S. 256, 259 (1968).
115. *U.S. v. McGee,* 426 F.2d 691 (1970).
116. *McGee v. U.S.,* 402 U.S. 479 (1971).
117. *Ibid.,* p. 488.
118. *Ibid.,* p. 492.
119. *Ehlert v. U. S.,* 422 F.2d 332 (1970).
120. *Ehlert v. U.S.,* 402 U.S. 99 (1971).
121. *Ibid.,* pp. 108–120.
122. *Commonwealth of Massachusetts v. Laird,* 400 U.S. 886 (1970).
123. *Ibid.*
124. *Ibid.*

3

Conscience and National Security (*ii*)

CONSCIENTIOUS OBJECTION AND NATURALIZED CITIZENSHIP

ANOTHER HISTORIC AREA OF CONFLICT between conscientious objectors to war and the public interest in national defense arises out of the requirement of the Naturalization Act of 1906 that applicants for citizenship declare under oath that they are willing to "support and defend the Constitution and laws of the United States against all enemies, foreign and domestic." [1] Mrs. Roszika Schwimmer, a 49-year-old Hungarian immigrant, filed a petition for naturalization in the District Court for the Northern District of Illinois in September, 1926. That court found her unable to take the prescribed oath of allegiance without mental reservation, and denied her application. After the Circuit Court of Appeals reversed the decree and directed the District Court to grant her petition,[2] the government sought and secured a review by the United States Supreme Court (*United States v. Schwimmer*).[3]

Question 22 of the preliminary form for naturalization

asks applicants whether they are willing to take up arms in defense of the United States. In reply, Mrs. Schwimmer admitted that she "would not take up arms personally," but denied that a woman's refusal to bear arms was a contradiction to the prescribed oath of allegiance.[4] She pointed to her devotion to American life and her competence to defend the United States against attacks by writing in foreign journals. She was unwilling to comply with any future requirement by the government that women take up arms in its defense, but she was willing to accept the same penalties which the government would administer to male citizens who are conscientious objectors. She also indicated in private correspondence that she was "an uncompromising pacifist" with "no sense of nationalism, only a cosmic consciousness of belonging to the human family." [5] In short, she was willing to do everything required of American citizens except fight.

Justice Butler, speaking for a majority of the Court, which included Chief Justice Taft and Justices McReynolds, Stone, Sutherland, and Van Devanter, reversed the decision of the court of appeals and reinstated the decree of the district court denying her position for naturalization. According to Justice Butler, aliens had only such rights to become citizens as Congress conferred upon them by statute and subject to the qualifications prescribed, and the "duty of citizens by force of arms to defend our government" against enemies when necessity should arise was declared to be "a fundamental principle of the Constitution." [6] Beliefs and behavior "indicating a disposition to hinder in the performance of that duty are subjects of inquiry under the statutory provisions governing naturalization and are of vital importance." [7] Moreover, "the influence of conscientious objectors against the use of military force in defense of the principles of our Government is apt to be more detrimental than their mere refusal to bear arms." [8] Thus "the fact that, by reason of sex, age, or other cause, they may be unfit to serve does not lessen their purpose or power to influence others." [9] Some seventeen years later, then-Chief Justice Stone indicated that he had concurred in the *Schwimmer* decision because he believed that petitioner Schwimmer not only would have refused to bear arms in defense of her country but would also have resisted such war efforts.[10]

Three Justices, Brandeis, Holmes, and Sanford, dissented.[11] Holmes, with Brandeis concurring, thought that the petitioner's pacifist views did not affect her ability to take the required oath of allegiance because she was a woman over fifty years of age at the time when the case reached the Supreme Court. It is interesting to note that neither the majority nor the minority considered seriously whether the oath of allegiance in fact required a pledge to bear arms in defense of the United States.

Mrs. Schwimmer was in a curious legal position as a result of this decision. By reason of her age and sex, she was not likely ever to be called on to bear arms as a citizen, but as an alien applying for citizenship, she was required to swear her willingness to take up arms in defense of the United States. Indeed, as an alien applying for citizenship, she was required to abjure all conscientious objection to combatant military service, while a citizen-member of a pacifist religious sect was entitled to an exemption on such grounds under the 1917 Selective Service Act. Since Mrs. Schwimmer was not affiliated with a pacifist religious sect, however, she would not have qualified for exemption under the World War I act even had she been a citizen called to service at that time.

Another alien applying for citizenship raised the issue whether even potential conscientious objection to a particular war on moral and religious grounds would bar him from taking the required oath of allegiance to "support and defend the Constitution and laws of the United States against all enemies, foreign and domestic." A Canadian immigrant, Douglas Macintosh, petitioned the federal District Court in Connecticut for naturalization in 1925. Since the petitioner would not promise in advance to bear arms in defense of the United States unless he believed the war to be morally justified, that court found that he was not attached to the principles of the Constitution and was, therefore, ineligible to take the oath of allegiance. The Circuit Court of Appeals reversed the decision of the District Court and directed that the petitioner be admitted to citizenship.[12] The government then sought and secured review by the United States Supreme Court (*United States v. Macintosh*).[13]

Macintosh was a Baptist minister, a professor of theology at the Yale Divinity School and Chaplain of the Graduate School, and had served as a chaplain with the Canadian Army in World War I. His personal character and conduct were beyond reproach, and he was not a pacifist. But in response to question 22 of the preliminary form for naturalization, Macintosh would not promise to support the government, right or wrong, in any dispute which might arise or to take up arms in its defense without knowing the cause for which the country might go to war. In a hearing before the District Court, he explained that he was ready to give to the United States all the allegiance he could give to any country, but that he could not put such allegiance above his allegiance to God. He did not anticipate a conflict between the two allegiances, but he preferred not to make any absolute promise about future wars.

Upon the basis of this reservation of final moral judgment by Macintosh, the Supreme Court denied his petition by a one-vote margin (5–4). Justice Sutherland, himself a naturalized citizen, spoke for a majority which included Justices Butler, McReynolds, Roberts, and Van Devanter, and found the case ruled by the *Schwimmer* decision. The petitioner, Sutherland argued, was unwilling "to leave the question of his future military service to the wisdom of

Congress where it belongs, and where every . . . citizen is obliged to leave it."[14] When he sought to put his allegiance to the will of God above his allegiance to the government, he meant "to make *his own interpretation* of the will of God the decisive test which shall conclude the government and stay its hand."[15] But "government must go forward upon the assumption . . . that unqualified allegiance to the nation and submission . . . to the laws of the land . . . are not inconsistent with the will of God."[16] The petitioner's attitude was, in effect, "a refusal to take the oath of allegiance except in an altered form."[17]

Chief Justice Hughes, joined by Justices Brandeis, Holmes, and Stone, dissented.[18] He pointed out that the question was not whether naturalization is a privilege, or whether Congress has the power to fix the conditions upon which the privilege is granted, or whether Congress may compel service in the armed forces at its discretion in time of war, or whether Congress may exact a promise to bear arms as a condition of its grant of naturalization. In his view, the question was a narrower one, namely, whether Congress had in fact exacted such a promise. According to Hughes, the implication of such an exaction could be implied neither literally nor historically from the prescribed oath of allegiance. The naturalization oath was substantially the same as that required of federal officeholders, and this oath was not interpreted to disqualify conscientious objectors to war from holding office. Moreover, by long-established practice, Congress had excused from combatant military service those whose religious convictions opposed it.

Hughes sharply distinguished the domain of government from the forum of conscience:

> When one's belief collides with the power of the state, the latter is supreme within its sphere, and submission or punishment follows. But in the forum of conscience, duty

> to a moral power higher than the state has always been maintained.[19]

Freedom of conscience "itself implies respect for an innate conviction of paramount duty," and the battle for religious liberty has been won "upon the very ground of the supremacy of conscience within its proper field."[20] What that field is

> presents in part a question of constitutional law and also, in part, one of legislative policy in avoiding unnecessary clashes with the dictates of conscience. There is abundant room for enforcing the requisite authority of law as it is enacted and requires obedience and for maintaining the conception of the supremacy of law as essential to orderly government without demanding that either citizens or applicants for citizenship shall assume by oath an obligation to regard allegiance to God as subordinate to allegiance to civil power.[21]

Accordingly, Hughes found no evidence that Congress intended to reverse its traditional policy in prescribing the general terms of the naturalization oath.

Justice Sutherland, like Justice Butler, rested the Court's decision without argument on the absolute duty of citizens to bear arms in defense of the United States; the minority in *Macintosh* challenged whether this duty could be inferred from the Congressional requirement of an oath of allegiance "to support and defend the Constitution and laws of the United States against all enemies, foreign and domestic." Sutherland thought that aliens applying for citizenship should be willing to profess an act of faith in the wisdom of Congressional exercise of its war-making power; Hughes thought that Congress had not exacted such a profession of faith and was prepared to admit sympathetically the possibility of a conflict between an individual citizen's moral judgment and a legal command by Congress. Ironically, Macintosh's troubles were largely of his own making. He was not a pacifist and had conditioned his allegiance only in the way most morally conscious citizens have always done, namely, he would not promise in advance to obey a legal command in serious conflict with moral conscience. His mistake was to make explicit a condition which most morally conscious citizens would have regarded as already implicit. Virtue is thus not always its own reward.

The political heterodoxy of Mrs. Schwimmer did not enhance her chances of qualifying for citizenship in the conservative and xenophobic 'twenties, and Macintosh's appeal to the supremacy of moral conscience over legal command sounded to Sutherland and his brethren of the majority like a call to anarchy. After the rise of Nazism and the Second World War, however, the court reviewed again the requirement of an alien applying for citizenship who was a conscientious objector to war to take the prescribed oath of allegiance. This time the climate of public and legal opinion was more favorable to such claims of conscience, and the Supreme Court ruled in favor of the applicant. Girouard, a native of Canada and a Seventh-Day Adventist, filed a petition for naturalization in the District Court of Massachusetts in 1943. He indicated his willingness to take the oath of allegiance and to accept noncombatant service in the armed forces in defense of the country but not to bear arms. Although the District Court admitted him to citizenship, the Circuit Court of Appeals reversed on the authority of *Schwimmer* and *Macintosh*.[22] Upon review, the Supreme Court in turn reversed the decision of the Court of Appeals and reinstated that of the District Court (*Girouard v. United States*).[23]

Justice Douglas, speaking for the new majority, echoed

the argument of dissenting Chief Justice Hughes in *Macintosh.* The question was one of statutory construction: the oath of allegiance did not specify a promise to bear arms, and the refusal to bear arms was no sign of disloyalty. Girouard's religious scruples would not have disqualified him from holding federal office, and there was "not the slightest suggestion that Congress set a stricter standard for aliens seeking admission to citizenship than it did for officials who make and enforce the laws of the nation and administer its affairs." [24]

Moreover, Douglas appealed to the Selective Service Act of 1940, in which Congress recognized that a conscientious objector to war may adequately discharge his obligations as a citizen by rendering noncombatant service, and to the Second War Powers Act of 1942, in which Congress relaxed certain requirements of naturalization for aliens who served honorably in the armed forces during World War II, whether as combatants or noncombatants. He deemed it a strange construction of Congressional intent to say that a substantially identical oath of allegiance demanded more of conscientious objectors who did not have the opportunity of noncombatant military service than of those who did. According to Douglas,

> The struggle for religious liberty has through the centuries been an effort to accommodate the demands of the state to the conscience of the individual. The victory for freedom of thought recorded in our Bill of Rights recognized that in the domain of conscience there is a moral power higher than the state.[25]

From the fact that Congress failed to overrule *Schwimmer* and *Macintosh,* Douglas refused to draw any conclusion: the inactivity of Congress was judged to be "as consistent with a desire to leave the problem fluid as . . . with an adoption by silence of the rule of those cases." [26]

And the affirmative action taken by Congress in 1942 denied any inference which otherwise might be drawn from its silence when the new Naturalization Act of 1940 re-enacted the oath in its pre-existing form.

Chief Justice Stone, joined by Justices Frankfurter and Reed, dissented.[27] Although he himself had opposed the statutory construction of the prescribed oath of allegiance in *Macintosh,* Stone argued that Congress had subsequently adopted and affirmed that construction. Despite persistent attempts in six successive congresses, the national legislature had never amended the law, and the Naturalization Act of 1940 made no change in the oath. Stone also interpreted the Second War Powers Act of 1942 only as a special favor and a recognition that most noncombatants could take the prescribed oath.

Douglas was joined, not surprisingly, by Justices Black, Murphy, and Rutledge, and by Justice Burton, who had replaced Justice Roberts. This change in the personnel of the Court was of crucial importance because Roberts had voted for the government with the majority in *Macintosh.* Moreover, despite the shift of Stone, the dissenters were weakened by the absence of one of their usual allies, Justice Jackson, who took no part in the case because he was serving as American prosecutor at the Nuremberg war trials.

The *Girouard* decision ended the anomalous legal situation in which a citizen who was a conscientious objector to war could qualify for exemption from combatant military service, but an alien with the same beliefs could not qualify for citizenship. In 1950, the Court extended the coverage of that decision in the case of a conscientious objector to even noncombatant military service (*Cohnstaedt v. Immigration and Naturalization Service*).[28] Martin Cohnstaedt, a German-born immigrant and a Quaker, was denied his petition for naturalization because he would not promise to accept noncombatant military service or even employment as a civilian in war industries.[29] He was willing, however, to perform medical service as a civilian, and the Supreme Court *per curiam* reversed the lower court ruling on the authority of *Girouard* (Chief Justice Vinson, Justice Clark, and Justice Reed, dissenting).

Since there were no opinions in *Cohnstaedt*, there is no way of knowing exactly why the justices voted as they did. But Justices Black, Burton, and Douglas voted for Cohnstaedt, as they had for Girouard, and their position seems to require no additional explanation. Justice Frankfurter's switch from dissent in *Girouard* to concurrence in *Cohnstaedt* was probably influenced by the principle of *stare decisis,* and the attitude of Justices Jackson and Minton may have been similar to Frankfurter's. Justice Reed was consistent both with his dissent in *Girouard* and his general unreceptiveness to claims of conscientious objectors to public laws, and Chief Justice Vinson's attitude may have been similar. Justice Clark, who later wrote the *Sicurella* and *Seeger* opinions, may have judged only that the public interest in exacting at least noncombatant military service from prospective citizens was of moderate enough order to sustain the requirement.

Justices of the majority in *Schwimmer* and *Macintosh* thought that the public interest in the willingness of prospective citizens to bear arms in any military conflict was of a high order, or at least so they seemed to say. Moreover, the issue for them was one of obedience to law, and they were unsympathetic to any exceptions for conscientious objectors. Justices of the majority in *Girouard,* however, rated the same public interest low with respect to universal pacifists. The dissenting justices in that case did not dispute the rank of the public interest at stake, but they were more deferential to the inactive role of the national legislature than the majority because of Congress' failure to amend the naturalization laws after *Macintosh.*

CONSCIENTIOUS OBJECTION AND WAR PROTESTS

The cases of conscientious objection to military service which we have considered have involved claims to immunity from coercion to act against conscience. Individuals and groups, however, may also claim a right to act according to conscience, and one such claim is to the expression and communication of a religious or moral viewpoint about war or a particular war. Although there were no federal cases before Vietnam which dealt with a conflict between an asserted right to express a specifically religious or moral viewpoint about war and an asserted national-security interest in its suppression, there were federal decisions which involved freedom of political speech in such circumstances.

Claims of conscience to the expression of a religious or moral viewpoint have also run into conflict with asserted interests of state and local governments in domestic public order, but these will be considered in the next chapter.[30] Here claims to freedom of political speech in the context of national-security interests will be introduced only to indicate what issues would be involved if those claims pertained specifically to rights of religious or moral conscience as well as generally to freedom of political expression. Indeed, every sincerely motivated and morally responsible claim to freedom of speech is in some sense a claim of conscience, and, conversely, every claim of conscience asserted on the basis of a right to freedom of speech may be viewed as an effort to transfer the claim of conscience to the morally neutral ground of constitutionally protected speech.

During World War I, Schenck and others were convicted of violating the 1917 Espionage Act by fomenting insubordination in the armed forces of the United States and by obstructing the draft. They printed and distributed leaflets which attacked the war effort and military conscription; the leaflets called on their readers not to be intimidated by a conscription act which violated the Thirteenth Amendment and to assert their rights. Justice Holmes, speaking for a unanimous Court, upheld the convictions (*Schenck v. United States*):

> The question in every case is whether the words used are used in such circumstances and are of such a nature as to create a clear and present danger that they will bring about the substantive evils that Congress has a right to prevent. It is a question of proximity and degree. When a nation is at war, many things which might be said in time of peace are such a hindrance to its effort that their utterance will not be endured so long as men fight, and that no court could regard them as protected by any constitutional right.[31]

Measured against this standard, Holmes concluded that the defendants had created a "clear and present danger" to national security interests and displayed the requisite intention to do so.

The Espionage Act of 1918 went far beyond the 1917 Act and made punishable any "disloyal, profane, scurrilous, or abusive language about the form of government, the Constitution, soldiers and sailors, flag or uniform of the armed forces" and any "word or act [favoring] the cause of the German Empire . . . or [opposing] the cause of the United States." [32] This law and its application were upheld by the Supreme Court in *Abrams v. United States*.[33] Abrams had distributed two leaflets which attacked Allied and American intervention in Russia after the October Revolution, told workers in ammunition factories that they were producing bullets to murder their fellow-workers, and exhorted all workers to a general strike. Justice Holmes, with Justice Brandeis, dissented principally on the ground that the statute of 1918 required proof, not shown by the government in the case of Abrams, of an actual intention not only to curtail war production but also "by such curtailment to cripple or hinder the United States in the prosecution of the war." [34] Holmes also argued—perhaps inconsistently with *Schenck*—that Abrams posed no demonstrably clear and present danger to the American war effort.

Both the *Schenck* and *Abrams* decisions involved questions of statutory construction rather than of constitutional interpretation. However, the "clear and present danger" formula was later accepted by the Court as the constitutional criterion to distinguish lawful from unlawful suppression of speech. This formula, of course, is no objective slide rule by which to measure the facts of particular cases, but it does place a stringent burden of proof on the government to justify its suppression of speech. In the words of Holmes' dissent in *Abrams,* American constitutional preference of free speech over its suppression is based on the proposition "that the best test of truth is the power of the thought to get itself accepted in the competition of the market." [35]

The involvement of the United States in Vietnam, unlike that in the two World Wars and in Korea, has provoked strong moral dissent and protest. One method of protesting that involvement has been the burning of draft cards, to which Congress reacted in 1965 by amending the Universal Military Training and Service Act of 1948 to provide penalties for the willful mutilation of Selective Service registration and classification certificates.[36] On March 3, 1966, David O'Brien, an opponent of the Vietnamese war on moral grounds, burned his registration certificate on the steps of the South Boston Federal Courthouse. He was indicted and convicted of willfully mutilating the certificate in violation of the 1965 amendment. When he appealed his conviction, the United States Court of Appeals declared the 1965 amendment an unconstitutional abridgment of free speech, but upheld O'Brien's conviction insofar as it included the lesser offense of non-possession of his registration certificate.[37] Both O'Brien and the government appealed to the Supreme Court, which granted certiorari.[38]

Chief Justice Warren, speaking for eight members of the Court, overruled the Court of Appeals and reinstated the decision of the District Court (*United States v. O'Brien*).[39] Since there is "nothing necessarily expressive" about the destruction of draft cards, Warren held that the 1965 amendment did not directly abridge freedom of speech.[40] But if there had been a "speech" element in O'Brien's act, its restriction would have been justified by a "sufficiently important governmental interest."[41] Such restriction would be justified, in Warren's view, if it falls within the constitutional power of the government, if it furthers an important or substantial governmental interest, if the governmental interest is unrelated to the suppression of speech, and if the restriction is no greater than essential to furtherance of the governmental interest.

Warren pointed out several ways in which registration certificates implemented Congress' power to raise armies: (1) they provide proof of an individual's registration; (2) the information they contain about the registrant's number and the address of the local board facilitates communication between the registrant and his board; and (3) they remind the registrant of his duty to notify the local board of any change of address. Moreover, mutilation would assist false representation of the registrant's status. The 1965 amendment protected "overlapping but not identical governmental interests" in the possession of draft cards because mutilation would be a "deliberate rendering of certificates unavailable for the purposes which they may serve," and because the mutilation of any certificate, whether the registrant's or another's, was prohibited.[42] Warren dismissed any judicial inquiry into the motives of Congress in adopting the amendment as inappropriate beyond its inevitable effect or transparent character.

Justice Harlan concurred but reserved the case where, although the Court's criteria were met, an enactment had the effect of preventing a "speaker" from reaching a significant audience with which he could not otherwise lawfully communicate.[43] Justice Douglas dissented because he felt that "the underlying and basic problem in this case . . . [is] whether conscription is permissible in the absence of a declaration of war."[44] He would have accordingly restored the case to the Court's calendar for reargument of that question.

Perhaps the most celebrated case involving dissent from the Vietnamese war was the trial of Dr. Benjamin Spock and his four codefendants, William Sloane Coffin, Michael Ferber, Mitchell Goodman, and Marcus Raskin, for conspiracy to obstruct the draft. After a lengthy trial, all but Raskin were convicted. The Circuit Court of Appeals, however, reversed the convictions on other than First Amendment grounds, summarily acquitting Ferber and Spock and ordering a new trial for Coffin and Goodman (*Spock v. United States*).[45] One judge would have relied on the First Amendment to acquit all the defendants. The government did not appeal the decision, and it did not retry Coffin and Goodman.

O'Brien argued that burning his draft card constituted symbolic speech, and the Spock defendants claimed immunity for their counsel to young men against the draft. But other dissenters on the Vietnamese war have gone beyond even potential claims of free speech. Some activists have poured animal blood on selective service files, others have burned them. Such activists may seek immunity for morally motivated acts against the use of the draft to support the war; their claims will be considered more fully in the next chapter as will those of other morally motivated dissenters opposed to domestic policies.[46] It should be noted here, however, that in the spring of 1970 the Supreme Court refused without dissent to review the convictions of several Roman Catholic activists for disturbing and destroying draft files.[47]

Had the activity of Schenck and Abrams been motivated by religious or moral considerations, their claims would have involved a general duty to oppose armed American intervention in Russia. To the extent that such a duty were perceived as specific rather than general because ordinary political processes were inadequate, at least in the short run, to redress the alleged evil, the claim might have been one of a moderate rank. Such was also the moral position of Dr. Spock and his fellow defendants. In the case of O'Brien and of other draft-card burners, the claims were in part explicitly of a moral character and directly reflected a despair with ordinary means of political advocacy and mobilization. (O'Brien himself was attacked by the crowd at the South Boston courthouse when he burned his draft-registration certificate.) In none of these cases, however, would the perceived moral obligations of the war protestors be of the highest rank because even activities perceived as relatively specific moral duties do not oblige individuals absolutely, but only if circumstances permit. Had matches or publicity been unavailable to O'Brien, for instance, presumably he would have felt himself guilty of no moral fault for failing to burn his draft card.

The public interest in national security against the claims of Schenck and Abrams was rated high by the Court, although Holmes and Brandeis dissented in the case of Abrams. The public interest in national security against the claim of Dr. Spock was rated low by the Court of Appeals. In the case of O'Brien, the court rated as moderate the public interest in the administrative convenience of maintaining registration certificates intact, and even Justice Douglas would not have disputed that rating if Congress had declared war or if the "war" were otherwise constitutional. Moreover, to the extent that war protestors by their "civil disobedience," that is, by their disobeying a particular law in order to protest the military activity or foreign policy of the government, implicitly challenge the legal system itself, courts are likely to rate high the public interest in national security and in internal public order, whatever the moral obligation perceived by the civil disobedients. At least the Court seemed to indicate such an attitude when it recently ruled without review and without dissent against two petitions for certorari by draft-file disrupters.

CONSCIENTIOUS OBJECTION AND STATE PENALTIES

Conscientious objectors to war have also been confronted with certain liabilities imposed by the states. The State of California required all students at its university to take a course in military science and tactics, and Hamilton and other minors who were conscientious objectors to war registered at the university in the fall of 1933. These students petitioned the university for exemption from the required course in military science because of their religious objection to war and to military training. When their petition was denied, and the Regents of the University refused to make the military-science course optional or to exempt them, they were suspended. Thereupon, they and their parents applied to the Supreme Court of California for a writ of mandate to compel the university to admit them without requiring of them the course in military science. When the writ was denied, they appealed to the United States Supreme Court for review under the guarantees of the Fourteenth Amendment.

The Supreme Court unanimously ruled against the appellants (*Hamilton v. Regents of State of California*).[48] Justice Butler, speaking for the Court, found that the appellants had not been deprived of their "privileges" as citizens of the United States because the "privilege" of attending the University of California had been conferred by the state, or of the "liberty" protected by the due-process clause because California did not require the appellants to attend the university. Thus "the fact that they are able to pay their way in this university but not in any other institution in California is without significance upon any constitutional or other question here involved." [49] Butler then cited approvingly *dicta* from *Schwimmer* and *Macintosh* on the duty of citizens to defend the government by force of arms against all enemies.

In a concurring opinion, Justice Cardozo, joined by Justices Brandeis and Stone, also argued that the appellants had not been required "in any absolute or peremptory way to join in courses of instruction that will fit them to bear arms." [50] The policy of the state requiring students who attend an institution of higher learning maintained at state expense to take such courses may be condemned as unfair to conscientious objectors, but Cardozo thought that more must be shown to upset the statute. Indeed, "never in our history has the notion been accepted or even . . . advanced that acts thus indirectly related to service in the camp or field are so tied to the practice of religion as to be exempt in law or in morals from regulation by the state." [51] If the rights of conscientious objectors were extended to include exemption from a course in military science required at a state university, they might also "refuse to pay taxes in furtherance of a war . . . or in furtherance of any other end condemned by conscience as irreligious or immoral." [52]

It is clear that both Justice Butler and Justice Cardozo considered attendance at a state university to be a privilege rather than a right of citizens of that state. Accordingly, a state might reasonably condition attendance at its university on a requirement to take a course in military science. The growth of the college-student population and state-university systems, however, may render this argument less convincing today. In *Brown v. Board of Education,* the Supreme Court declared in 1954 of primary and secondary education that "education is perhaps the most important function of state and local government," that it is "the very foundation of good citizenship," and that "such an opportunity, where the state has undertaken to provide it, is a right which must be made available to all on equal terms." [53] It requires no great imagination to think that what the Court there said of primary and secondary education may be applicable today to higher education.

Hamilton's conscientious objection was not to the performance of the primary act which he considered immoral, namely, the waging of war and military service, but rather to cooperation with such activity by taking a course in military science prescribed at a state university. Justice Butler made this point when he remarked that students required by the Regents' order to take the prescribed course were not obliged to "serve in the army or in any sense become a part of the military establishment of the United States." [54] Justice Cardozo was even more explicit: the prescribed course was "without the duty or the pledge of service" and only "indirectly related to service in the camp or field." [55] But since there was no indication that Hamilton and the others falsely represented the state of their consciences, their claims to perceive courses in military science as too closely connected with war activities to permit them morally to participate should have been accepted at face value. This, of course, would still leave open the question of the strength of the countervailing national-security interest against the recognition of their claims.

In another case ten years later, the Supreme Court of Illinois refused to allow Clyde Summers, a conscientious objector to war, to practice law before the courts of Illinois because of what the court described as an inability to take in good faith the required oath to support the state constitution. The justices of the Illinois Supreme Court ruled that officers charged with the administration of justice were obliged to take an oath to support the state constitution and interpreted the oath to require a willingness to perform military service in time of war.[56] Since the petitioner was unable to take such an oath, the Illinois court reasoned, he lacked the moral character and fitness to function as an officer of the Illinois courts.

By a one-vote margin (5–4), the United States Supreme Court affirmed the decision of the Illinois Supreme Court (In re *Summers*).[57] The *Summers* decision antedated that of *Girouard,* and Justice Reed argued for the majority that the Illinois requirement that lawyers profess a willingness to perform military service in time of war did not violate the principle of religious freedom secured by the Fourteenth Amendment against state action "when a like interpretation of a similar oath as to the federal Constitution bars an alien from national citizenship." [58] Reed was joined by Chief Justice Stone and Justices Frankfurter, Jackson, and Roberts. Since Stone dissented in *Girouard,* his adhesion to the conservative bloc in this case may have also been influenced by the failure of Congress to amend the naturalization laws after *Macintosh.*

Justice Black, joined by Justices Douglas, Murphy, and Rutledge, dissented.[59] Although Black maintained that Illinois had the constitutional power to draft conscientious objectors for war duty and to punish them for a refusal to serve as soldiers, he thought that a state could not constitutionally use a test oath of religious beliefs to bar Summers from practicing law. Black also pointed out that the Illinois constitution itself excused from militia duty persons "exempted by the laws of the United States," and that Summers had been classified as a conscientious objector under the Selective Training and Service Act of 1940. Thus the likelihood that the petitioner would ever be called to serve in a war was said to have "little more reality than an imaginary quantity in mathematics." [60] In view of the narrowness of the majority and the subsequent reversal of *Schwimmer* and *Macintosh* by *Girouard,* the present validity of the *Summers* decision is doubtful.

In both these cases, conscientious objectors to war claimed rights incidental to the performance of what they perceived as absolute religious duties. There were no claims that the States of California and Illinois directly coerced Hamilton and Summers, respectively, to act against their consciences, but rather that denial of the educational opportunities of a state university at lower financial cost and of the practice of law would indirectly coerce the conscientious objectors to do so. Their claims were accordingly of a moderately high order. Against their claims, the public interest in national security would seem to be of a low order, especially since the claimants would have qualified for exemption from combatant military service under the Selective Service Act of 1917 and all military service under the Act of 1940. Yet a unanimous Court overruled Hamilton's claim and this rejection reflected, in part, a narrow conception of a citizen's "right" to attend a state university. Of the majority in the *Summers* case, at least Justices Frankfurter, Jackson, Reed, and Roberts were consistent with their general philosophy of wide judicial deference to legislative judgments by states in matters of civil liberties and of economic regulation.

NOTES

1. 54 Stat. 1157, 8 U.S.C. #735 (b).
2. *Schwimmer v. U.S.*, 27 F.2d 742 (1928).
3. *U.S. v. Schwimmer,* 279 U.S. 644 (1929).
4. *Ibid.*, p. 647.
5. *Ibid.*, p. 648.
6. *Ibid.*, p. 650.
7. *Ibid.*, p. 651.
8. *Ibid.*

9. *Ibid.*
10. *Girouard v. U.S.* 328 U.S. 61, 72 (1946).
11. *U.S. v. Schwimmer,* p. 653 (Holmes with Brandeis) and p. 655 (Sanford).
12. *Macintosh v. U.S.,* 42 F.2d 845 (1930).
13. *U.S. v. Macintosh,* 283 U.S. 605 (1931).
14. *Ibid.,* p. 624.
15. *Ibid.,* p. 625; italics in original.
16. *Ibid.*
17. *Ibid.,* p. 626.
18. *Ibid.,* p. 627.
19. *Ibid.,* p. 633.
20. *Ibid.,* p. 634.
21. *Ibid.*
22. *U.S. v. Girouard,* 149 F.2d 760 (1945).
23. *Girouard v. U.S.,* 328 U.S. 61 (1946).
24. *Ibid.,* pp. 65–66.
25. *Ibid.,* p. 68.
26. *Ibid.,* p. 70.
27. *Ibid.*
28. *Cohnstaedt v. Immigration and Naturalization Service,* 339 U.S. 901 (1950).
29. *Cohnstaedt v. Immigration and Naturalization Service,* 167 Kan. 456, 207 P.2d 425 (1949).
30. *Infra,* pp. 82–90.
31. *Schenck v. U.S.,* 249 U.S. 47, 52 (1919).
32. 40 Stat. 553.
33. *Abrams v. U.S.,* 250 U.S. 616 (1919).
34. *Ibid.,* p. 626.
35. *Ibid.,* p. 630.
36. 50 U.S.C. App. #462 (b).
37. *O'Brien v. U.S.,* 376 F.2d 538 (1967).
38. *U.S. v. O'Brien,* 389 U.S. 814 (1967).
39. *U.S. v. O'Brien,* 391 U.S. 367 (1968).
40. *Ibid.,* p. 375.
41. *Ibid.,* p. 376.
42. *Ibid.,* p. 380.
43. *Ibid.,* p. 388.
44. *Ibid.,* p. 389.
45. *Spock v. U.S.,* 416 F.2d 165 (1969).
46. *Infra,* pp. 90–93.
47. *Berrigan v. U.S.,* 397 U.S. 909 (1970) and *Moylan v. U.S.,* 397 U.S. 910 (1970); cf. 417 F.2d 1009 and 1002 (1969).
48. *Hamilton v. Regents of the University of California,* 293 U.S. 245 (1934).
49. *Ibid.,* p. 262.
50. *Ibid.,* p. 266.

51. *Ibid.*, p. 267.
52. *Ibid.*, p. 268.
53. *Brown v. Board of Education of Topeka,* 347 U.S. 483, 493 (1954).
54. *Hamilton,* p. 259.
55. *Ibid.*, p. 267.
56. Since the proceedings were not treated as judicial by the Illinois Supreme Court, there was no official record. In re *Summers,* 325 U.S. 561, 563 (1945).
57. In re *Summers,* 325 U.S. 561 (1945).
58. *Ibid.*, p. 573.
59. *Ibid.*
60. *Ibid.*, p. 577.

4

Conscience and Public Order

BESIDES CONFLICTING with national security interests, claims of conscience may also run counter to various interests in domestic public order, interests which have traditionally been protected by state and local governments rather than by the federal government. Although the United States Supreme Court before the Civil War held that the Bill of Rights of the federal Constitution was not applicable to the states,[1] passage of the Fourteenth Amendment had the effect of nationalizing the First Amendment. In *Gitlow v. New York,* the Court opened the door to comprehensive review of state action affecting the personal liberties embodied in the First Amendment.[2] The Court there assumed "that freedom of speech and of the press—which are protected by the First Amendment from abridgement by Congress—are among the liberties protected by the due process clause of the Fourteenth Amendment from impairment by the states."[3] In 1940 the Court extended the protection of the Fourteenth Amendment to guarantee freedom of religious exercise against infringement by state action, and in 1947 the Court completed the absorption of

First Amendment freedoms under the Fourteenth by interpreting the due-process clause to preclude an "establishment of religion" by the states.[4]

PREVENTION OF VIOLENCE

As we have seen in the *Schenck* and *Abrams* cases which involved national security interests, every sincerely motivated and morally responsible claim to freedom of speech is in some sense a claim of conscience, and, conversely, every claim of conscience asserting a right to freedom of speech may be seen as an attempt to transfer that claim to the morally neutral ground of constitutionally protected speech.[5] For our purposes, however, we shall consider only those claims to freedom of speech which are explicitly concerned with the expression of a religious or moral point of view and shall treat them formally as claims of conscience.

The most serious interest in public order at the local level which may run counter to the rights of individuals to freedom of speech—religious or other, of course—is breach of the peace or the threat of such breach. A case of this sort specifically involving religious speech was reviewed for the first time by the Supreme Court in 1940 (*Cantwell v. Connecticut*).[6] Jesse Cantwell, a Jehovah's Witness, was arrested and convicted in New Haven, Connecticut, on a charge of breach of the peace. In the course of sidewalk proselytizing, he stopped two men and with their permission played the record "Enemies," a record which attacked the Roman Catholic Church and all organized religion. The two men, Roman Catholics, were incensed by the content of the record, and they told the defendant to go away. The defendant was not offensive to the listeners, entered into no argument with them, and upon their objection picked up his materials and walked away. The defendant was not convicted of violating a statute which specifically regulated street discussion of religious affairs in order to prevent disorders or one which specifically regulated the playing of phonographs on streets in the interests of the public's comfort or privacy, but of the common-law offense of breach of the peace.

Speaking for a unanimous Court, Justice Roberts overturned the conviction. Although he admitted that the common-law offense of breach of the peace included not only violent acts but also acts or words likely to produce violence in others, he argued that such provocative language, to be considered an invitation to a breach of the peace, must consist of profane, indecent, or abusive remarks directed to the person of the hearer. In the instant case, he found no assault or bodily harm, no truculent bearing, no intentional discourtesy, and no personal abuse. Indeed, the defendant, when challenged, simply picked up his materials and walked away. Nor was the sound of the phonograph shown to have disturbed residents of the street, to have drawn a crowd, or to have impeded traffic. Justice Roberts acknowledged that the contents of the record, not unnaturally, aroused animosity, but he ruled that, in the absence of a statute narrowly drawn to define and punish specific conduct constituting a clear and present danger to a substantial interest of the public, the defendant's communication raised no menace to public peace and order which would render him liable to conviction of the common-law offense of breach of the peace, and his action was accordingly protected by the First and Fourteenth Amendments of the federal Constitution.

Two years later, the Court upheld the conviction of another Jehovah's Witness on a charge of breaching the peace (*Chaplinsky v. New Hampshire*).[7] Chaplinsky was distributing religious literature on a Saturday afternoon at a busy intersection in Rochester, New Hampshire, and denouncing organized religion as a "racket." [8] When complaints were lodged with the city marshal, he told the complainants that Chaplinsky's activities were lawful, but he also warned the Witness that the crowd was getting restless. A disturbance ensued, and the traffic officer on duty at the intersection started with Chaplinsky to the police station but did not inform the Witness that he was under arrest or about to be arrested. On the way to the station, they met the city marshal, who had been advised that a riot was in progress and was en route to the scene. The marshal repeated his warning to Chaplinsky, and the latter responded by calling the marshal a "damned racketeer" and a "damned Fascist." [9] (Chaplinsky claimed that the marshal initiated the use of invective language.) Thereupon Chaplinsky was arrested and convicted of a breach of the peace under a New Hampshire statute which made it a crime to "address any offensive, derisive, or annoying word to any other person who is lawfully in any street or other public place." [10] The state courts had previously held the statute applicable only to the use in a public place of face-to-face words likely to cause a breach of the peace by the person to whom the words were addressed.

Speaking for a unanimous Court, Justice Murphy upheld the conviction:

> There are certain well-defined and narrowly limited classes of speech, the prevention and punishment of which have never been thought to raise any constitutional problem. These include the lewd and obscene, the profane, the libelous, and the insulting or "fighting" words—those which by their very utterance inflict injury or tend to incite an immediate breach of the peace.[11]

Murphy added that the state court's exclusion of evidence which Chaplinsky sought to introduce to show provocation and prove the truth of his statements about the city marshal was constitutionally unobjectionable. Since the state court was competent to decide what constituted a defense or mitigated punishment under the statute, the statute on its face and as applied did not violate the First and Fourteenth Amendments of the federal Constitution.

In 1948 a federal district court dismissed an action by Jehovah's Witnesses against a sheriff to restrain and redress deprivation of rights they claimed to freedom of speech, assembly, and worship.[12] It found, *inter alia,* that the sheriff acted "within the scope of his authority and properly" in denying the Witnesses access to the town in the belief that such a course was necessary to prevent riot and bloodshed.[13] But the Court of Appeals, reversing the decision of the lower court (*Sellers v. Johnson*), found it "somewhat difficult" to accept the theory "that a group of individuals may be deprived of their constitutional rights of assembly, speech, and worship if they have become so unpopular with, or offensive to, the people of the community that their presence in a public park to deliver a Bible lecture is likely to result in riot or bloodshed." [14] The Court of Appeals did not rest its decision on this point, however, because it judged that there was "no substantial evidence" to support the conclusion that the proposed meetings actually constituted any serious danger to the peace and welfare of the community; it regarded the circumstances of the case as fully "consistent with the hypothesis that the [threatened] disorder was due to the failure of the local and state authorities to police the park." [15] The Supreme Court denied certiorari.[16]

Thus there were two main issues in the *Sellers* case: an issue of fact, namely, whether the dangers of violence and disorder were grave and imminent; and an issue of law, namely, to what extent local authorities were constitutionally obliged to protect the speaker of unpopular views. Two subsequent cases, *Terminiello v. Chicago* and *Feiner v. New York,* which did not involve claims of conscience to the expression of religious or moral viewpoints but rather claims by citizens to the expression of political or social viewpoints, presented both these issues again to the

Supreme Court for review.[17] In the first case Terminiello "vigorously, if not viciously," criticized various political and racial groups, and a surging, howling mob gathered in protest outside the auditorium in which he was speaking to his followers.[18] He called his adversaries "slimy scum," "snakes," "bedbugs," and the like.[19] Those outside the auditorium yelled "Fascists, Hitlers" at those attending the meeting, tried to tear clothes off those who entered, broke 28 windows, and threw stink bombs.[20] Terminiello was arrested and convicted of breaching the peace.

By a one-vote margin (5–4), the Court reversed the conviction. Speaking for the majority, Justice Douglas did not reach the questions whether Terminiello uttered "fighting words," whether epithets uttered to a favorable audience inside the auditorium could be considered provocative of a hostile audience outside, whether the police were able to control the disturbance, or to what extent the police were obliged to protect Terminiello and his followers. The decision rested on the narrow ground of the trial judge's charge to the jury, which defined "breach of the peace" to include speech which "stirs the public to anger, invites dispute, brings about a condition of unrest or creates a disturbance." [21] The Court struck down the ordinance, thus broadly construed, considering it to be a function of free speech to invite dispute and ruling that free speech "may indeed best serve its high purpose when it induces a condition of unrest, creates dissatisfaction with conditions as they are, or even stirs people to anger." [22] Terminiello's speech was accordingly held entitled to constitutional protection against punishment "unless shown likely to produce a clear and present danger of a serious substantive evil that rises far above public inconvenience, annoyance, or unrest." [23]

The *Terminiello* decision rested on technical grounds, but that of *Feiner* reached substantive issues in a conflict between the rights to free speech and the requirements of public order. Over loud-speakers mounted on a car, Feiner made a speech on a street corner in a predominantly Negro residential section of Syracuse, New York. A crowd of 75 to 80 persons, blacks and whites, gathered around him, and several pedestrians were forced to use the street in order to pass by. In the course of his speech, Feiner referred to President Harry Truman as a "bum," to the American Legion as a "Nazi Gestapo," and to the mayor of Syracuse as a "champagne-sipping bum." [24] He also indicated in an excited manner that "Negroes don't have equal rights," and that "they should rise up in arms and fight for their rights." [25] Shortly after he started speaking, two policemen arrived on the scene. Feiner's statements "stirred up a little excitement," one man indicating that "if the police did not get the s—o—b off his box-stand, he would do so himself." [26] Although there was not yet a disturbance, there was, according to police testimony, "angry muttering" and "pushing." [27] After disregarding two requests to stop speaking, Feiner was arrested by one of the officers, who said that he had "stepped in to prevent it from resulting in a fight." [28] Feiner was convicted of the misdemeanor of disorderly conduct.

Speaking for seven members of the Court, Chief Justice Vinson affirmed the conviction. He admitted that "ordinary murmurings and objections of a hostile audience cannot be allowed to silence a speaker," although he was "mindful of the possible danger of giving overzealous police officials complete discretion to break up otherwise lawful public meetings." [29] But "when, as here, the speaker passes the bounds of argument or persuasion and undertakes incitement to riot," he thought that the police were not or ought not to be "powerless to prevent a breach of the peace." [30] Justices Black and Douglas dissented. Black thought it "farfetched to suggest that the 'facts' showed any imminent threat of riot or uncontrollable disorder." [31] Moreover, assuming that the "facts" indicated a critical situation, Black rejected what he said was the Court's opinion "that the police has no obligation to protect petitioner's constitutional right to talk." [32] If, in the name of preserving order, police "ever can interfere with a lawful public speaker, they first must make all reasonable efforts to protect him." [33] He pointed out that the officers had made no attempt to quiet the restless crowd, no effort to clear a path on the sidewalk for those forced by the crowd to walk in the street, and had done nothing to discourage the threat to assault Feiner.

Vinson and Black clearly disagreed about the interpretation of the "facts" of the case. Vinson thought that there had been a grave and imminent threat of violence and disorder and that Feiner was inciting to riot; Black, however, thought that there had not been an imminent threat of riot and that the threat of disorder was controllable. Vinson and Black relied on different but not necessarily contradictory legal standards by which to judge conflicts between rights to free speech and the requirements of public order. Since Vinson thought that Feiner had incited to riot and that the threat of violence and disorder was imminent, the Chief Justice did not hold the police responsible for keeping the speaker's audience in check. When Black assumed *arguendo* that the "facts" indicated a "critical situation," he did not include a stipulation that Feiner intended to incite a riot, and he held the police responsible under those circumstances for the protection of the speaker. This difference between the intended incitement by the speaker to riot found by the majority in *Feiner* and the threat of riot resulting from the unintended reactions of the audience found by the Court of Appeals in *Sellers* may serve to distinguish the two decisions and to delineate the constitutional responsibilities of the police toward a speaker facing a hostile audience.

In another case decided the same day as *Feiner*, *Kunz v. New York*, the Court overturned the conviction of a sidewalk preacher for violation of an ordinance which made it unlawful to hold a religious meeting on the streets of the City of New York without first obtaining a permit from the police commissioner.[34] Carl Kunz, an ordained Baptist minister, had applied for and obtained a permit under the ordinance in question. In November, 1946, his permit was revoked after a hearing by the police commissioner on evidence that Kunz had ridiculed and denounced other religious beliefs at his meetings. The preacher applied for another permit in 1947 and again in 1948, but was notified each time that his application had been denied; he was given no reason. On September 11, 1948, Kunz was arrested for speaking at Columbus Circle without a permit, and subsequently convicted.

Again speaking for the Court, Chief Justice Vinson reversed the conviction on the ground that the ordinance allowed the police commissioner to exercise discretion on the basis of his own interpretation of what he deemed to be conduct condemned by the ordinance and thus gave "an administrative official discretionary power to control in advance the right of citizens to speak on religious matters on the streets of New York." [35] In ruling that the ordinance was an invalid prior restraint of First Amendment rights, he indicated that there were appropriate public remedies to protect the peace and order of the community if Kunz's speeches resulted in violence or disorder, but that the instant case involved suppression of speech rather than punishment for its unlawful use. Justice Jackson, the sole dissenter, argued that Kunz had used "fighting" words which had resulted in disorder at previous sidewalk meetings, that New York City might legitimately take into consideration the preacher's past conduct to determine whether he would receive a permit to use the city streets for religious meetings, and that Kunz accordingly was not deprived of the constitutional right of free speech.[36]

With the exception of Terminiello and Feiner, defendants in these cases were evangelists who claimed rights to specific modes of implementing a general religious duty to preach the gospel according to their particular lights, and in comparison with other claims of conscience, theirs were of low rank. Actually these claims by religiously motivated individuals did not differ significantly from those made by secularly motivated individuals to rights of free speech. In most of these cases, the Court rated low or held as prematurely invoked the countervailing public interest against breaches of the peace by a unanimous or near-unanimous vote. Only in *Chaplinsky* did the Court rate the countervailing public interest high, and Chaplinsky could hardly claim that invective language was a means of preaching the gospel. In *Feiner,* of course, a majority of the Court rated high the countervailing public interest against breaches of the peace, but Feiner had advanced a claim to a right of freedom of political rather than religious expression.

CIVIL DISOBEDIENCE

In addition to claims of conscience to rights of expression, there are also claims of conscience to immunity of action. Thus varieties of "civil disobedience" in efforts to achieve rights for Negroes or better conditions for the poor can represent claims of conscience to immunity for morally motivated actions in contravention of local laws, and, similarly, the claims of dissenters on the Vietnamese war to immunity for morally motivated actions in contravention of federal or local laws. There are two central elements in "civil disobedience": disobedience and civility, and the latter element poses particularly difficult problems of philosophical analysis and definition. Should the act of disobedience always be performed openly? Should the act always be planned and not spontaneous? How concrete should the objective of public reform be? How far should the disobedient go to exhaust existing legal remedies before the act of disobedience is undertaken? Should the disobedient always use nonviolent means to achieve his objective? How far should the disobedient respect the person and property of others? How close a relation should exist between the law violated and the objective of dissent? To what extent should the disobedient submit to the legal consequences of his act? For our purposes, however, these questions may be left unresolved, provided only that the effects of disobedience on the public, especially concerning the means employed, are recognized.

The element of disobedience is less difficult to define. Although most challenges to local laws by civil-rights partisans in the early 'sixties involved claims that those laws mandated segregation in violation of the Fourteenth Amendment of the federal Constitution or that enforcement of private segregation by public authorities was prohibited by the same amendment, Supreme Court decisions and the passage of the 1964 Civil Rights Act have vindicated most of these claims. Thus "civil disobedience" is now often directed at the local level against laws of unquestioned constitutionality. At issue is not the right to immunity for actions in contravention of allegedly unconstitutional laws or even of laws necessarily regarded as unfair, nor only the right to immunity for the expression and communication of views opposed to local laws or policies. Rather, the issue is one of an asserted right to immunity for actions in contravention of laws whose validity (or even propriety) may be admitted in order to achieve reform of a system of laws or a public policy.

The National Commission on the Causes and Prevention of Violence defined the purpose of civil disobedience in the contemporary context as one which will "influence community action by harassing or intimidating the members of the community into making concessions to a particular point of view." [37] The Commission admitted that the available evidence was insufficient to demonstrate that acts of civil disobedience of a more limited kind inevitably lead to an increased disrespect for law or propensity toward crime on the part of participants, but it also found that such conduct has a seriously adverse effect on other people and especially the system of laws upon which society depends.[38] Citing the example of India, the Commission argued that civil disobedience tends to impair the operation of democratic processes even though disobedients do not intend to do so.

Many advocates of civil disobedience do not assert any legal rights to immunity for their actions. They recognize the threat of their doctrine to the democratic legal system and accordingly profess willingness to accept penalties for their actions. This, they argue, demonstrates the civility of their disobedience. But since they assert that their actions are based on dictates of conscience and are justified by the evils they seek to remedy, and since other disobedients claim legal rights to immunity for their morally motivated actions, both groups represent potential or actual claims of conscience to immunity. From this perspective, the legal claims of civil disobedients are based on the perception of a positive moral duty to remedy conditions of social injustice. Moreover, since these individuals feel themselves unable to alter government policy or to persuade the mass of their fellow-citizens by ordinary means of political action, at least in the short run, they may perceive various types of disobedience (nonviolent to violent) as relatively specific moral obligations, and such moral obligations would be of a moderately high order.

But whatever the degree of moral obligation which they perceive, civil disobedients' acts constitute threats to the legal system and run counter to what judges are likely to consider one of the highest public interests, the general observance of law. Thus morally motivated disobedients—however civil—are unlikely to have their claims of conscience legally vindicated. Prosecutors, of course, may take good motives into account when they make the choice whether to prosecute, and judges may take good motives into account when they impose sentence.

Although courts, as part of the larger political and social systems, can innovate and have innovated by adapting elastic legal prescriptions to new demands, they cannot recognize the validity of direct challenges to the legal system itself, however morally motivated. But civil disobedience is more than a challenge to the legal system; it is also, and primarily, a challenge to the political system. Civil disobedience, in proportion to its incidence, is evidence both that the demands of minorities are not being adequately met, and that representative democratic institutions are not responsive enough to them. Moreover, civil disobedience has proved to be a very effective means for minorities to achieve their demands, although it may have now reached a point of counterproductivity.

USE OF PUBLIC FACILITIES

Prevention of breaches of the peace is not the only public interest to be protected when speakers seek to use streets as a forum to express their religious or moral points of view. In *Cox v. New Hampshire,* the Supreme Court in 1941 upheld the right of a locality to require permits for parades when the limited objective of the statute was construed to define the duty of the licensing authority and the rights of applicants "with regard only to considerations of time, place, and manner so as to conserve the public convenience." [39] Without applying for a permit, 88 Jehovah's Witnesses in groups of 15 to 20 persons marched on a Saturday evening through various parts of the business district of Manchester, New Hampshire. They carried placards denouncing organized religion and inviting the public to a later meeting of the sect. Sixty-eight of the marchers were arrested and convicted of holding a parade without the required permit. Evidence was introduced at their trial to show that on Saturday nights in an hour's time 26,000 persons passed one of the intersections where the defendants had marched, and that the marchers had interfered with normal sidewalk travel. The Supreme Court unanimously affirmed the convictions as a valid exercise of the state's police powers to regulate the use of streets in the interest of public convenience.

In addition to regulation of the use of streets to secure public convenience in travel, local communities may undertake to regulate the use of parks to secure public convenience in areas of recreation. In *Niemotko v. Maryland,* the city of Havre de Grace had a "practice" or custom—but no ordinance—whereby the park commissioner and city council exercised authority to grant permits for the use of a city park.[40] Although permits had always been issued for religious organizations and Sunday-school picnics, the city council denied two Jehovah's Witnesses, Niemotko and Kelley, a permit to use the park because members of the city council disliked, or disagreed with, the Witnesses and their religious views. When Niemotko and Kelley later spoke at the park, they were arrested and convicted of disturbing the peace, but it was clear that the conviction rested only on the fact that they lacked the permit required by the city's "practice."

The Supreme Court unanimously reversed the convictions. Speaking for the Court, Chief Justice Vinson found that, under the amorphous "practice" of Havre de Grace, "no standards appear anywhere, no narrowly drawn limitations, no circumscribing of . . . absolute power, no substantial interest of the community to be served."[41] Moreover, the case clearly showed "unwarranted discrimination" in the refusal to issue a permit to the Witnesses.[42] Accordingly, Vinson held that the city's "practice" was a prior restraint of freedom of speech in contravention of the

First and Fourteenth Amendments, and that the "completely arbitrary and discriminatory" refusal to grant the permit was a denial of equal protection.[43] Under these circumstances, Vinson held irrelevant the argument, whatever its validity, that state and city officials should have the right to exclude religious groups as such from the use of public parks.

A similar case involving the use of public parks for religious meetings was presented to the Court two years later (*Fowler v. Rhode Island*).[44] The city of Pawtucket prohibited addresses at any political or religious meetings in a public park. Jehovah's Witnesses assembled in Slater Park in Pawtucket for a religious meeting, and Fowler addressed the group. He was convicted and fined $5.00 for violation of the ordinance. Speaking for a unanimous Court, Justice Douglas reversed the conviction on the ground that other church services were allowed in the park, and those services involved preaching. "To call the words which one minister speaks to his congregation a sermon immune from regulation and the words of another minister an address subject to regulation is merely an indirect way of preferring one religion over another."[45] The effect was thus to violate First Amendment guarantees of freedom of speech and religion and the Fourteenth Amendment guarantee of equal protection under law. Justice Frankfurter concurred exclusively on the basis of the equal-protection clause.

In another case decided the same year, *Poulos v. New Hampshire,* the Court ruled on a different aspect of the right to hold religious meetings in public parks.[46] Poulos applied for a license to conduct religious services in a public park as required by state law. When the license was refused six weeks before the scheduled meeting, Poulos conducted the meeting without a license. The New Hampshire Supreme Court found the refusal of the license "arbitrary and unreasonable," but held that Poulos' proper remedy was to seek review of the unlawful refusal rather than to raise the illegality of the refusal as a defense in a subsequent prosecution.[47] The United States Supreme Court agreed. Speaking for seven members of the Court, Justice Reed rejected the contention that the city council's unlawful refusal to issue a license to Poulos was a defense against prosecution for violating a valid ordinance. Since the ordinance was valid on its face and only the arbitrary refusal to issue the license unlawful, the Court held that the state could require Poulos to seek redress through appropriate judicial procedure before speaking in the park. "Delay is unfortunate, but the expense and annoyance of litigation is a price citizens must pay for life in an orderly society."[48] Justices Black and Douglas dissented on the ground that Poulos should not be liable to prosecution for speaking without a license when he had been refused that license unlawfully and that the validity of the ordinance was irrelevant to Poulos' plight.[49]

Poulos had approximately six weeks from the denial of the license to the date of his scheduled speech to seek relief by court action, and New Hampshire's extraordinary-writ proceedings were expeditious. The *Poulos* decision may thus be read narrowly to hold that a speaker cannot proceed without a license when he has failed to demonstrate the inadequacy of his civil remedies against arbitrary administration of an ordinance which is valid on its face. In fact, *Cox, Niemotko, Fowler,* and *Poulos* can be read together to uphold the power of local communities to insure the orderly use of public facilities by requiring permits of speakers but to deny to local communities any power to discriminate among users of public facilities with respect to the content of their speech. It should be noted that in none of the latter three cases did the Court say that citizens have a right to use public parks for speeches and meetings or that local communities may not ban such activity. In this respect, the right to use public streets for purposes of communication may be significantly broader than the right to use public parks for the same purposes.

The claim of conscience to the communication of a religious or moral viewpoint has also run into conflict with the public interest in keeping streets clean. In *Jamison v. Texas,* the Supreme Court unanimously held that local communities may not ban the distribution on public streets of all handbills of a religious nature which incidentally invite the purchase of books.[50] Justice Black, speaking for the Court, objected to the universality of the ban, that is, its coverage of all times, all places, and all circumstances. Black distinguished the case from one of the preceding year in which the Court unanimously upheld a total ban on the distribution of commercial handbills on public streets, in spite of an incidental civic appeal appended to the handbills "with the intent and for the purpose of evading the prohibition of the ordinance" (*Valentine v. Christensen*).[51] The *Jamison* case is interesting because the claim of conscience to immunity for the distribution of religious handbills prevailed there over the public interest in clean streets, while a parallel claim by a distributor of commercial handbills failed. Since the public interest against distribution at stake in both cases was the same, it is clear that the Court preferred Jamison's claim to that of the commercial distributor. Of course, the reasoning in *Jamison* is applicable to all claims to freedom of noncommercial expression, and thus the decision did not recognize a specific exemption for claims of religious or moral conscience.

In 1946 the Court extended the right of itinerant evangelists to distribute religious literature to company towns (*Marsh v. Alabama*) and federal housing projects (*Tucker v. Texas*).[52] In both these cases, Justice Frankfurter joined Justices Black, Douglas, Murphy, and Rutledge to form the majorities. Frankfurter was evidently influenced by the principle of *stare decisis*. In *Marsh,* he argued that, as long as the *Murdock* decision represented the law of the land, he was "unable to find legal significance in the fact that a town . . . happens to be company-owned." [53] In *Tucker*, he argued that it was even less desirable to make freedoms of religion and speech "turn on gossamer distinctions about the extent to which land has been 'dedicated' to public uses." [54] Justice Reed, joined by Chief Justice Stone and Justice Burton, dissented on the grounds that the premises of the company town and the housing project were not open to general use by the public.[55] (Justice Jackson was serving in Nuremberg and did not participate in the decisions.) But the Court declined two years later to review a New York decision upholding the right of private apartment-house owners to exclude itinerant evangelist-distributors of religious literature from entering their building unless invited by tenants (*Watchtower Bible and Tract Society v. Metropolitan Life Insurance Co.*).[56] Only Justices Douglas and Murphy would have granted certiorari.

In all these cases, the claims of conscience were to rights to specific modes of implementing what was perceived as a general religious duty to preach the word of God, and of relatively low rank in comparison with other claims of conscience. The claims of Cox and Poulos were held by the Court to run counter to at least moderate public interests in the orderly use of public facilities, but allegations of similar public interests against Niemotko and Fowler were held to be null because they were discriminatory. The claim of a public interest in clean streets, presumably of low rank, was held to be inadequate to justify limitations on Jamison's religious expression. The claim of Jehovah's Witnesses in the *Watchtower* case were held to run counter to a moderate public interest in the protection of private property, but claims of similar public interests in the protection of the "private" property of company towns and federal housing projects against Marsh and Tucker, respectively, were rejected by the Court and presumably rated low.

PREVENTION OF FRAUD

Breach of the peace was not the only charge against Jesse Cantwell; he, his father, and his brother were also convicted of soliciting donations for a religious cause without the certification by a welfare official which was required by statute. The statute was designed to protect the public against fraud and imposition in the solicitation of funds in the name of religion, but the Supreme Court unanimously reversed the convictions on this charge as well. Since a local official was empowered by the statute to determine whether a solicitor's cause was "religious," Justice Roberts held that the statute was a prior restraint upon the exercise of religious freedom guaranteed by the First Amendment and included in the liberty protected by the Fourteenth. He pointed out that penal laws were available to punish fraud and that the state might protect its citizens from fraudulent solicitation by requiring the identification of solicitors. "But to condition the solicitation of aid for the perpetuation [*sic*] of religious views or systems upon a license, the grant of which rests in the exercise of a determination by state authority as to what is a religious cause," placed a prior and prohibited restraint upon the exercise of religious freedom.[57]

Four years after the *Cantwell* decision, the Court reviewed another case involving a conflict between the claim of individuals to religious freedom and the interest of the public in protection against fraud, a case of two criminal convictions for the use of the mails to solicit by false and fraudulent representation funds for, and membership in, a purportedly religious movement (*United States v. Ballard*).[58] Donald and Edna Ballard were indicted for representing falsely that they had been selected as divine messengers for communicating the teachings of the "I Am" movement, that they had the power to heal and even to cure diseases the medical profession considered incurable, and that they had cured hundreds of afflicted persons. The indictment charged that the defendants knew that these claims were false and that the claims were made with the intention of cheating and defrauding the public.

From the beginning, the defendants objected that their religious beliefs were being attacked and that the government was attempting to restrict their religious freedom in violation of the First Amendment. The trial court, however, disregarded these contentions and restricted the Ballards' defense with respect to their religious beliefs to the question of their good faith. When the case went to the jury, the trial judge instructed it not to consider the truth or falsity of the defendants' claims of supernatural powers but only whether the defendants believed their claims in good faith. The jury found the defendants guilty, but the Court of Appeals reversed the convictions and ordered a new trial, ruling that the Ballards were entitled to submit to the consideration of the jury a defense based on the asserted truth of their religious beliefs.

The Supreme Court divided three ways. Justice Douglas, speaking for five justices, held that the trial court correctly excluded the question of the truth or falsity of the defendants' religious beliefs but remanded the case to the Court of Appeals to review other issues. According to the majority, "heresy trials are foreign to our Constitution," and men "may not be put to the proof of their religious doctrines or beliefs." [59] Thus religious beliefs cannot be submitted to a jury charged with finding their truth or falsity.

Chief Justice Stone, joined by Justices Frankfurter and Roberts, dissented. Stone argued first that some counts in the indictment had charged the Ballards with fraudulent procurement of money by knowingly making false statements about their religious experiences and that these counts were susceptible to negative proofs. If one of the defendants asserted that he had had a religious experience in San Francisco on a certain day, Stone did not doubt that it would be open to the government to submit to the jury proof that he had never been there. Or if one of the defendants asserted that he had in fact cured hundreds of persons by the use of his spiritual powers, the government might introduce evidence to show that no such cures had ever been effected. But Stone's main argument was that the case went to the jury on the single issue of whether the Ballards believed that the religious experiences they claimed had in fact incurred, and the jury had found against them. Since "the state of one's mind is a fact as capable of fraudulent misrepresentation as is one's physical condition or the state of one's bodily health," Stone argued that none of the defendants' constitutional rights had been violated.[60] They were prosecuted for the fraudulent procurement of money "by false representation as to their beliefs, religious or otherwise," and so the jury's judgment of guilty should be simply reinstated.[61]

Justice Jackson, the other dissenting member of the Court, would have dismissed the indictment altogether and "have done with this business of judicially examining other people's faiths." [62] Thus Jackson would not have allowed the jury to consider even the issue of the defendants' good faith, but he would not bar the government from prosecuting religious leaders for fraud if they made false representations about matters other than their religious beliefs or experience—if, for example, they represented that funds were solicited to construct a church when in fact they were converted to personal use. Jackson raised four main points to support his position: (1) religious insincerity cannot be dissociated from religious truths because what a person may believe depends on what he considers to be believable; (2) any inquiring into the intellectual honesty of a man's religious beliefs raises the psychological barrier that unbelievers among his judges are likely not to understand or believe him; (3) religious belief implies the possibility of doubt, and government is not competent to determine what degree of skepticism or disbelief in a religious representation amounts to actionable fraud; and (4) members of a sect get what they pay for, and the wrong they may suffer is not the money they part with so much as the mental and spiritual poison they may get, "precisely the thing the Constitution put beyond the reach of the prosecutor." [63]

A recent California case raised an issue of fraud similar to that in *Ballard*. David Supple left a substantial portion of his estate to various Roman Catholic charities, which bequests a grandnephew contested on the grounds that the will had been obtained by fraud and undue influence. The allegation was that the Catholic Church promised to shorten the periods of purgation which the testator and deceased relatives would be otherwise obliged to undergo after death to expiate their sins in exchange for the performance of certain good works, which included gifts to the church and affiliated agencies, and that this representation was in fact false. A lower court admitted the will to probate, and the California Court of Appeals affirmed the judgment (In re *Supple's Estate*).[64] Following the majority in the *Ballard* case, the appellate court held that California would not allow inquiry into the truth or falsity of religious beliefs and pointed out that no allegation had been made that Roman Catholic churchmen did not actually believe the teachings attributed to them, that is, that there was no allegation of bad faith. This decision raises the prospect that, had such an allegation been made, the Roman Catholic beneficiaries of Supple's will would have had to argue the sincerity of their beliefs in a court of law—if they wanted to receive the bequests made to them under the contested will.

Another recent California case involved Dr. Merle E.

Parker and the Foundation for Divine Meditation, of which Parker was the sponsor and director. Besides conducting religious services and sponsoring recreational activities, Parker published tracts and a newspaper, *The National Christian Crusader,* which promoted the other publications. Some of Parker's publications promised their readers financial profit if they undertook such projects as growing Ysabel Ming trees and raising earthworms. Parker and the Foundation did a thriving business, grossing $207,-000 one year and $290,000 another. In the light of these and other facts, the United States Court of Appeals held that the evidence supported a ruling of the Tax Court that the Foundation was engaged in activities which were substantially nonexempt (*Parker v. Commissioner of Internal Revenue*).[65] Although the Court of Appeals admitted that religious organizations need not lose their tax-exempt status simply because they offered their literature for sale and that the services of worship and associated recreational activities were religious in nature, it held nonetheless that Parker's organization evidenced a nonreligious purpose in the extent and scope of its profit-making circulation, the methods of promotion, the generally nonreligious subject matter of some of the publications, the large annual profits, the substantial accumulation of earnings, and the statements made by Dr. Parker himself.

The criminal prosecution of the Ballards and the contested will of Supple illustrate the difficulty of adjudicating claims of fraud in the solicitation of funds by organizations which purport to be religious. In the light of the constitutional guarantee of freedom of religious exercise, Justice Jackson's solution is administratively the simplest and perhaps politically the wisest: a rule of *caveat emptor* between buyers and sellers of religious doctrines. As Jackson pointed out, it is difficult to distinguish between religious sincerity and religious truth, and the main loss to consumers deceived by religious frauds is psychological rather than financial. The issue is more complicated when the interest of a third party is at stake, as when Supple's grandnephew was effectively disinherited by the alleged fraud influencing Supple's testamentary dispositions. But even in that case, of course, the grandnephew had no vested right to inherit, and the issue of fraud was essentially one of buyer and seller between Supple and the religious organizations he chose to benefit.

Although there was no allegation of fraud in the *Parker* case, his claim to tax-exempt status did run directly counter to a claim by the government to the collection of taxes. Since tax exemption for religious organizations is a privilege created by statute, contests concerning eligibility for that status will arise here as in other areas of tax law, and courts will be forced to rule on them. In the *Parker* case, the Court of Appeals made commercial activity a criterion of ineligibility, and the decision would appear to harmonize with the purpose of the exemption and to involve no determination of the truth or the sincerity of religious beliefs.

The Cantwells claimed a right to implement a general religious duty to preach the gospel by incidentally soliciting funds on the sidewalks of New Haven, Connecticut. Against that claim, the State of Connecticut alleged a public interest in the requirement of a license to prevent fraudulent solicitation of funds under the guise of religion. Although the Cantwells' claim was of a relatively low order from the specific perspective of moral obligation and not significantly different from any other claim to freedom of expression, the Court held unanimously in favor of the Cantwells because Connecticut sought to protect the public interest against fraud by what the Court considered a constitutionally invalid means, one with substantial risk of prior censorship. The Ballards similarly claimed a right to implement a general duty to preach their religious beliefs by soliciting funds through the mails. Against that claim, the government alleged that the Ballards were guilty of fraudulently misrepresenting themselves and their cause. Only Justice Jackson thought the public interest against the Ballards' claim of low rank; the other eight members of the Court agreed that the public interest against fraud was at least moderate enough to sustain the Ballards' convictions if they misrepresented their actual beliefs.

Supple's executors claimed, in effect, that a testator has a right to implement a general religious duty to expiate his sins by making charitable contributions. Against that claim, Supple's grandnephew asserted a public interest against enforcing bequests obtained by fraud or undue influence. The courts held the public interest alleged by Supple's grandnephew to be legally null because he had not proved conscious misrepresentation, an essential element in fraud. Parker claimed a right to implement a general duty to promote his religious beliefs by commercial enterprises. Against that claim, the government alleged a public interest in revenue. The courts held the public interest moderate enough to justify the collection of general revenue taxes.

Sabbatarians seek immunity from the financial loss indirectly imposed on them by the restrictions of Sunday laws. The effect of Sunday laws on Sabbatarian entrepreneurs will be considered in the next chapter in connection with countervailing public-welfare interests in common rest and recreation.[66] Here, however, in connection with a public interest asserted against the risk of fraud, belongs the claim of Mrs. Sherbert, a Seventh-Day Adventist, who could not obtain employment because she would not accept work on Saturday, a day on which the tenets of her religion prohibited labor. She applied for unemployment compensation but was denied it on the ground that she failed, without good cause, to accept "suitable" work when it was offered her. The South Carolina Supreme

Court upheld the decision of the state's Employment Security Commission, and Mrs. Sherbert appealed to the United States Supreme Court. Although South Carolina did not command Mrs. Sherbert to work on Saturday under threat of criminal penalties, its denial of unemployment benefits threatened her with severe financial penalties if she did not accept work on Saturday and thus forced her to act against her religious beliefs. Accordingly, her claim of conscience was of a relatively high order.

The state's main argument for disqualifying Mrs. Sherbert from unemployment compensation was that to grant her claim would open the workers' fund to unscrupulous applicants who might feign religious objections to work on Saturday. The public interest thus asserted against allowing Mrs. Sherbert's claim was principally to administrative convenience in preventing fraudulent access to the fund, although the state did argue incidentally that recognition of Mrs. Sherbert's claim might hinder employers from scheduling Saturday work.

Justice Brennan, speaking for six members of the Court, found no compelling interest on the part of South Carolina in disqualifying Mrs. Sherbert from eligibility as a recipient of unemployment compensation (*Sherbert v. Verner*).[67] Justice Stewart concurred separately, although he insisted that the *Sherbert* decision was inconsistent with *Braunfeld*.[68] This majority held the state's claim of a public interest against fraudulent access to its unemployment compensation fund to be of too low an order to justify the financial pressure that denial of Mrs. Sherbert's application would exert against her fulfillment of what she perceived as a religious duty not to work on Saturday. Justices Harlan and White, dissenting, pointed out—correctly—that the effect of the Court's decision was to give applicants for unemployment compensation unwilling to work on Saturdays for religious reasons a standing superior to that of those unwilling to work then for other reasons.[69]

The case is thus a clear example of exemption from a restrictive public law in favor of individual conscience.

But the requirement of work on Saturdays for public construction workers apparently satisfies the compelling-interest formula where Sabbatarians are involved. The State of California dismissed Thomas Stimpel, a Seventh-Day Adventist, from a construction job when he refused to accept work on Saturdays for religious reasons, and he lost his suit to recover his job in the courts of that state (*Stimpel v. State Personnel Board*).[70] Over the sole dissent of Justice Douglas, the United States Supreme Court refused to grant certiorari, and thus apparently accepted as sufficiently compelling the public interest of California in requiring work on Saturdays from all its construction employees.[71]

TAXES ON THE INCIDENTS OF RELIGIOUS PROSELYTISM

As we indicated earlier in connection with the use of public facilities, the Supreme Court in the *Cox* case upheld the power of a municipality to require a license for street parades "with regard only to considerations of time, place, and manner so as to conserve the public convenience."[72] Also involved in that case was the validity of the license fees charged, which ranged from $300.00 to a nominal amount. The Court affirmed their validity, accepting a construction of the state's statute to require "a reasonable fixing of the amount of the fee" dependent on the public expense of policing the parade licensed.[73] The fees were accordingly held not to constitute a revenue tax but one to meet expenses incidental to maintaining public order for the parade licensed. Moreover, the Court found no evidence that the statute had been administered in other than a fair and nondiscriminatory manner.

Since the defendants in *Cox* had not applied for the license, the issue of license fees for the exercise of First

Amendment rights could be raised only in an abstract form. But it is not difficult to imagine the hardships which the license fees potentially at stake in the *Cox* case might impose on less affluent noncommercial groups seeking to influence the public. This situation was forcefully presented to the Court one year later when Jehovah's Witnesses contested local license taxes on persons selling, or canvassing for the sale of, printed matter (*Jones v. Opelika*).[74] The taxes under attack varied from $15.00 per year in Opelika, Alabama, to $25.00 per month, $10.00 per week, and $2.50 per day in Fort Smith, Arkansas. The Witnesses, convicted of violating the ordinances which required the licenses, complained that application of the fees to their missionary activities abridged their freedom of religious exercise in violation of the First and Fourteenth Amendments.

A sharply divided court (5–4) upheld the convictions. According to Justice Reed, who was joined by Justices Byrnes, Frankfurter, Jackson, and Roberts, the sole constitutional question presented to the Court was "whether a nondiscriminatory license fee, presumably appropriate in amount," may be imposed on sellers of religious literature,[75] and he held that "the First Amendment does not require a subsidy in the form of fiscal exemption" for such sellers.[76] Chief Justice Stone, dissenting with Justices Black, Douglas, and Murphy, saw the question as "whether a flat tax, more than a nominal fee to defray the expenses of a regulatory license, can constitutionally be laid on a noncommercial, nonprofit activity devoted exclusively to the dissemination of ideas, educational and religious in character, to those persons who consent to receive them." [77] In Stone's judgment, a flat license tax unrelated to the defendants' activities or the receipts derived from them restrained in advance the freedom taxed and tended to suppress its exercise. Stone also stressed the cumulative effort of such local taxes on the missionary activities of itinerant evangelists.

One year later, after Justice Rutledge had succeeded Justice Byrnes, the Court marshaled a 5–4 majority for the position of the dissenters in *Jones,* in a substantially identical Pennsylvania case (*Murdock v. Pennsylvania*).[78] Justice Douglas, speaking for the new majority, repeated the arguments of Stone in the *Jones* case and commented that "the mere fact that religious literature is 'sold' by itinerant preachers rather than 'donated' does not transform evangelism into a commercial enterprise." [79] He held accordingly that "the constitutional rights of those spreading their religious beliefs through the spoken and printed word are not to be gauged by standards governing retailers or wholesalers of books." [80] The Court thus recognized an exemption from general revenue license taxes in favor of itinerant evangelists incidentally selling religious literature.

The following year the Court extended the *Murdock* principle to exempt from payment of a similar license fee a Jehovah's Witness who both maintained his home in the taxing municipality and earned his entire living by means of the sale of religious literature (*Follett v. McCormick*).[81] Justice Douglas, joined by Chief Justice Stone and Justices Black, Murphy, and Rutledge, argued that the books offered for sale were religious in nature and that the commercial aspects of Follett's activities were irrelevant; since freedoms of the press and religion were involved, the license fee was held to constitute a tax on the exercise of a constitutional privilege. Justice Reed also joined the majority in this case. Accepting the *Murdock* decision as "now the law of the land," he saw "no difference in respect to the exercise of religion between an itinerant distributor and one who remains in one general neighborhood or between one who is active part-time and another who is active all of his time." [82]

The dissenters, Justices Frankfurter, Jackson, and Roberts, argued that the decision went beyond *Murdock* because residents, unlike transients, have clear responsibilities to bear their share of the community's common burden.[83] If resident evangelist-sellers of religious literature were exempted from flat license fees, then other vendors of books could not be so taxed without creating an extensive exemption for the religiously motivated sellers. Moreover, those pursuing other vocations might seek exemption from general revenue taxes by claiming that their work was an exercise of religion. Thus the dissenters stressed the extent of the exemption recognized by the Court for evangelist-sellers of religious literature.

The claim of the Witnesses in these cases was to a right to sell religious literature as an incident of a general religious duty to preach their message. Against that claim, local governments asserted principally a public interest in the raising of general revenue. It should be noted that the governments in these cases did not claim that the fees charged were required to defray the administrative cost of regulating the activities licensed. Both the Witnesses' claims of conscience and the countervailing public interests in revenue were of relatively low order, and the ultimate decisions favored the claims of conscience. As in the flag-salute cases to be considered in Chapter 6,[84] this dispute reflected in part a disagreement on judicial philosophy concerning the degree of deference owed to local legislative judgment, and in part a refusal to make exceptions for claims of conscience from otherwise admittedly valid public laws. But the dispute also reflected disagreement on the extent to which the commercial activities of the Witnesses could be dissociated from their acts of religious proselytism. In this respect, the claim of Follett was clearly the weakest in the series of cases.

MISCELLANEOUS

Mrs. Owen Jenison refused to serve on a jury because of her religious conviction that the Bible commanded her not to judge other human beings (see Mt 7:2). She was convicted of contempt of court and sentenced to thirty days in prison. The Minnesota Supreme Court affirmed her conviction,[85] but the United States Supreme Court reversed the conviction *per curiam* and remanded the case to the state court "for further consideration in the light of *Sherbert v. Verner*" (In re *Jenison*).[86] Mrs. Jenison's claim of conscience, if truly represented, was of the highest order; her conscience absolutely forbade her to serve on a jury. Since the Court had already ruled in the *Sherbert* case that the government must show a "compelling" public interest to justify restrictions on conscientious objectors, it required Minnesota to review Mrs. Jenison's conviction in the light of that ruling. The Court clearly indicated by its reversal and remand that it thought that jury service did not constitute such a "compelling" public interest.

Recurring and often bitter conflicts between different groups of church members have cast courts in the role of referee in the adjudication of property rights. Insofar as parties to these conflicts base their claims on conscience, they claim property rights incidental to their duties of religious worship. The conflicts, however, are not between individuals and governments but rather between claims of conscience by different individuals. The Supreme Court has consistently ruled that governments have no constitutionally valid public interests in these conflicts except to clarify title and that legislatures and courts cannot interpret religious doctrine or interfere with church governing bodies.[87]

NOTES

1. *Barron v. Baltimore,* 32 U.S. 243 (1833).
2. *Gitlow v. New York,* 268 U.S. 652 (1925).
3. *Ibid.,* p. 666.
4. *Cantwell v. Connecticut,* 310 U.S. 296 (1940) and *Everson v. Board of Education,* 330 U.S. 1 (1947). The useful Tables in

Henry J. Abraham, *Freedom and the Court* (New York: Oxford University Press, 1967), pp. 194–200, may be consulted for a graphic presentation of the decisions of the Supreme Court in the area of freedom of religion. (I regret that the second edition [1972] appeared too late to be used.)

5. *Supra,* p. 67.
6. See n. 4.
7. *Chaplinsky v. New Hampshire,* 315 U.S. 568 (1942).
8. *Ibid.,* p. 570.
9. *Ibid.,* p. 569.
10. *Ibid.*
11. *Ibid.,* p. 572.
12. *Sellers v. Johnson,* 69 F.Supp. 778 (1946).
13. *Ibid.,* p. 788.
14. *Sellers v. Johnson,* 163 F.2d 877, 881 (1947).
15. *Ibid.,* p. 889.
16. *Johnson v. Sellers,* 332 U.S. 851 (1948).
17. *Terminiello v. Chicago,* 337 U.S. 1 (1949) and *Feiner v. New York,* 340 U.S. 315 (1951).
18. *Terminiello,* p. 3.
19. *Ibid.,* pp. 17–22.
20. *Ibid.,* p. 16.
21. *Ibid.,* p. 3.
22. *Ibid.,* p. 4.
23. *Ibid.*
24. *Feiner,* p. 330.
25. *Ibid.*
26. *Ibid.,* pp. 317 and 324.
27. *Ibid.,* p. 324.
28. *Ibid.,* p. 317.
29. *Ibid.,* p. 320.
30. *Ibid.,* p. 321.
31. *Ibid.,* p. 325.
32. *Ibid.,* p. 326.
33. *Ibid.*
34. *Kunz v. New York,* 340 U.S. 290 (1951).
35. *Ibid.,* p. 293.
36. *Ibid.,* pp. 295–314.
37. *To Establish Justice, to Insure Domestic Tranquility: The Final Report of the National Commission on the Causes and Prevention of Violence* (New York: Bantam, 1970), p. 86.
38. *Ibid.* All members of the Commission agreed to this finding, but they split sharply on the moral justification and ultimate consequences of civil disobedience.
39. *Cox v. New Hampshire,* 312 U.S. 569, 575–76 (1941).
40. *Niemotko v. Maryland,* 340 U.S. 268 (1951).
41. *Ibid.,* p. 272.

42. *Ibid.*
43. *Ibid.*, p. 273.
44. *Fowler v. Rhode Island,* 345 U.S. 67 (1953).
45. *Ibid.*, p. 70.
46. *Poulos v. New Hampshire,* 345 U.S. 395 (1953).
47. *Ibid.*, p. 400.
48. *Ibid.*, p. 409.
49. *Ibid.*, pp. 421–26.
50. *Jamison v. Texas,* 318 U.S. 413 (1943).
51. *Valentine v. Christensen,* 316 U.S. 52, 55 (1942).
52. *Marsh v. Alabama,* 326 U.S. 501 (1946); *Tucker v. Texas,* 326 U.S. 517 (1946).
53. *Marsh,* p. 510.
54. *Tucker,* p. 521.
55. *Marsh,* p. 511; *Tucker,* p. 521.
56. *Watchtower Bible and Tract Society v. Metropolitan Life Insurance Co.,* 334 U.S. 886 (1948).
57. *Cantwell v. Connecticut,* 310 U.S. 296, 307 (1940).
58. *U.S. v. Ballard,* 322 U.S. 78 (1944); cf. 35 F.Supp. 105 (1940) and 138 F.2d 540 (1943).
59. *U.S. v. Ballard,* 322 U.S. 78, 86 (1944).
60. *Ibid.*, p. 90.
61. *Ibid.*
62. *Ibid.*, p. 95.
63. *Ibid.*
64. In re *Supple's Estate,* 55 Cal. Rptr. 542 (1966).
65. *Parker v. Commissioner of Internal Revenue,* 365 F.2d 792 (1966).
66. *Infra,* pp. 135–141.
67. *Sherbert v. Verner,* 374 U.S. 398 (1963).
68. *Ibid.*, p. 413.
69. *Ibid.*, p. 418.
70. *Stimpel v. State Personnel Board,* 6 Cal. App.3d 206, 85 Cal. Rptr. 797 (1970).
71. *Stimpel v. State Personnel Board of California,* 400 U.S. 952 (1970); but cf. *Dewey v. Reynolds Metal Co.,* 300 F.Supp. 709 (1969), 429 F.2d 324 (1970), and 400 U.S. 1008 (1971).
72. See n. 39.
73. *Ibid.*, pp. 576–77.
74. *Jones v. Opelika,* 316 U.S. 584 (1942).
75. *Ibid.*, p. 593.
76. *Ibid.*, p. 599.
77. *Ibid.*, p. 604.
78. *Murdock v. Pennsylvania,* 319 U.S. 105 (1943).
79. *Ibid.*, p. 111.
80. *Ibid.*
81. *Follett v. McCormick,* 321 U.S. 573 (1944).

82. *Ibid.*, p. 578.
83. *Ibid.*, p. 579.
84. *Infra,* pp. 164–169.
85. In re *Jenison,* 265 Minn. 96, 120 N.W.2d 515 (1963).
86. In re *Jenison,* 375 U.S. 14 (1963).
87. Cf. *Watson v. Jones,* 80 U.S. 697 (1872); *Gonzalez v. The Roman Catholic Archbishop of Manila,* 280 U.S. 1 (1929); *Kedroff v. Saint Nicholas Cathedral,* 344 U.S. 94 (1952); *Kreshik v. St. Nicholas Cathedral,* 363 U.S. 190 (1960); *Presbyterian Church in the United States v. Mary Elizabeth Blue Hull Memorial Presbyterian Church,* 393 U.S. 440 (1969); and *Maryland and Virginia Eldership of the Churches of God v. The Church of God at Sharpsburg, Inc.,* 396 U.S. 367 (1970).

5

Conscience and Public Welfare

PROTECTION OF LIFE

CLAIMS OF CONSCIENCE may also run counter to the interests of state and local governments in the protection of public welfare, and prominent among such interests are those involving the health of citizens. *Harden v. State* is a case which was never reviewed by the Supreme Court, but which illustrates the type of conflict which can arise between individual conscience and public interest in this area.[1] In the course of the religious services of a denomination known as the "Holiness Church," some members who had been "anointed" and admitted into the "Paragon of Truth" handled poisonous snakes and wrapped them around their necks and bodies as a test and proof of the sincerity of their religious faith and practice.[2] They believed that those so "anointed" would not be bitten by the snakes or, if bitten, would suffer no adverse physical effects. Moreover, in accordance with the protection promised in Mk 16:18 ("they will pick up serpents"), they believed that the handling of the snakes in their services was a necessary method of evangelism in order to convert nonbelievers to Christianity and to move those weak in Christian faith to its practice. Ten members of the church conducted the snake ritual in the manner described and were convicted of violating a Tennessee statute which prohibited the handling of any poisonous snake "so as to endanger the life or health of any person." [3] On appeal, the Supreme Court of Tennessee affirmed the convictions.

Appellants argued in the first place that the statute did not apply to religious services conducted in a church. The Tennessee court noted, however, that rattlesnakes were commonly known to be poisonous and that the Holiness Church recognized this danger by the practice of stretching a rope in front of the stage to prevent any of the audience from coming onto it and by stationing guards at intervals along the rope to turn back any straying snake. In fact, there was evidence to show that at least one person in the audience crossed the rope, and that one worshiper, bitten while handling the snakes, died from the effects within a few hours. Given this danger shown by the evidence, the court found nothing in the language of the statute to infer that the legislature had intended to exempt anyone from its provisions. Appellants argued in the second place that if the statute did apply to religious services conducted in a church, it violated the freedom of their religious exercise guaranteed by both federal and state constitutions. To this argument the court rejoined that the appellants were free to believe without any fear of punishment that handling poisonous snakes in their religious services would be harmless to the participants and an incentive to the religious faith and practice of the audience, but that their right to act according to such belief was limited by society's right to protect itself from acts, religious or otherwise, which might be dangerous to human life and health.

"Anointed" of the Holiness Church claimed a relatively

specific religious duty to handle snakes as part of their public worship. Like the Mormon practice of polygamy, to be considered in Chapter 6,[4] the claim was not to an absolute duty since the unavailability of snakes would effectively prevent their use, presumably without any perception of moral fault by members of the Holiness Church. But the duty was conceived as relatively specific, insofar as handling the snakes was considered a means of preaching the gospel prescribed by Scripture. Accordingly, it was a claim of moderate rank. The counterclaim of Tennessee to an interest in public health was based on two distinct, though related, grounds: (1) the participants' actions were without adequate safeguards for their audience and thus potentially hazardous to their lives; and (2) the participants' actions were hazardous to their own lives. The first interest was clearly a matter of public health. With respect to the second, the cumulus of even voluntarily assumed risks to life by participants in the religious services might lessen the state's reservoir of able-bodied citizens, and the potential brutalization of public attitudes toward human life resulting from the exhibition of such risks might run counter to a legislatively determined interest in public morals. The Tennessee court did not evaluate the two interests separately, but rated high the combined public interests in the lives of participants and audience and preferred these to the worshipers' claims of conscience.

Claims of public-health interest may also conflict with claims of individuals to bodily integrity. In *Jacobson v. Massachusetts,* the Supreme Court reviewed a regulation by the Board of Health of Cambridge, Massachusetts, which, under the authority of a state statute, required all persons resident in the city to be vaccinated against smallpox.[5] Jacobson refused to comply with the regulation and was convicted of violating it. His conviction was sustained by the Supreme Judicial Court of Massachusetts, and he appealed to the Supreme Court of the United States.

Jacobson did not specifically object to the compulsory vaccination law on the ground that it violated his freedom of religious exercise, and his failure to do so may be related to the fact that the Court had not yet declared the religious-exercise clause of the First Amendment to be binding on state governments through the due-process clause of the Fourteenth Amendment. But Jacobson did argue (in the Court's paraphrase of his words) that the compulsory vaccination law was "unreasonable, arbitrary, oppressive, and hostile to the inherent right of every freeman to care for his own body and health in such a way as to him seems best," and that the execution of such a law against one who objected to vaccination was an assault upon his person.[6]

The Court overrode Jacobson's objections. Justice Harlan, speaking for a seven-man majority, pointed out that a society which allowed each individual to be a law unto himself would be confronted with disorder and anarchy, and that a community has the right to protect itself against the threat of an epidemic of disease. The Court acknowledged that some of the medical profession at that time attached little or no value to vaccination as a means of preventing the spread of smallpox, but the Court held that local governments might reasonably proceed upon the theory that vaccination was an effective means to suppress the threat of a smallpox epidemic to their populations. Justices Brewer and Peckham dissented.[7]

Jacobson did not object to compulsory vaccination on specifically religious or moral grounds, but rather on an asserted right of the individual to complete bodily integrity. As such, his claim was based on a radically limited concept of the individual's relation to society rather than on any rights or duties of conscience. Had Jacobson objected to compulsory vaccination on religious or moral grounds, he might have claimed that he himself would have been forced to submit to something against his conscience and to cooperate in an activity deemed immoral by complying, actively or passively, with the regulation. If such were the moral perception of an individual, his claim of conscience would be of a high order. But since the vaccination would be ordered by the board of health and performed by another (the doctor), the individual need not perceive his cooperation as so intimately linked to the vaccination that it imputes to him any moral responsibility for it. Individual perceptions, even within a common set of religious beliefs, may differ on issues of cooperation, and it would be necessary to investigate such perception on a case-by-case basis in order to assess their subjective strength.

Against Jacobson's asserted right as a freeman to his bodily integrity, the Commonwealth of Massachusetts claimed a right to protect the public against the threat of an epidemic of smallpox. Although the Court did not explicate how Jacobson's failure to submit to vaccination would have constituted such a threat to others besides those who, like himself, refused to be vaccinated, it is evident enough that he could have become a carrier of the germ and a consequent threat both to infants not yet immunized and to newcomers who had not had sufficient time to obtain the vaccination prescribed by the regulation. In this connection, the relatively high mobility of American society is particularly relevant to the potential threat. The Court made clear that the probable validity of the theory underlying the regulation was sufficient to justify the action of the state and city.

Related to Jacobson's claim to bodily integrity against compulsory vaccination is the objection of Jehovah's Witnesses to compulsory blood transfusions. They believe that to receive a blood transfusion is to "eat blood," an act prohibited by the Old Testament (Lev 7:26). In the case of In re *Brooks' Estate,* the Supreme Court of Illinois refused to approve a lower court order for a blood transfusion to save the life of an adult Witness who objected to receiving it, clearly realizing that her death would probably result.[8] The patient had no minor children, and the Illinois high court held that there was no danger to public health, welfare, or morals such as to support government intervention in conflict with the patient's free exercise of her religion. A similar result was reached by a New York court in a case which involved a completely competent adult patient with no minor children (*Erickson v. Dilgard*).[9] These courts thus found no public interest in health, welfare, or morals to justify government action restricting the individual patients' claims of religious conscience not to be forced to submit to the blood transfusion necessary to save their lives; the only possible claim of the state in these cases was to the preservation of individual lives, and this claim was considered insufficient to override the individuals' claims of conscience.

But the results have been different when minors were involved. The Supreme Court of Illinois, for example, approved a lower court order for a blood transfusion in the case of a minor, a transfusion which doctors testified to be necessary to prevent the child's death or permanent injury and to which his parents, Jehovah's Witnesses, objected on religious grounds (*People* ex rel. *Wallace v. Labrenz*).[10] The court relied on the right of the state to intervene as *parens patriae* to protect the health of minors when their parents fail to do so, and the United States Supreme Court denied certiorari.[11]

The interest of minors may also affect the disposition of cases which involve blood transfusions for adults. Thus, in *United States v. George,* a federal district court judge in Connecticut ordered a blood transfusion for an adult patient, the father of four children.[12] Although the patient, a Jehovah's Witness, was completely rational and coherent, the court ordered the transfusion on the rationale that the state had a right to intervene as *parens patriae* to prevent the patient from abandoning his children by death. The court added that the patient had voluntarily submitted himself to medical treatment, and he could not subsequently invoke his religious beliefs to dictate to the doctors a course of action which might be held to amount to malpractice. Such a threat to the doctors and the hospital involved may not have been substantial in view of the fact that the patient was completely rational at the time of his objection to the blood transfusion.

In another case, *Application of President and Directors of Georgetown College, Inc.*, a woman suffering from a hemorrhaging ulcer was brought to Georgetown University Hospital in Washington, D.C., for emergency treatment.[13] When the doctors attending her declared that blood transfusions were necessary to save her life, both she and her husband, Jehovah's Witnesses, refused to consent because of their religious beliefs. The university's attorneys brought a judge of the District of Columbia Court of Appeals into the hospital, and he immediately issued an order for the transfusions. In an opinion written some months later, he justified his order on several grounds: (1) the patient was in no better mental condition to decide whether to consent to a blood transfusion than a child would have been; (2) the patient was the mother of a seven-month-old child whom the government had a right as *parens patriae* to protect from abandonment by the patient's death; (3) the hospital and doctors had assumed legal responsibility for the patient when they admitted her; and (4) suicide may be a crime in the District of Columbia, and in that case the refusal of necessary medical assistance might be held to abet the commission of a crime. Of these grounds, the first two distinguish the result in this case from that in other cases in which courts refused to order blood transfusions for adult patients over their religious objections, and the last ground was tenuous because the patient did not deliberately intend to kill herself. On the patient's appeal for a rehearing, the Court of Appeals, sitting *en banc*, declared the case moot, although three judges argued that the hospital did not have a sufficient interest to make the original application for a court order, and that there was accordingly no "case or controversy" properly within judicial cognizance.[14] The Supreme Court denied certiorari.[15]

In the *George* case, the judge first assured the patient that the court would not force him to submit to a blood transfusion, but issued the order after the patient stated that he would not physically resist the doctors once the order was signed. In the *Georgetown* case, the judge ascertained from the patient and her husband that they would not feel that they had acted against their religious beliefs if the court took the responsibility for authorizing the transfusions. As we suggested in connection with the claim of Jacobson, there is a question whether acts mandated by public authorities but performed by others force the individuals affected to do anything contrary to their consciences or at least need to be so perceived by them. At most it would seem to involve their passive cooperation in an act deemed immoral by nonresistance and submission to the physical power of others.

The public interest in the health and welfare of minors at stake in cases in which adults refuse to receive blood transfusions for religious reasons may involve unborn children as well as those already born. A married woman suffering from complications developed in the course of a seven-and-a-half-month pregnancy was brought to a hospital in New Jersey. Doctors there warned her that she was in grave danger of death unless she received a blood transfusion, and that she might thereby bring death to her unborn child. As a Jehovah's Witness, she refused to consent to the transfusion on religious grounds. Hospital attorneys then obtained an order from the New Jersey Supreme Court (*Raleigh Fitkin–Paul Morgan Memorial Hospital v. Anderson*) under which a special guardian was appointed for the child with authority to "consent to such blood transfusions as may be necessary to preserve the lives of the mother and the child." [16] The court's action was grounded specifically on the right of the unborn child to the protection of the state, even though the mother rather than the child would receive the transfusion(s). Again the United States Supreme Court refused to grant certiorari, although Justice Douglas indicated that he would have granted the writ.[17]

In a recent case on the subject of conscientious objection to public authorization of blood transfusions (*Jehovah's Witnesses v. King Co. Hospital*), Jehovah's Witnesses in the State of Washington sought a declaratory judgment and an injunction against the application of a state statute to themselves as individuals and as a class.[18] Dismissing aspects relating to adults as beyond its jurisdiction, a three-judge federal district court upheld the application of the relevant statutes to juveniles whose parents or guardians belonged to the sect. On appeal, the Supreme Court affirmed the judgment *per curiam,* citing the *Prince* decision.[19] Justices Douglas and Harlan, however, would have noted probable jurisdiction and set the case down for oral argument. Harlan did not indicate why he joined Douglas in this case but not in *Anderson,* but it is possible that he was reluctant to pass judgment on the second case because the patient there was in a short-term danger of death, and a final judicial decision was not likely to be forthcoming before the danger passed and the patient had no further need of transfusions.

Jacobson's potential claim of conscience against compulsory vaccination and those of Jehovah's Witnesses against compulsory blood transfusions involved duties not to cooperate actively (Jacobson) or passively (Jacobson and the Witnesses) with actions deemed by the individuals to be immoral. If so, they were of a high order. Judges in at least two of these cases, those of *George* and of *Georgetown Hos-*

pital, made inquiries of the patients to ascertain whether and to what extent they would feel morally obliged to resist court-ordered transfusions and found the patients to have no moral objection to submission if the courts assumed responsibility. But in every case where courts judged that there was a serious interest in the health of the general public (as in the case of *Jacobson*), or in the life of minors (as in the case of *Wallace* and *King Co. Hospital*), or in the life of an unborn child (as in the case of *Anderson*), or in the welfare of minor children (as in the cases of *George* and *Georgetown Hospital*), the decisions were favorable to the public interest.

Some opponents of restrictive abortion legislation also raise claims of conscience against a public interest in the protection of at least potentially human life. Pregnant women may perceive abortions as important or even essential to the well-being of their home life and children. Thus they may perceive abortions as relatively necessary moral duties. Against such claims of conscience, the public has traditionally asserted an interest in protecting the lives of unborn children. Other expectant mothers, of course, perceive abortions only in terms of moral rights unrelated to moral duties, and the public debate—both legislative and judicial—is taking place in this context.

Similar to the objections of Jehovah's Witnesses to blood transfusions are those of Christian Scientists to the use of medicines, and these objections may conflict with public law when, for example, local authorities fluoridate water supplies. Such individuals are coerced to act against judgments of their consciences by financial and other costs of nonparticipation; their only morally acceptable options within the context of their religious beliefs would appear to be to buy unfluoridated water for drinking purposes or to move out of the locality. The locality, however, cannot accommodate the conscientious objections of Christian Scientists without forgoing the entire program of fluoridation.

Thus, in the case of fluoridation, there is no room for an individual conscience to claim immunity from public law; the policy of fluoridation itself is at issue. Although recognition of Christian Scientists' objections to fluoridation might deny only small benefits to individual citizens, the cumulative value of fluoridation to the public as a whole might be considered of moderate rank by courts.

EUGENICS AND POPULATION CONTROL

An issue of compulsory sterilization reached the United States Supreme Court as early as 1927 (*Buck v. Bell*).[20] In that case, lawyers for Carrie Buck, a feeble-minded patient in a state hospital whose mother and illegitimate daughter were also feeble-minded, challenged a Virginia statute providing for the compulsory sterilization of institutionalized mental defectives. It was their principal contention that the law deprived the persons affected of their liberty without the due process of law required by the Fourteenth Amendment, but they also argued that the treatment afforded institutionalized patients differed without cause from that afforded mental defectives outside state institutions, and that such discrimination violated the equal-protection clause of the same Amendment.

Justice Holmes, speaking for eight members of the Court, upheld the law against both contentions. On the due-process issue of whether it is within the constitutional power of a state to deprive mental defectives of their physical powers of reproduction, Holmes declared sweepingly: "The principle that sustains compulsory vaccination is broad enough to cover cutting the Fallopian tubes. . . . Three generations of imbeciles are enough." [21] Since "the public welfare may call upon the best citizens for their lives," *a fortiori* it should be able to "call upon those who already sap the strength of the state for those lesser sacrifices, often not felt to be such by those concerned, in order to prevent our being swamped with incompetence."[22] On the equal-protection issue, "the usual last resort of constitutional arguments," Holmes pointed out that the law does all that is needed when it does all that it can "so far and so fast as its means allow."[23]

Since Carrie Buck was a Catholic, her lawyers might have challenged the Virginia law on the ground that submission to sterilization was against her conscience. In fact they did not do so, but had this issue been raised, Buck's complaint would have been analogous to Jehovah's Witnesses' against court-ordered blood transfusions. Thus, her claim of conscience would have been to a moral duty not to submit to an action deemed immoral. From the viewpoint of moral consciousness, it would be an objection to cooperating with an act deemed immoral to the extent that the individual submits without resistance to the physical power of state officials, and, if so, it would be of a high order. But, as Holmes intimated, mental defectives like Buck may not even cross the threshold of moral judgment prerequisite for a conflict of conscience with the sterilization law. Thus, whatever the justice or propriety of compulsory sterilization of mental defectives, there may be no issue involving coercion of the individual mental defective to act against his conscience.

The public interest in the sterilization of mental defectives is, of course, dependent on genetic evidence of the transmission of mental defects. Although the genetic theory behind the Virginia law in the *Buck* case is dubious, the growing capacity of science in the sophisticated control of the reproductive process may result in eugenic legislation. Moreover, compulsory sterilization may be judged to serve public interests other than eugenics. In 1966, for example, the welfare mother of two children, one illegitimate, was arrested and convicted in California on the misdemeanor charge of being in a place where narcotics were used with her knowledge.[24] The municipal judge offered her the choice of imprisonment for six months or probation if she agreed to submit to sterilization, and the judge intimated that he offered the option of sterilization because he did not consider the defendant a fit mother. The defendant refused to agree to sterilization and was jailed. On appeal, however, the sentence was reversed, and probation granted without condition because the law made no provision for such a requirement.[25]

With the high cost of welfare and the large number of illegitimate children supported by welfare, there may be attempts to reduce these expenditures by making public support conditional on sterilization operations or the practice of birth control. Or expansion of population at home and abroad beyond the available food-supply may lead to various forms of compulsory population control, including sterilization after a family has two or three children. If so, the integrity of the individual's reproductive process will again be an issue of public policy and its relation to a dissenting religious or moral conscience. Indeed, even currently existing voluntary public programs of birth control and sterilization raise problems of conscience for public employees who deem them immoral but who may be charged with administering them.

CONTROL OF DRUGS

An unusual, and to most Americans unorthodox, claim of conscience is one to the use of drugs in religious rites. Claims of public health and morals are ranged against this claim. The religious ceremonial of the Native American Church, influential among Indians of the West, for example, makes use of "buttons" of the dried peyote plant, a ceremony in which participants chew peyote, four "buttons" at a time because four is considered a magical number. The peyote used in the rite induces visions, and these inspire singing and prayer in which the plant is reverentially linked to the Holy Trinity of traditional Christianity. California is one of the few states which prohibit the use of peyote, and in April, 1962, three Navahos were arrested while they participated in a peyote service.

Although the Navahos were found guilty after a two-day trial, the California Supreme Court reversed their convictions in 1964 (*People v. Woody*).[26] The court found that members of the Native American Church considered use of the drug in their rites a sacrament. Indeed, they considered peyote even more than a sacrament because they directed prayers to it as to a Deity and condemned nonreligious use of peyote as sacrilegious. The court admitted that the government may restrict practices which purport to be religious, as in the case of Mormon polygamy, but the court argued that this may be done only if a compelling public interest is demonstrated which outweighs the individual's interest in religious freedom. In the instant case, the court held that the state had failed to demonstrate such a public interest; the evidence did not show that the use of peyote worked permanent injury, or that it led to narcotic addiction, or that the Indians used the drug in place of medical care, or that minors participated in the rites.

When Dr. Timothy Leary was tried on a charge of illegal transportation of marijuana in 1966, he advanced a defense similar to that of the Indians who use peyote in their religious rites. Leary testified that he used the drug for religious and scientific purposes and contended that to deny him the right to use it would be a violation of his religious freedom. He also introduced evidence to show that marijuana plays an important role in the rituals of the Brahma-Krishna sect of Hinduism. After a jury in a federal district court found him guilty, he was sentenced to imprisonment for thirty years and fined $40,000. Six months after his conviction and a year before the circuit court ruled on his appeal, Leary announced the foundation of a new religion based on the sacramental use of LSD, marijuana, and peyote, and claimed that this League of Spiritual Discovery already had 411 members.

The United States Court of Appeals unanimously upheld his conviction on September 29, 1967 (*Leary v. United States*).[27] Against Leary's claim to immunity on religious grounds, the court ruled that the use of marijuana was not a prerequisite to the practice of Hinduism because the evidence showed that only some Hindus make use of the drug as an aid to expanding their religious consciousness. (Since Leary was tried and convicted before he formed his own religious society and constituted the use of certain drugs as essential to its members' religious experience, the court did not rule on that state of facts.) Moreover, the court refused to examine the question whether marijuana is in fact a harmful drug, although Leary had introduced evidence at the trial to show that the drug is harmless; it was sufficient for the court that Congress had demonstrated "beyond doubt" by constituting traffic in marijuana a crime subject to severe penalties "that it believed marijuana is an evil in American society and a serious threat to its people." [28] The Supreme Court subsequently reversed Leary's conviction but without reviewing the First Amendment claim.[29]

The appellate court in the Leary case challenged whether his activity was essential to the practice of his religion. But such a question seems more theological than legal, and courts would do well to assume that the sincere individual is best qualified to interpret what constitutes a religious duty for him. Accordingly, the federal Court of Appeals in the Leary case should have assumed that the defendant, if sincere, fairly represented his perception of a duty of religious worship, and should have followed the example of the California Supreme Court in the peyote case by inquiring only into the public interest in prohibiting traffic in marijuana to Leary. The essential questions for the court to have asked in such an inquiry were two: (1) Was there sufficient evidence for Congress to judge that the drug was in fact an evil requiring the penalties assigned? and (2) If so, was there a compelling public interest in refusing to grant Leary immunity from the regulation so that he might follow his conscience in matters of religious worship? Had the court answered the first question affirmatively and the second negatively, a serious question about Leary's sincerity in the representation of his religious beliefs might still remain, and the court might have remanded the case to the lower court for a determination of that fact. The question whether Leary's claim to immunity for the use of marijuana as a type of sacrament in a religious rite was sincere or whether religion was invoked simply to justify secularly motivated activity may be best left unasked in criminal prosecutions when there is no risk of loss to a third party or to the government outside of the regulatory prohibition itself.

These two cases involving the use of drugs in religious rites illustrate the importance of assessing both the weights to be attached to claims of individual conscience and those of public interest. On the one hand, if Leary's claim is taken at face value, then both he and the members of the Native American Church in the California case were laying claims to an immunity for their actions. Like Harden, they claimed that the actions for which they sought immunity were religious duties relatively indispensable to their moral integrity. Although these claims are not absolute and specific, as is the case of negative prescriptions of conscience against the performance of acts commanded by public law, they are nonetheless claims to duties which leave no choice of means to the individuals perceiving them. In this respect, such duties morally oblige the individual more severely than those general duties which leave a choice concerning the means and degree of implementation, such as "give to the poor" or "preach the gospel."

On the other hand, if a compelling public interest is required to justify restrictions on such religious duties, assessment of the public interest at stake will involve a two-fold consideration: the public interest as applied to the public generally, and the public interest as applied to the individual claiming exemption for reasons of conscience. Accordingly, the state would have a burden of proof in the case of Leary and that of the Indians to show not only public interests sufficient to justify the regulations involved as applied to the public generally but also *compelling* public interests as applied to the claimants of conscience to exemptions. The appellate court in the case of the Indian peyote rite adhered to this method of analysis, but the appellate court in the Leary case did not. Had it done so, it might have reached the same result against Leary on the basis of evidence sufficient to sustain the judgment of Congress that any use of marijuana would result in serious harm to the public.

REST AND RECREATION

On the same day on which the United States Supreme Court invalidated the flat license taxes on the incidental sale of religious literature by itinerant evangelists (*Murdock v. Pennsylvania*),[30] the court affirmed the right of Jehovah's Witnesses evangelists to distribute from door to door handbills advertising a meeting, despite a city ordinance (*Martin v. Struthers*).[31] An ordinance of Struthers, Ohio, forbade knocking on the door or ringing the doorbell of a private residence in order to deliver a handbill, and the city argued that the ordinance was designed to prevent crime and to assure privacy in an industrial community where many citizens worked on night shifts and slept during the day. But the Court held that these reasons were insufficient to justify the ordinance.

Justice Black, speaking for the majority, found that the ordinance controlled the distribution of literature and substituted community judgment for that of the individual householder. Although Black accepted the validity of "reasonable police and health regulations of the time and manner of distribution" of literature to protect the leisure of citizens against intrusion and their property against burglary, he thought that the Ohio ordinance curtailed the freedoms of speech and of the press too broadly.[32] He pointed out that the law of trespass protected the householder who posted his residence against uninvited distributors, and that the registration and licensing of distributors for purposes of identification could control abuse by criminals. In a separate opinion, Justice Murphy, joined by Justices Douglas and Rutledge, agreed with Black but argued further that "freedom of religion has a higher dignity under the Constitution than municipal or personal convenience."[33] Thus, although Black and Chief Justice Stone were content to rest the decision on the freedoms of speech and of the press, Justices Murphy, Douglas, and Rutledge cited as well the freedom of religious exercise. Justice Frankfurter accepted the decision insofar as it struck down an invidious discrimination against distributors of literature in favor of ordinary vendors.[34] But Frankfurter would have extended the total prohibition of bell-ringing and door-knocking even to the "door-to-door vending of phylacteries or rosaries or of any printed matter."[35]

Justice Reed, joined by Justices Jackson and Roberts, dissented.[36] He argued that the ordinance did not prohibit the distribution of literature but only of handbills, circulars, and other printed advertisements, and he did not consider the classification discriminatory because the irritations arising from distribution of the latter materials might be judged more serious than those arising from distribution of other materials or from the activities of ordinary vendors.

The nature of the Witnesses' claim of conscience in this case is clear: they claimed the right to implement their general religious duty to preach their beliefs and proselytize nonbelievers by door-to-door solicitation. They were not compelled by the ordinance to act against their consciences nor impeded from the performance of a religious duty which was specific about means; rather they were denied one useful means of carrying on the proselytism which they conceived as religious duty.

The public interests which the ordinance sought to secure were at best of low to moderate weight. The prohibition of all door-to-door distribution of handbills bore only a tenuous relation to the prevention of crime since the municipality could require salesmen and distributors of handbills to register and obtain a license for a nominal fee. More substantial was the public interest in securing the privacy of residents against the nuisance of door-to-door distributors of handbills, but the Court split sharply on the value to be assigned to this public interest in relation to the counterclaim by the Witnesses to freedoms of speech, of the press, and of religion. The majority argued that an individual desiring privacy could assure it by posting a prohibition of uninvited visitation, and that the rights to freedom of expression overrode whatever public interest was at stake. The dissenters argued that the ordinance was the most efficient way to protect the privacy of residents, and that the legitimacy of such a public interest was sufficient to justify the limitation on freedom of expression.

Black and Stone assimilated the Witnesses' claim of conscience to the more general freedoms of speech and of the press. Although Douglas, Murphy, and Rutledge cited freedom of religion in their separate opinion, they agreed that freedoms of speech and of the press were at issue. And Frankfurter's qualified concurrence rested on the requirement of reasonable classification by the equal-protection clause of the Fourteenth Amendment. Thus, the six justices of the majority did not create an exemption for religiously motivated distribution of handbills from door to door but rather established a principle applicable to all noncommercial distributors of handbills as well. Moreover, since Frankfurter defended the right of a municipality to prohibit all uninvited solicitation, the division of the justices was basically the same as in *Murdock*. The justices disagreed in both cases about the standard to be applied in First Amendment conflicts between individual claims and public regulations; the majority, consisting of Black, Douglas, Murphy, Rutledge, and Stone, required local governments, in effect, to show compelling public interests to justify limitations of First Amendment rights, and the minority, consisting of Frankfurter, Jackson, Reed, and Roberts, were willing to sustain any arguably reasonable legislative determination of even a low public interest against claims to First Amendment rights.

The *Martin* decision permitted noncommercial distributors of handbills to summon occupants to the door despite an ordinance to the contrary, but it did not affect the validity of the prohibitory regulation with respect to commercial distributors. Eight years later, in 1951, the Court specifically upheld an ordinance of Alexandria, Louisiana, which forbade entrance to the property of private residences to solicit orders for the sale of goods without prior consent of the owners or occupants (*Breard v. Alexandria*).[37] Breard, an agent of a Texas corporation, was fined for violating the ordinance when he solicited subscriptions for magazines and periodicals in Alexandria. Speaking for the majority upholding the ordinance, Justice Reed was joined by Justices Burton, Clark, Frankfurter, Jackson, and Minton. Reed found that the ordinance did not represent a violation of the due-process clause in classification by the prohibition on door-to-door selling or any discrimination against, or undue burden on, interstate commerce. With respect to the *Martin* precedent, he argued that there had been no "element of the commercial" present in that case.[38] Justice Black, joined by Justice Douglas, dissented on the grounds that First Amendment freedoms enjoyed a preferred constitutional status, that freedom of the press was involved here, and that freedom of the press included the freedom to circulate magazines and periodicals.[39] Chief Justice Vinson dissented solely on the ground that the ordinance discriminated against, and unduly burdened, interstate commerce.[40]

Another and more general conflict between private claims of religious conscience and the public interest in the protection of leisure is that of Sabbatarian entrepreneurs against the restrictions imposed on them by Sunday laws. Forty-nine states make illegal on Sunday some form of conduct which would be lawful if performed on weekdays.[41] Fifteen states forbid only one or several activities, while thirty-four have enacted a comprehensive ban on Sunday labor and sales.[42] Of these thirty-four states, twenty-two make an exception from the ban against Sunday labor for Sabbatarians, but only eleven extend the exemption to Sunday sales.[43] In all, thirty-seven states maintain some form of restrictive legislation on Sunday labor or sales or both without exempting conscientious Sabbatarians.

Although the United States Supreme Court had refused in 1951 to review the constitutionality of the New York Sunday law "for want of a substantial federal question" (*Friedman v. New York*),[44] conflicting decisions by federal district courts of the first and third circuits in 1959 induced the Court to review similar laws of Massachusetts and Pennsylvania.[45] At the same time, two cases from a federal district court in Pennsylvania and the Court of Appeals of Maryland were granted review in 1960.[46] Over the sole dissent of Justice Douglas, the Supreme Court ruled in the spring of 1961 in favor of the contested Sunday laws of

Massachusetts, Pennsylvania, and Maryland (*McGowan v. Maryland*).[47] Chief Justice Warren, speaking for the majority, rejected the contention that the Sunday laws in dispute were religious legislation. The Chief Justice conceded that these laws were "undeniably religious in origin" and "still contained references to the Lord's Day." [48] But he found that the basis for the Sunday legislation before the Court was no longer exclusively or even primarily religious, and that the statutes in question had been "divorced from the religious orientation of their predecessors." [49]

The Sunday laws at issue were designed to provide a periodic respite from work for all citizens and simultaneously to insure fair conditions of retail competition. Against the contention that a day-of-rest purpose would be adequately fulfilled by a regulation which prescribed a one-day-in-seven rest, the Chief Justice observed that "it seems plain that the problems involved in enforcing such a provision would be exceedingly more difficult than those in enforcing a common day-of-rest provision." [50] Even more important is the Chief Justice's argument that, in addition to providing a one-day-in-seven work stoppage, the states sought by Sunday legislation "to set one day apart from all others as a day of rest, repose, recreation, and tranquillity—a day which all members of the family and community have the opportunity to spend and enjoy together." [51] One effect of the legislation, of course, was to prefer the orthodox Christian day of rest, but Warren thought it "unrealistic for enforcement purposes and perhaps detrimental to the general welfare to require a state to choose a common day of rest other than that which most persons would select of their own accord." [52]

The Sabbatarians before the Court in two of these cases (*Braunfeld v. Brown* and *Crown Kosher Super Market v. Gallagher*) contended further that states with Sunday laws are obliged at least to exempt from the Sunday labor and sales ban those who conscientiously observe another day of the week as a day of rest.[53] Such an exemption, they argued, would achieve the state's interest in a day of rest for all citizens and simultaneously relieve Sabbatarians of the economic burdens imposed on them by Sunday laws. Since a state can achieve the secular purposes of Sunday law without imposing an indirect burden on their religious observance, the Sabbatarians argued that the application of Sunday laws to them was invidiously discriminatory and constitutionally invalid.

The central question thus presented was whether the state could in fact achieve the secular goal of Sunday laws if it extended exemptions to conscientious Sabbatarians. Chief Justice Warren pointed out several ways in which exemptions might adversely affect the secular aims of Sunday laws. First, enforcement problems would be more difficult since there would be two or more days to enforce rather than one. Moreover, to "allow only people who rest on a day other than Sunday to keep their businesses open on that day might well provide these people with an economic advantage over their competitors who must remain closed on that day." [54] Because of the potential competitive advantage, unscrupulous entrepreneurs might assert that religious convictions compelled them to close on a less profitable day, and a state might object to conducting an inquiry into the sincerity of merchants' religious beliefs. Exempted employers might hire only employees whose religious beliefs qualified them for the exemption, and a state might legitimately oppose the injection of a religious factor into the employment picture. Finally, if exemptions for conscientious Sabbatarians did indeed assure a day of rest for all citizens without upsetting the balance of competition or creating other problems, they would still undermine the common day of rest and recreation which the Sunday laws were also designed to provide.

Justice Douglas dissented from the decision of the Court in all four cases.[55] In his view, the Sunday laws in dispute constituted religious legislation and hence an establishment prohibited by the First and Fourteenth Amendments. Moreover, Sunday laws "put an economic penalty on those who observe Saturday rather than Sunday as the Sabbath," and hence constitute state interference with the free exercise of religion.[56] The American ideal of religious liberty, in Justice Douglas' view, demands absolute respect for the "religious regime of every group . . . unless it crosses the line of criminal conduct." [57] And Sunday labor or sales are intrinsically "wholesome and not antisocial." [58]

Justices Brennan and Stewart dissented only in the two cases in which Sabbatarians complained of an infringement of the free exercise of their religious beliefs.[59] Justice Brennan admitted that Sunday laws do not compel overt affirmation of a repugnant belief, that the effect of Sunday laws on the religious observance of Sabbatarians is indirect, that the granting of exemptions to Sabbatarians would "make Sundays a little noisier and the task of the police . . . a little more difficult," and that the exempted "non-Sunday observers might get an unfair [competitive] advantage." [60] But the mere convenience of having everyone rest on the same day could not justify making one or more religions economically disadvantageous. The free exercise of religion, in Brennan's view, is a "preferred" freedom and may be infringed—even indirectly—only to prevent the grave and imminent dangers of criminal actions or other substantive evils.

Opponents of Sunday laws also objected that the legislative classifications of permissible and prohibited occupations were arbitrary and thus violated the Fourteenth Amendment guarantee of equal protection. Classifications of and exemptions from prohibited occupations have been subject to pressure from almost every lobby. Yet the general rationale of Sunday laws is fairly clear: the legislatures wished to establish a day of rest by more or less comprehensively forbidding unnecessary business on Sunday. If account is taken of the recreational opportunities proper to a day of rest, many of the apparent anomalies of classification dissolve. But even if there remain substantial anomalies of classification, legislatures may recognize degrees of harm and act accordingly. To exercise discretion in the choice of means to combat the evils of uninterrupted labor or to express belief concerning the degree of harm in certain business activities is part and parcel of the legislative function of classification. For these reasons, Chief Justice Warren concluded that "on the record before us we cannot say that these statutes do not provide equal protection of the laws."[61]

The nature of the Sabbatarians' claims of conscience involved in these cases was not in dispute. The Sunday laws at issue did not demand that Sabbatarians work on the Sabbath, but only that they abstain from commercial activity on Sunday. In this respect, their claims differed from those of Mrs. Sherbert, whom South Carolina required to accept work on Saturday under penalty of losing eligibility for unemployment compensation.[62] Nor did the Sunday laws prohibit outright any religious practice or any implementation of general religious or moral duties. But the effect of the Sunday laws was that Sabbatarian entrepreneurs were not permitted to practice their religion and their trade simultaneously without incurring substantial economic loss by remaining closed for business on both Saturday and Sunday. The Sabbatarians' claims of conscience in these cases, therefore, were to a right to engage in commercial activity on Sunday because their religious duties obliged them to refrain from such activity on Saturday.

Like Jones, Murdock, and Follett, the Sabbatarian entrepreneurs did not claim that their consciences prescribed commercial activities as religious duties,[63] but rather that they had a right to engage in such activities because they were economically incidental to the observance of religious duties. But the Sabbatarians' claims of conscience against the restrictions of the Sunday laws were more pressing than those of the Jehovah's Witnesses in *Jones*, *Murdock*, and *Follett*; the effect of the Sunday laws was to coerce the former by financial penalties to act against negative, specific, and absolute prescriptions of conscience, while the effect of the flat license fees exacted from the latter incidental to their itinerant evangelism was to impede the implementation of a general religious duty to proselytize unbelievers. Hence the moral integrity of the Sabbatarian entrepreneurs was more threatened by Sunday laws than that of the Jehovah's Witnesses by the flat license fees, and the moral claims of the former are of moderate rank in comparison with those of the latter.

The nature and legitimacy of the public interest protected by Sunday laws were also not strongly disputed. Only Justice Douglas thought that the laws preferred orthodox Christianity by selecting Sunday as a common day of rest, and that there was accordingly no constitutionally permissible public interest to justify the laws. The rest of the Court identified the public interest in these cases with the secular goal of common rest and recreation and defended its sufficiency for the general regulation of business. These eight members of the Court further agreed that the public interest against a grant of exemption to Sabbatarian entrepreneurs was also based on the likelihood in such a case of administrative difficulties and competitive imbalance.

But Justices Brennan and Stewart dissented (1) from the values assigned by the Court to common rest and recreation, administrative convenience, and competitive balance against a grant of exemptions to Sabbatarian businessmen from the restrictions of Sunday laws, and (2) from the Court's constitutional criterion for deciding between the conflicting claims of the state and the Sabbatarians. On the first point, the dissenting justices thought much less of the values of common rest and recreation, administrative convenience, and competitive balance than did the majority of the Court; they thought that the public interests in the denial of exemption to Sabbatarians were of relatively low value, while the majority apparently thought them of at least moderate value.

On the second point, Justice Brennan thought that the constitutional criterion to determine the legitimacy of state regulation of commercial activity against claims of conscience to exemption on the basis of economic consequences was the presence of a compelling public interest, and Justice Stewart thought that Sunday closing laws involved a choice "which no state can constitutionally demand," at least "in the interest of enforced Sunday togetherness."[64] Chief Justice Warren, however, was satisfied to rest the case against a grant of exemption to Sabbatarians on a distinction between direct and indirect burdens on the freedom of religious exercise:

> To strike down, without the most critical scrutiny, legislation which imposes only an indirect burden on the exercise of religion, i.e., legislation which does not make unlawful the religious practice itself, would radically restrict the operating latitude of the legislature.[65]

The Chief Justice mentioned specifically the indirect burdens which limited tax-deductions for religious contributions imposed on those whose religion required larger donations and the indirect burden which the closing of the courts on Saturday and Sunday imposed on lawyers who observe another day of the week as a day of religious rest.

The subsequent *Sherbert* decision clarified the positions of Justice Brennan and Chief Justice Warren in the Sunday-closing cases. Justice Brennan indicated that he was willing to interpret the decision in those cases as resting on a finding of a substantial, "compelling" public interest in the denial of exemption to Sabbatarian entrepreneurs;[66] but Chief Justice Warren and his associates in the Sunday-closing cases (except Harlan) joined Brennan's opinion and acquiesced in his requirement of a "compelling" public interest to justify the imposition of even indirectly serious economic consequences upon the exercise of religious conscience. Thus Brennan and Warren in *Sherbert* narrowed their disagreement in *Braunfeld* to one of evaluation rather than of criterion, namely, whether denial of exemptions from Sunday laws to Sabbatarians protected low or moderate to high public interests. Concurring Justice Stewart, however, adhered to his view in the Sunday-closing cases that the state may not put an individual to the choice between his religion and his business, and that the decision in *Sherbert* was inconsistent with the decisions in the previous cases of Sabbatarian claims of conscience.[67]

MISCELLANEOUS

Several other claims of conscience have been or might be asserted against assorted claims of public-welfare interests. One of these was involved in a professed agnostic's claim of a right to serve as a notary public despite a requirement by the State of Maryland that all officeholders declare their belief in the existence of God. Torcaso had been appointed to the office of notary public by the governor but was refused a commission because he would not declare such a belief. Although the state courts upheld the requirement, the United States Supreme Court ruled unanimously in favor of Torcaso (*Torcaso v. Watkins*).[68] Justice Black, speaking for the Court, held that the Maryland requirement that officeholders declare a belief in the existence of God unconstitutionally invaded Torcaso's freedom of religion contrary to the guarantees of the First and Fourteenth Amendments. The Court reaffirmed the interpretation of the establishment clause in *Everson* to the effect that "neither a state nor the federal government can constitutionally force a person 'to profess a belief or disbelief in any religion' " and added that "neither can constitutionally . . . impose requirements which aid all religions as against nonbelievers." [69]

Although Torcaso's legal claim was phrased principally as an absolute challenge to the legitimacy of the Maryland requirement, his claim may also be understood as one of conscience. Since the political penalty and incidental financial loss were relatively light, and since Torcaso was not compelled in any case to hold the office of notary public, he could not claim that he was directly coerced by the state to act against his conscience and to repudiate his conscientiously held beliefs. Rather, his claim was potentially to a right not to be politically penalized for adhering to his beliefs and so indirectly pressured into acting against them. Thus it was a potential claim of conscience to a right incidental, if peripheral, to the fulfillment of a negative duty not to profess as true those beliefs which he held to be false.

The claim of a public interest in the declaration by officeholders that they believe in the existence of God was presumably akin to the argument of Locke that atheists are not to be trusted because "promises, covenants, and oaths, which are the bond of human society, can have no hold upon an atheist." [70] Such an argument is unsupported by any empirical evidence, and the Court found the public interest at stake totally deprived by the establishment clause of any constitutional standing. Torcaso's claim of conscience may have been only of a moderate rank in comparison with other such claims, but the countervailing public interest was held to be null because it was entirely excluded from any protection by government action.

Several decades ago, Miss Vivian Kellems dramatically refused to pay her income taxes because she claimed that the progressive features of those taxes constituted an "immoral" confiscation of her property for redistributive purposes.[71] Miss Kellems did not claim an exemption from the exactions of federal income taxes; she challenged the legitimacy of the entire system. Her claim and those of others opposed to regulatory and redistributive functions of the welfare state dispute the nature and general purposes of government, and essentially these claims involve matters of political philosophy rather than of moral imperatives.

Miss Kellems did not claim that progressive income taxes coerced her to act against any prescription of conscience. Nor did she claim that such taxes hindered her from carrying out any moral duty. Nor did she claim a moral duty to oppose progressive income taxes in behalf of others. She claimed only that the existing tax laws operated unjustly on her. Similarly, other complaints against alleged injustices by government policies of economic regulation and redistribution do not typically pose a conflict between the moral imperatives of individuals and the legal imperatives of society but rather a challenge to the validity of the legal imperatives themselves. And unlike the objection of Jehovah's Witnesses to blood transfusions, money rather than bodily integrity is at stake.

Objections to regulatory schemes affecting public morals are frequently similar to those of Miss Kellem. Those who oppose legal prohibition of the use of alcohol or marijuana, for instance, are likely to argue on philosophical rather than constitutional grounds that such regulations are "no business of the government." Assuming, as in Miss Kellems' case, that these objections qualify as moral claims to freedom of choice and action, however, they are not claims to immunity from legal coercion contrary to negative prescriptions of conscience. Nor are they claims to immunity from legal coercion which would impede the execution of positive moral duties. Nor are they even claims of rights or privileges incidental to the execution of moral duties. Rather they are claims that the objectionable regulatory laws invade the individual's freedom of moral choice. As in the case of Miss Kellems, the claims are not to exemptions or exceptions for the individuals affected from the regulatory schemes but to the legitimacy of the regulations themselves. Thus these claims do not represent a conflict between moral and legal imperatives but a challenge to the validity or wisdom of the legal imperatives themselves.

NOTES

1. *Harden v. State,* 188 Tenn. 17, 216 S.W.2d 708 (1948).
2. *Harden,* 188 Tenn. 20, 216 S.W.2d 709.
3. *Ibid.*
4. *Infra,* pp. 150–156.
5. *Jacobson v. Massachusetts,* 197 U.S. 11 (1905).
6. *Ibid.*
7. *Ibid.,* p. 39 (without opinion).
8. In re *Brooks' Estate,* 32 Ill.2d 316, 205 N.E.2d 435 (1965).
9. *Erickson v. Dilgard,* 44 Misc.2d 27, 252 N.Y.S.2d 705 (1962).
10. *People* ex rel. *Wallace v. Labrenz,* 411 Ill. 618, 104 N.E.2d. 769 (1952).
11. *Labrenz v. Ill.* ex rel. *Wallace,* 344 U.S. 824 (1952).
12. *U.S. v. George,* 239 F.Supp. 752 (1965).
13. *Application of President and Directors of Georgetown College, Inc.,* 331 F.2d 1000 (1963).
14. *Application of President and Directors of Georgetown College, Inc.,* 331 F.2d 1010 (1964).
15. *Jones v. President and Directors of Georgetown College, Inc.,* 377 U.S. 978 (1964).
16. *Raleigh Fitkin–Paul Morgan Memorial Hospital v. Anderson,* 42 N.J. 421, 424, 201 A.2d 537, 538 (1964).
17. *Anderson v. Raleigh Fitkin–Paul Morgan Memorial Hospital,* 377 U.S. 985 (1964).
18. *Jehovah's Witnesses v. King Co. Hospital,* 278 F.Supp. 488 (1967).
19. *Jehovah's Witnesses v. King Co. Hospital,* 390 U.S. 598 (1968); cf. *Prince v. Massachusetts* 321 U.S. 158 (1944) and Chap. 6, pp. 156–159.
20. *Buck v. Bell,* 274 U.S. 200 (1927). Only Justice Butler dissented.
21. *Ibid.,* p. 207.
22. *Ibid.*
23. *Ibid.,* p. 208.
24. *The New York Times,* May 24, 1966, p. 39.

25. *The New York Times,* June 9, 1966, p. 51.
26. *People v. Woody,* 40 Cal. Rptr. 69, 394 P.2d 813 (1964).
27. *Leary v. U.S.,* 383 F.2d 851 (1967).
28. *Ibid.,* p. 861.
29. *Leary v. U.S.,* 395 U.S. 6 (1969).
30. *Murdock v. Pennsylvania,* 319 U.S. 105 (1943); see Chap. 2, p. 109.
31. *Martin v. Struthers,* 319 U.S. 141 (1943).
32. *Ibid.,* p. 147.
33. *Ibid.,* pp. 151–52.
34. *Ibid.,* p. 152.
35. *Ibid.,* p. 154.
36. *Ibid.*
37. *Breard v. Alexander,* 341 U.S. 622 (1951).
38. *Ibid.,* p. 643.
39. *Ibid.,* p. 649.
40. *Ibid.,* p. 645.
41. Alaska is the only state with no Sunday legislation. See Appendix II of Justice Frankfurter's concurring opinion in *McGowan v. Maryland,* 366 U.S. 420, 551–60 (1961).
42. *Ibid.*
43. *Ibid.* New York has joined the ranks of those states which since 1961 have been granting exemptions to Sabbatarians. Only one state with a selective sales ban, Wisconsin, provides exemption for Sabbatarians.
44. *Friedman v. New York,* 341 U.S. 907 (1951).
45. *Crown Kosher Super Market v. Gallagher,* 176 F.Supp. 466 (1959) and *Two Guys From Harrison–Allentown, Inc. v. McGinley,* 179 F.Supp. 944 (1959), respectively. For the Supreme Court's grant of review, see 362 U.S. 960 (1960).
46. *McGowan v. State,* 220 Maryland 117, 151 A.2d 156 (1958) and *Braunfeld v. Brown,* 184 F.Supp. 352 (1960), respectively. For the Supreme Court's grant of review, see 362 U.S. 959 and 987 (1960), respectively.
47. *McGowan v. Maryland,* 366 U.S. 420 (1961).
48. *Ibid.,* p. 446 and *Gallagher v. Crown Kosher Super Market of Massachusetts,* 366 U.S. 617, 626 (1961), respectively.
49. *Gallagher,* p. 626.
50. *McGowan,* p. 451.
51. *Ibid.,* p. 450.
52. *Ibid.,* p. 452.
53. See nn. 46 and 45, respectively.
54. *Braunfeld v. Brown,* 366 U.S. 599, 608–609 (1961).
55. *McGowan,* pp. 561–81.
56. *Ibid.,* p. 577.
57. *Ibid.,* p. 575.
58. *Ibid.*
59. *Braunfeld,* pp. 610–16 and 616, respectively.

60. *Braunfeld,* pp. 614–15.
61. *McGowan,* p. 428.
62. *Supra,* pp. 105–107.
63. *Supra,* pp. 108–110.
64. *Braunfeld,* p. 616.
65. *Ibid.,* p. 606.
66. *Sherbert v. Verner,* 374 U.S. 398, 406 (1963).
67. *Ibid.,* pp. 413–19.
68. *Torcaso v. Watkins,* 367 U.S. 488 (1961).
69. *Ibid.,* p. 495; cf. *Everson v. Board of Education of Ewing Township, N.J.,* 330 U.S. 1, 15–16 (1947).
70. John Locke, *A Letter Concerning Toleration* in *The Works of John Locke* (12th ed.; London: Rivington, 1824), V, 47.
71. See, e.g., *The New York Times,* January 17, 1949.

6

Conscience, Family, and Education

In the preceding four chapters, conflicts between individual conscience and public interests in national security, internal order, and public welfare have been considered. All these conflicts involved moral issues at bottom and in the broadest sense. The claims of individual conscience were *ex professo* moral; the claims of society were based ultimately on value judgments about what is good or bad for citizens. As Aristotle observed over two thousand years ago:

> Lawgivers make the citizens good by inculcating [good] habits in them, and this is the aim of every lawgiver; if he does not succeed in doing that, his legislation is a failure. It is in this that a good constitution differs from a bad one.[1]

But the legal concept of "public morality" in modern times has the narrower meaning of legal restrictions on the behavior of citizens which are directly aimed at their character-formation rather than their physical well-being, and such restrictions have been challenged in the name of conscience by members of minority religious groups outside the dominant American consensus.

Some of the conflicts between individual conscience and public law previously considered involved issues of public morality in the narrower sense. The use of drugs is an example of this, not only with respect to those who, like Leary, claim to use drugs for religious reasons but also with respect to one principal justification alleged for the restrictions.[2] Similarly, court-ordered blood transfusions for parents with religious objections to them may involve an issue not only of their physical well-being but also of the moral well-being of children who would be otherwise deprived of their parents' love and care.[3] But legislation regulating marriage, family, and education aims specifically, if partially, at the character-formation of citizens, and conflicts between such legislation of public morality and dissenting consciences are the subject of the present chapter.

MARRIAGE

In the second half of the nineteenth century, there was a bitter conflict between Mormons settling in the West, especially in Utah, and the federal government administering the territories. Between 1870 and 1890, 573 Mormons were convicted of the crime of plural marriage or unlawful cohabitation.[4] In the first of the cases involving this conflict to reach the full Supreme Court (*Reynolds v. United States*), a Mormon named George Reynolds had been convicted of bigamy.[5] On appeal, Reynolds claimed that he should have been acquitted since he sincerely believed that the practice of polygamy was commanded by the tenets of his religion. A unanimous Court, through Chief Justice Waite, accepted the allegation of the plaintiff in error that he was a member of the Mormon Church, that "it was the duty of male members of said church, circumstances permitting, to practice polygamy," that "the failing or refusing to practice polygamy by such male members of said church, when circumstances would admit, would be punished," and that "the penalty for such failure and refusal would be damnation in the life to come." [6] The issue thus joined was whether the federal statute forbidding bigamy as applied to Mormons abridged the First Amendment guarantee of the freedom of religious exercise.

Against Reynolds' claim, the Court cited the preamble to the Virginia Statute of Religious Liberty, in which its drafter, Jefferson, conceded that government might rightfully "interfere when [religious] principles break out into overt acts against peace and public order." [7] Moreover, after the United States had adopted the Constitution and the Bill of Rights, Jefferson interpreted the First Amendment in his letter to the Danbury Baptist Association as establishing a "wall of separation" between church and state. But, the Court noted, President Jefferson in the same letter expressed his conviction that there was "no natural right in opposition to . . . social duties." [8] Since Jefferson was the "acknowledged leader" of advocates of the Amendment, the Court argued, the Danbury statement "may be accepted almost as an authoritative declaration of the scope and effect of the Amendment." [9] Accordingly, "Congress was deprived of all legislative power over mere opinion but was left free to reach actions . . . in violation of social duties or subversive of good order." [10] The court then pointed to the long legal tradition against the practice of bigamy, indicating, in particular, that all the colonies had had laws against bigamy, and that the same Virginia Legislature which had enacted the Statute of Religious Liberty also passed a statute against bigamy, which included the death penalty.

Considering the public interest served by the legislation against bigamy, the Court observed with a flourish of Anglo-Saxon superiority that the practice had always been "odious among the northern and western nations of Europe and, until the establishment of the Mormon Church, was almost exclusively a feature of the life of Asiatic and of African people."[11] The Court recognized marriage not only as a "sacred obligation" but also as a civil contract subject to regulation by law.[12] Society was said to be built upon the foundation of marriage and the family, and principles of government to be related to the kind of marriage unions prevailing. Citing a Professor Lieber in a very rare use of sociological jurisprudence for the period, the Court argued that polygamy led to a patriarchal principle which would fetter people in "stationary despotism," while monogamy led in the opposite direction, the direction of democracy.[13] The Court conceded that an exceptional colony of polygamists might exist for a time without disturbing the social conditions of the majority, but held that its suppression for the general welfare was within the legitimate scope of every civil government to determine.

The only question remaining to be settled by the Court was whether those who practice polygamy as a religious duty were entitled by the First Amendment to an exception from the operation of the regulatory federal statute. The Court ruled that to make such an exception would introduce a new element into criminal law with respect to actions, which, unlike opinions, the government may regulate. To permit an exception for the Mormons would be to make their religious doctrines superior to the law of the land and "permit every citizen to become a law unto himself."[14] The Court bolstered its argument by asking rhetorically whether religious beliefs would be thought to excuse those who performed human sacrifices in their rites or those wives who attempted to immolate themselves upon the funeral pyres of their husbands.

In a postscript little noted by commentators on the *Reynolds* case, the Court on a petition for rehearing vacated the sentence of the trial court.[15] The Court held that the trial court was in error to impose upon Reynolds a sentence of imprisonment at hard labor and remanded the case with instructions to impose a sentence of imprisonment without the specification of hard labor. This action at least suggests how courts can take into account the motivation of a wrongdoer in the matter of the penalties to be imposed even if no exception with respect to criminal liability is considered expedient.

Eleven years after *Reynolds*, the Court again confronted a conflict between the Mormon practice of polygamy and federal law (*Davis v. Beason*).[16] This time the issue involved the right of Mormons to vote in the Territory of Idaho. Davis, a Mormon, was indicted for conspiracy to obstruct the administration of the laws of the territory by seeking to register as a voter and taking the legally prescribed oath in spite of the fact that he knowingly belonged to an organization prohibited by the oath to prospective voters. The oath required voters in the territory to disavow, *inter alia,* the practice of bigamy or polygamy and membership in any organization "which teaches, advises, counsels, or encourages its members, devotees, or any other person to commit the crime of bigamy or polygamy . . . as a duty."[17] In a collateral attack on the indictment, Davis sought a writ of habeas corpus to obtain his freedom. He argued principally that the territorial requirements for voting and the companion oath constituted an "establishment of religion" prohibited by the First Amendment because they in effect proscribed membership in the Mormon Church.

Justice Field, speaking for a unanimous Court, noted first that the issue posed by the petition for a writ of habeas corpus was a narrow one, namely, the issue of jurisdiction. Therefore the Court considered only whether, if the allegations were taken as true, an offense had been committed for which the territorial court had jurisdiction to try the defendant. The Court did not weigh arguments against the oath on the basis of rights to speech or assembly, nor did it appeal to a doctrine of estoppel to preclude Davis from challenging the legality of the oath in view of his presumed perjury. Rather, the Court reviewed only the legality of Idaho's restriction of the right to vote to those who would promise not to teach or counsel the practice of polygamy, as applied to Mormons like Davis.

On this point, the Court thought that there could not be any "serious discussion or difference of opinion." [18] Bigamy and polygamy were said to be crimes "by the laws of all civilized and Christian countries," by the laws of the United States, and by the laws of Idaho, and the Court argued that bigamy and polygamy would "tend to destroy the purity of the marriage relation, to disturb the peace of families, to degrade woman, and to debase man." [19] If bigamy and polygamy were crimes, "then to teach, advise, and counsel their practice" would aid in their commission, and such activities were thus "themselves criminal and proper subjects of punishment, as aiding and abetting crime are in all other cases." [20] The Court argued further that the First Amendment was never intended "as a protection against legislation for the punishment of acts inimical to the peace, good order, and morals of society," [21] and pointed out that there had been religious sects which, as part of their tenets, denied the existence of any marriage tie or required human sacrifices on special occasions. Should a sect of either kind attempt to carry out its doctrines, the Court did not doubt that "swift punishment would follow," and that "no heed would be given" to the religious motivations of the wrongdoers.[22]

The Mormons' claims of conscience in these cases were to a positive religious duty with respect to the practice of polygamy since the Mormon religion at that time prescribed plural marriage as a religious duty for its male members. The prescription was not absolute because "circumstances" might not permit its fulfillment, and one authority estimates that its actual practice by Mormons never exceeded 15 per cent.[23] Unlike a negative injunction of conscience, where the failure to follow the injunction in matters considered sufficiently important would be compatible with the preservation of moral integrity only by conditions eliminating personal responsibility, a positive prescription of conscience is intrinsically dependent on the circumstances necessary for its fulfillment. Thus in the case of the Mormons, the practice of polygamy was at least contingent upon the availability and consent of potential spouses. One expert has concluded that only 8 per cent of Mormon families in Utah practiced polygamy in the last decade of the nineteenth century;[24] the relative balance between men and women in the state and the poverty of new immigrants probably operated to restrict the practice as much as the opposition of the federal government.

But the religious duty of Mormons to practice polygamy was specific. Unlike a religious duty "to preach the gospel" or "to give to the poor," where the prescription is general and the means unspecified, the religious duty of Mormons to practice polygamy was specific in the conduct prescribed, and its performance, if possible, was presumably regarded as essential to their religious and moral integrity. The moral obligation thus imposed on Mormons by their religious consciences was of a moderately high order. From the viewpoint of the coercion effected by the restrictive legislation on Mormons to forgo what they conceived as a religious duty, the moral plight of Reynolds was probably worse than that of Davis; the former was imprisoned for the practice of polygamy, while the latter, had he not taken the oath, would have lost only the right to vote.

The public interest against the practice of polygamy was based primarily on the moral effects of the practice on those involved, including children. The Court in these cases thought the public interest involved to be a serious one and did not see how an exception could be made for the Mormons without undermining the institution of monogamous marriage in the territory. As Justice Field indicated briefly, polygamy was thought to undermine the value of personal union in marriage, to reduce women to the status of chattels, and to exacerbate the potential for conflict within families. This is a plausible argument against the general practice of polygamy, and there is some evidence that the specific practice of polygamy by Mormons created considerable strains on the participants.[25]

Although the practice of polygamy in the conventional sense was not likely to flourish in modern American society for economic reasons, the practice of taking successive wives did come into prevalence in the twentieth century. Although generally narrow grounds for divorce in most states in the early days of this century undoubtedly caused hardships for those who desired divorces, they did not in the typical case cause conflicts of conscience for the individuals involved. Some may indeed have regarded divorce and remarriage as a moral duty, but this was not likely to have been typical. Individuals in such circumstances were, for the most part, akin to all those who in any period disagree with the objectives of legislation affecting public morals for reasons of personal desire or philosophy of government. At any rate, the issue is no longer a pressing one in American society.

CHILD WELFARE

Although parents are considered by American law to have the primary responsibility for preparing children to assume an adult role in society, the state may intervene as *parens patriae* to restrict parents' control in order to safeguard the public interest in the well-being of children. The leading case on this point is that of *Prince v. Massachusetts.*[26] Mrs. Sarah Prince, a Jehovah's Witness, had legal custody of her nine-year-old niece, Betty Simmons. Although Mrs.

Prince had been warned by a school official on a previous occasion not to do so, she took Betty with her on the evening of December 18, 1941, to preach and to distribute the pamphlets *Watchtower* and *Consolation* on the sidewalk of a street intersection in Brockton, Massachusetts. Betty held up copies of the pamphlets for passersby to see, and although no one accepted a copy from Betty or gave her money, a canvas magazine bag hung from her shoulder on which was printed "*Watchtower* and *Consolation*, 5¢ per copy." Mrs. Prince was convicted of violating Massachusetts child-labor laws, which forbade boys under 12 and girls under 18 to "sell, expose, or offer for sale any . . . periodicals . . . in any street or public place" and made parents and guardians criminally liable if they compelled or permitted minors under their control to work in violation of the prohibition.[27] The Supreme Judicial Court of Massachusetts upheld Mrs. Prince's conviction, and she appealed to the United States Supreme Court.

Mrs. Prince's appeal rested squarely on the freedom of religious exercise guaranteed by the First Amendment and made applicable to the states by the Fourteenth, and she buttressed her appeal by a claim of parental right as secured by the due-process clause of the latter Amendment. Thus she claimed two liberties, one for herself as parent to teach her ward the tenets and practices of her faith, and the other for the child to observe these by preaching the gospel and distributing religious pamphlets in conformity with the scriptural suggestion that "a little child shall lead them." [28] In a 5–4 decision, the Supreme Court upheld Mrs. Prince's conviction.

Speaking for the narrow majority, Justice Rutledge acknowledged the rights of children to exercise their religion and the right of parents to encourage children's exercise of their religious beliefs. But neither the rights of religious exercise nor the rights of parental control were said to be without limitations. According to Rutledge, the state's authority over children's activities is broader than that over similar activities of adults, and, to assure "the healthy, well-rounded growth of young people," the state may seek to avert "the crippling effects of child employment, more especially in public places, and the possible harms arising from other activities subject to all the diverse influences of the street." [29] Specifically, the "exercise of the right to engage in propagandizing the community, whether in religious, political, or other matters, may and at times does create situations difficult enough for adults to cope with and wholly inappropriate for children." [30] Such employment of children, Rutledge argued, might cause "emotional excitement and psychological or physical injury." [31]

Justice Murphy, speaking for the dissenters, admitted that the power of the state to control religious and other activities of children is greater than its power over similar activities of adults, but he argued that, in dealing with direct or indirect restrictions of religious freedom, the burden is on the state to prove the compelling interests protected by its legislation: "If the right of a child to practice its religion . . . is to be forbidden by constitutional means, there must be convincing proof that such a practice constitutes a grave and immediate danger to the state or to the health, morals, or welfare of the child." [32] In his opinion, the state had failed completely to sustain its burden of proof, and the mere possibility of harm from the distribution of religious literature was insufficient justification for restricting Betty's freedom of religious exercise. Moreover, he thought that such religiously motivated activity under the supervision of a guardian was likely to be immune from the usual harmful influences of the street corner.

Mrs. Prince's claim of conscience as guardian was to a right to allow and encourage her niece to distribute religious literature on street corners as part of a general duty to "preach the gospel." Since there were available to Mrs. Prince's ward other methods of implementing this duty, such as the visiting of private homes or the public distribution of handbills unconnected with the solicitation of funds, Mrs. Prince's claim of conscience was not pressing from the viewpoint of the threatened impact of the child-labor laws on her own religious or moral integrity or that of her ward. This is not to say that Mrs. Prince's claim was trivial in all respects, merely that she and her ward had options by which they could fulfill their obligations both to their consciences and to the law.

The public interest at stake in the *Prince* case involved the child's welfare, and this interest was asserted to be not only generic with respect to the effects of child labor but specific with respect to the proselytizing activities of Betty. Since Mrs. Prince claimed an exemption for the religiously motivated activities of her ward from regulations which her lawyers conceded to be valid for identical, secularly motivated, activities, the public interest to be weighed against Mrs. Prince's claim had to rest specifically on the harmful results of Betty's participation in her aunt's proselytizing activities. Although the majority expressed concern for Betty's physical well-being, the main emphasis seems to have been concern for her psychological and moral development. For its part, the minority attempted to show that there was no proof of any danger to Betty's physical safety, mental health, or moral virtue.

In summary, then, Mrs. Prince's claim of conscience was of a relatively low order. In the view of the minority, the public interest against Mrs. Prince's claims of exemption for her niece's proselytizing activities was unproved and accordingly rated low. But in the view of the majority, the public interest in denying her an exemption from the child-labor laws of Massachusetts was of moderate rank and superior to her claim.

EDUCATION: PAROCHIAL SCHOOLS AND CIVIC VIRTUE

Schools in modern American society are perhaps the most influential institution, after the family, in the character-formation of citizens. It is understandable, therefore, why there are so many controversies over the value-orientation of education, especially in primary and secondary schools. One such controversy involves the question of public support for church-related schools. Much of this controversy, especially as expressed in court opinions, has focused on the religious-establishment clause of the First Amendment, but it is not the purpose of this work to study judicial interpretations of that clause.[33] The controversy over public support for church-related schools, however, can be interpreted in terms of a conflict between individual conscience and public law. In fact, there are two such conflicts, one between the individual who feels a religious or moral duty to send his child to a church-related school and the laws which deny him financial aid, and the other between the individual who objects to the expenditure of "his" taxes to support religiously oriented education and the laws which grant various financial aids to church-related schools or their pupils.

Related to the first conflict is the case of *Pierce v. Society of Sisters.*[34] In that case, the Supreme Court struck down an Oregon statute which would have obliged all children to attend public schools. Justice McReynolds, speaking for the unanimous Court, argued that "the child is not the mere creature of the state," and that "those who nurture him and direct his destiny have the right, coupled with the high duty, to recognize and prepare him for additional obligations."[35] Although the issue directly involved in the *Pierce* case was whether the Sisters had a vested property right to operate their private school, that issue was reducible to a claim of conscience by parents of a right to choose a religiously oriented education for their children; the countervailing public interest at stake was one of fostering democratic values by attendance at common schools. In the opinion of the Court, the claim of conscience by parents to a right to implement their duty to educate their children in religious values by attendance at church-related schools was superior to the public interest in the attendance of all children at common schools. The primary target of the Oregon law was the Roman Catholic parochial school system. Since, however, the law was applicable to all private schools, the Court did not examine the validity or strength of a public interest against any alleged threat to civic virtue posed specifically by that system.

The Roman Catholic parents in the *Pierce* case may even have perceived a specific religious duty imposed on them by church rules to send their children to the church-related school. Moreover, their claim may have been strengthened by the importance of schooling for religious formation in modern society. The claim of Oregon that public schools were essential to the transmission of democratic values and the achievement of social unity, on the other hand, was rejected by the Court. Thus perhaps a moderately pressing claim of conscience by the parents of children attending parochial schools was vindicated against what the Court regarded as a low public interest in the moral formation of citizens by compelling their attendance at common schools under threat of criminal penalties.

There is no Supreme Court decision involving claims by parents of children in church-related schools to compel public support, and the reason for this is apparent enough. A claim alleging the failure of public authorities to appropriate money can only succeed if the plaintiff can cite a constitutional guarantee or statutory mandate in his favor, and courts are reluctant to specify what legislatures are obligated to do in the general appropriation of public funds. Since, however, the absence of public support for pupils attending church-related schools can be assumed to reflect a public policy and a public interest, it can be examined as such, and parents' claims to financial support from state and federal governments can be considered for what they are in part, namely, claims of conscience. The claims of parochial school patrons, of course, also involve claims of distributive justice, but for present purposes they can be considered only from the viewpoint of perceived moral obligation.

The claim of parents seeking public support for the education of their children in church-related schools is similar to that fundamentally represented by the Sisters in the *Pierce* case. As in the *Pierce* case, parents may even base their claim of conscience to public support for their children's education at church-related schools on a specific duty imposed by church rules. Or they may assert a right to financial support, not merely a duty to send their children to church-related schools without criminal penalties, thereby claiming a right instrumental to what they perceive as a duty to give their children a religiously oriented education.

One public interest asserted against such financial support is the necessity of attendance at common schools for the transmission of democratic values and the development of social cohesion. But denial of public support for church-related schools may also be based on the effect of such aid on the maintenance of an institutional separation of church and state. Indeed, since church-related schools undeniably include secular subjects in their curricula, a public policy against financial aid to these schools may even reflect a fear that the presence of some or any religious values in education constitutes a threat to civic virtue. (Whatever may be said of the danger which publicly supported church-related schools pose to the separation of church and state or particular religious orientations to democratic values, it would seem clear that an objection to the presence of religious values in the education of youth *qua* religious values would be radically inconsistent with the purposes of the First Amendment.) Thus, the public interest against public support of church-related schools would appear to be ranked higher by most legislators and judges than the interest asserted against the right of such schools to exist; a moderate public interest is seen by them to run counter to claims to public support based on claims of conscience, at most moderate in rank, by the patrons of parochial schools.

When financial aid is given by public laws to church-related schools or their pupils, a different conflict between dissenting individuals and the laws arises. Here the conflict is between those who object to public support of religiously oriented schools and the laws authorizing such support. It is difficult, however, to classify the objections of these dissenters strictly as claims of conscience; they attack the legitimacy of the appropriations in terms of distributive justice and undesirable institutional "entanglements" of church and state rather than in terms of constraints on their dissenting consciences—at least in the short run. (Of course, public support of church-related schools may operate psychologically and socially over time against the integrity of dissenters' beliefs.) They are indeed compelled to pay taxes which will be used for purposes to which they object, but whatever the unfairness or undesirability of such appropriations, dissenters are not coerced to act in any way against their consciousness of their own religious or moral duties, at least in the short run. There is a moral issue at the root of the objections to public support of church-related schools or their pupils, but it is an issue of the legitimacy of such support rather than an immediate issue of coercing the consciences of the individuals who object to it. From this point of view, it is immaterial whether the public support is for bus rides (*Everson v. Board of Education*), or textbooks (*Board of*

Education v. Allen), or more substantial items like teachers' salaries.[36]

EDUCATION: PUBLIC SCHOOLS AND PATRIOTIC EXERCISES

Public schools, because they are publicly created and supported, are subject to greater control by state legislatures than are private schools. In particular, many states require patriotic exercises in public schools, such as those of saluting the flag and of pledging allegiance to the United States, and these exercises have led to one of the sharpest controversies on the rights of conscience in the history of American law. A board of education in Minersville, Pennsylvania, had mandated a program of flag-salute and pledge of allegiance for all teachers and students. When two children, Lillian and William Gobitis, refused for religious reasons to salute the flag, they were expelled from the public schools of the municipality. (The Gobitises were Jehovah's Witnesses, and they believed that to salute the flag would be to worship a "graven image" contrary to the Biblical prohibition of Ex 20:4–5.) Since the children were of an age for which Pennsylvania compelled school attendance, their parents were forced to send them to a private school. Because of the heavy financial burden thereby entailed, the father of the children brought suit in a federal district court to enjoin the local authorities from continuing to exact participation in the flag-salute ceremony as a condition of his children's attendance at the Minersville school. When the district court granted the injunction and the Circuit Court of Appeals affirmed the action, the state appealed to the United States Supreme Court for review.

Justice Frankfurter, speaking for eight members of the Court, overturned the decision of the district court and upheld the validity of the Minersville requirements (*Minersville v. Gobitis*).[37] The year of the *Gobitis* decision was 1940, and the conflict between the Court and Congress and the states in matters of social and economic legislation before 1938 was still a vivid memory. Frankfurter preferred a philosophy of judicial restraint, "to fight out the wise use of legislative authority in the forum of public opinion and before legislative assemblies rather than to transfer such a contest to the judicial arena," and the only question for Frankfurter was one of the legitimacy or reasonableness of the Pennsylvania program.[38] Since a free society is founded on "the binding tie of cohesive sentiment . . . fostered by all those agencies of the mind and spirit which may serve to gather up the traditions of a people, transmit them from generation to generation, and thereby create the community of a treasured common life which constitutes a civilization," Frankfurter said, it may use the educational process to inculcate that sentiment.[39] Against the claim of the Witnesses that they should have an exception or immunity from participation in the flag-salute ceremony because of their conscientious objections to it, Frankfurter argued that such an exception "might introduce elements of difficulty into school discipline" and "might cast doubts in the minds of other children which would themselves weaken the effect of the exercise." [40]

The sole dissenter in the *Gobitis* case was Justice Stone. In his view, the law sustained by the Court as applied to the Gobitis children did more than suppress freedom of speech and prohibit the free exercise of religion: "For by this law the state seeks to coerce these children to express a sentiment which . . . violates their deepest religious convictions." [41] If the guarantees of civil liberty —guarantees of the freedom of the human mind and spirit —are to have any meaning, Stone argued, they must be deemed "to withhold from the state any authority to compel belief or the expression of it where that expression violates religious convictions, whatever may be the legislative view of the desirability of such compulsion." [42] Of the role of the Court in review of the legislative determination of the issue, Stone defended "a searching judicial inquiry into the legislative judgment where prejudice against discreet and insular minorities may tend to curtail the operation of . . . political processes ordinarily to be relied on to protect minorities." [43] And Stone pointed out that the Court had not hitherto hesitated "similarly to scrutinize legislation restricting the civil liberty of racial and religious minorities, although no political process was affected." [44]

The lopsided margin of the *Gobitis* decision should not have encouraged an expectation that it would be reversed in the short period of three years. Yet sharp criticism of the decision by the press and especially by the law journals led three members of the Court to reconsider their views, and when the first *Jones* case was decided in 1942, Justices Black, Douglas, and Murphy stated in dissent that they had become convinced that *Gobitis* was "wrongly decided." [45] With now-Chief Justice Stone, this made four members of the Court who were known to oppose the *Gobitis* ruling. Moreover, Justice Jackson had been appointed to the Court at the time of Chief Justice Hughes' retirement, and Justice Rutledge replaced Justice Byrnes in February, 1943. Thus critics took hope that the *Gobitis* decision would be overruled if a proper case were presented to the Court, and they did not have long to wait.

A year and a half after the *Gobitis* decision in 1940, the West Virginia State Board of Education ordered that the salute to the flag become a regular part of the program of activities in the public schools of the state, and that all teachers and pupils participate in the salute. Failure by pupils to conform was considered "insubordination" to be dealt with by expulsion; some children of the Jehovah's Witness faith actually were expelled from school, and others were threatened with expulsion, for failure to participate in the ceremonies. Officials also threatened to send such children to reformatories for juvenile delinquents, and their parents were prosecuted, or threatened with prosecution, for causing delinquency. A number of these parents then brought suit to enjoin enforcement of the West Virginia regulation against themselves, their children, and other Witnesses. The federal District Court issued the injunction, and the Board of Education appealed directly to the United States Supreme Court.

This time the Witnesses won their case in the high court (*West Virginia v. Barnette*).[46] Justice Jackson, speaking for six members of the Court, noted that the compulsory flag-salute required an "affirmation of a belief and an attitude of mind," [47] and Jackson held that legislatures had no constitutional power to require such an affirmation:

> If there is any fixed star in our constitutional constellation, it is that no official, high or petty, can prescribe what shall be orthodox in politics, nationalism, religion, or other matters of opinion or force citizens to confess by word or act their faith therein. . . . We think the action of the local authorities in compelling the flag salute and pledge transcends constitutional limitations on their power and invades the sphere of intellect and spirit which it is the purpose of the First Amendment . . . to reserve from all official control.[48]

Since there was no power to make the flag-salute a legal duty in the first place, Jackson accordingly did not find it necessary to inquire whether nonconformist beliefs would exempt the Witnesses from the duty to salute. Against the judicial restraint urged by Frankfurter, he argued that "the very purpose of the Bill of Rights was to withdraw certain subjects from the vicissitudes of political controversy, to place them beyond the reach of majorities and officials, and to establish them as legal principles to be applied by the courts." [49]

Jackson thus restated the issue in the flag-salute cases as one of freedom from compulsion of any expression rather than one of freedom from words or acts prohibited by an individual's religious or moral conscience. But Justices Black and Douglas, concurring, emphasized that claim of conscience: "Neither our domestic tranquillity in peace nor our martial effort in war depend on compelling little children to participate in a ceremony which ends in nothing for them but a fear of spiritual condemnation." [50] And Justice Murphy, also concurring, insisted that "official compulsion to affirm what is contrary to one's religious beliefs is the antithesis of freedom of worship." [51] For his part, Justice Frankfurter in dissent repeated his view that the only issue was whether legislators could reasonably prescribe the flag-salute at all.[52] Since the requirement of West Virginia was admittedly not designed to be discriminatory, he would not strike it down because it hurt or offended dissidents.

The claim of conscience represented by Gobitis and Barnette was the same: a claim that the act of flag-saluting required by the state was prohibited to them by a specific, negative, and absolute moral judgment. As such, the claim was of the highest order because there was no way for the individual to obey the law and at the same time preserve his moral integrity. The penalties for nonconformity in the two cases were different, at least in the short run; Gobitis was penalized by the financial costs of private schooling for his children, while Barnette was threatened with imprisonment. But Gobitis might have been forced into Barnette's position in the long run, and, in any case, the penalties coercing both to conform were severe.

The countervailing public interest asserted in these cases, of course, was to the development of patriotic attitudes in the young, and even Frankfurter thought the flag-salute exercises to be at best of moderate utility for this purpose. The *Gobitis* majority did not rest its decision on the high value of flag-salutes to national unity but rather on a judicial philosophy of deference to legislative judgment and an unwillingness to make exceptions for dissenters from laws otherwise deemed valid, although these laws promote only a low to moderate public interest. Jackson's majority opinion in *Barnette* assumed a broader role for the Court in review of legislation affecting civil liberties and avoided a grant of exemptions for conscientious objectors to flag-salutes by invalidating any compulsion of such expression from pupils unwilling to do so for whatever reason or motive. Thus Jackson in effect held the compulsion of flag-salutes to represent no constitutionally valid public interest.

Jehovah's Witnesses might object to even a voluntary program of patriotic exercises in public schools which included flag-salutes because of the socially coercive effects on their nonparticipating children. The claim has never been litigated, but it is similar to that of those parents who objected to voluntary programs of religious exercises in public schools, a claim to be considered in the next section. It would be a claim by the parents to a right not to have their children subjected to the social pressure of publicly sponsored patriotic exercises, a right instrumental to what they would perceive as an absolute duty for their children not to participate. As such, the claim would be against the indirect effect of the exercises and so of moderate rank. Since the claim, if vindicated, would require the elimination of the exercises, the overall public interest in promoting patriotic attitudes in young citizens by the exercises would probably be rated moderate enough to be preferred over the claim of the dissenters.

The public interest in the education of children beyond the eighth grade has been directly challenged by members of the Amish religious sect as a corrupting involvement in "worldliness." The Amish people, who live in tightly knit farm communities, have been prosecuted in several states for refusing to obey laws which require children to attend school until the age of sixteen. The Supreme Court of the

State of Wisconsin has ruled that the compulsory education law, as applied to the Amish, violates the First Amendment's guarantee of the free exercise of religion.[53] The State of Wisconsin petitioned for certiorari, which was granted.[54]

Chief Justice Burger, speaking for the Court, upheld the decision of the Wisconsin Supreme Court in favor of the Amish parents (*Wisconsin v. Yoder* et al.).[55] According to Burger, there was ample evidence that ordinary secondary education contravened the basic religious tenets and practice of the Amish faith, for both the parents and the children, and the state's claim to act as *parens patriae* did not override this claim to the free exercise of religion. The Amish parents had indicated their willingness to provide vocational training with a few hours of formal study each week as an alternative to conventional high-school education, but the state refused to accept the alternative.[56] Under these circumstances, the state had the burden of demonstrating that the loss of one or two years' secondary education would impair the physical or mental health of the children or render them unable to support themselves as adults or detract from their ability to discharge the duties and responsibilities of citizenship. This burden the state failed to sustain to the Court's satisfaction. The Court avowed that its holding did not resolve questions of potential conflict between the wishes of parents and their offspring, although it noted the strong legal tradition in favor of parental rights in the upbringing of their children. And the Court took pains to distinguish the Amish claims from those based on philosophical and personal choice.

Justice Stewart, joined by Justice Brennan, concurred in the judgment and opinion of the Court but emphasized that the decision involved no questions regarding the rights of Amish children to attend public or private high schools if they wished to do so against the will of their parents.[57] Justice White, joined by Justices Brennan and Stewart, also concurred in the judgment and opinion of the Court but only after concluding that the state had not demonstrated the inability of Amish children who leave school after the eighth grade to acquire further academic skills if they later abandon their parents' faith.[58] Justice Douglas concurred in the case of one Amish parent whose child testified that her religious views were opposed to high-school education, but he dissented in two other cases in which the children had not testified; he would have remanded the latter cases for new hearings on the religious views of the children, which views he would have made dispositive of the cases.[59] Douglas also disagreed with the Court's attempt to reserve exemption from compulsory secondary education to those motivated by religious views in the traditional sense. The newly appointed Justices Powell and Rehnquist, who had not heard the oral argument, did not participate in the consideration or decision of the cases.[60]

The claims of conscience by the Amish parents in these cases, which were assumed by all the justices except Justice Douglas to be identical with that of their children, were of the highest order—namely, that they not be coerced into sending their children to participate in schooling which they deemed seriously immoral. Against these claims of the Amish parents, the Court held the public interest in compelling one or two years' formal secondary education beyond grade school to be of low priority. But Justice Douglas would ascertain the wishes of children in every case, and Justices Brennan and Stewart would re-examine the public interest in the welfare of children in properly presented cases of conflict between them and their parents. The Court's attempt to distinguish religious claims to exemption from those based on philosophical views does not appear to be consistent with the *Seeger* and *Welsh* decisions, but perhaps Chief Justice Burger wished only to distinguish opposition to compulsory secondary education based on a concept of moral duty, whether conventionally religious or not, from that based on views about what is educationally desirable. In any case, the Court here recognized a claim of conscience—and only a claim of conscience—to exemption from the prescriptions of an otherwise valid law.

EDUCATION: PUBLIC SCHOOLS AND RELIGIOUS EXERCISES

Another source of conflict between individual conscience and public law in connection with state control of public schools arises from various efforts to include religious exercises or instruction within the educational framework of these schools. Let us take first the case of religious exercises sponsored by public authorities. Even were such exercises to qualify as "nonsectarian," they would still exert obvious coercion on the children of nonbelievers to participate if attendance were compulsory and subtle pressure on them if attendance were voluntary. (It is, of course, highly doubtful whether any religious exercise can avoid some sectarian implications, and sectarian religious exercises under public auspices in the school, whether compulsory or voluntary, would run directly counter to the First Amendment's prohibition of a religious establishment.) If attendance at "nonsectarian" religious exercises were compulsory, the children of nonbelievers would be coerced by law to attend the exercises and probably be influenced by group pressure to participate. If attendance at the exercises were voluntary in the sense that those children would be excused whose parents so requested, children not participating would be effectively stigmatized and thus influenced to conform. Even if attendance at the exercises were completely voluntary—without records of attendance—the authority of the state behind the exercises might generate social pressures to conform, especially in the lower grades.

The claim by the children of nonbelievers (or more precisely, by their parents in their behalf) is that religious exercises sponsored by public authorities operate to coerce them through the social pressure of other children's participation to act against the dictates of their consciences, that is, to participate passively or even actively in religious exercises in which they do not believe. Their claim of conscience is accordingly based on a moral duty not to affirm what they regard as false. More precisely, their claim of conscience is to a right instrumental to fulfillment of that duty, namely, a right not to be pressured socially into conformity by the publicly sponsored religious exercises of others.

This claim is similar to that of Gobitis and Barnette, but in the case of voluntary religious exercises, the coercion is one of social pressure indirectly produced by the voluntary, if publicly sponsored, actions of other students rather than by the direct threat by public authorities of at least severe financial loss against Gobitis or of imprisonment against Barnette. Thus the social pressure alleged by nonbelievers to coerce their children to violate their conscience in the matter of religious exercises in public schools is not as immediate or severe as the coercion in the flag-salute cases. Moreover, the threat of social pressure by voluntary religious exercises may be exaggerated by nonbelievers: it is not self-evident that publicly sponsored religious exercises would significantly add to already existent social pressure to conform; in fact, the dominant social pressure in many areas of contemporary America may be against participation in voluntary religious exercises. This is not to say that the conscientious objections of nonbelievers to the exercises are trivial, especially in the long run, merely that their moral dilemma is of a lesser order than that of Gobitis and Barnette, that is, of only moderate rank.

The countervailing public interest asserted in favor of religious exercises is their value in promoting the moral character of citizens. But the principle of the *Barnette* decision would presumably invalidate any program of compulsory religious exercises, at least if they compelled public recitation, and the Supreme Court in *Engel v. Vitale* (Justice Stewart dissenting) and *Abington v. Schempp* held even voluntary, publicly sponsored religious exercises not to represent, in terms of the First Amendment religious-establishment clause, any constitutionally valid public interest.[61] Thus, though public authorities may sponsor voluntary patriotic exercises in public schools after *Barnette*, they may not do the same for voluntary religious exercises after *Engel* and *Abington*. In conflicts between the claims of dissenting conscience and the public interest in voluntary religious exercises, the former have prevailed over the latter primarily not because of the intrinsic merits of the former but because of the legally null value attributed to the latter by a nearly unanimous Court in the two key cases. Perhaps precisely because the claims of dissenting conscience against publicly sponsored religious exercises in the schools were based on the indirect psychological and social pressures to conform, the Court preferred to rely on the religious-establishment clause to resolve the issue.

Another claim of conscience was advanced by parents in behalf of their children's right to recite a prayer aloud in a public school cafeteria. In that case, a group of young children chanted the following prayer at a mid-morning snack: "God is great, God is good, and we thank Him for our food." When the principal ordered an end to the practice, fifteen parents of the children brought suit in a Federal District Court to stop his action. The District Court ruled for the parents,[62] but the Circuit Court of Appeals reversed the decision (*Oshinsky v. Stein*).[63] Assuming for the sake of argument that the children's prayer did not violate the religious-establishment clause of the First Amendment, and that it was initiated by the children rather than by their teachers, the Circuit Court held that the free-exercise and free-speech clauses of the same

Amendment nonetheless did not compel public school authorities to permit it.

Insofar as the claim of the parents in behalf of their children was one of conscience, it was based on what was perceived as a religious duty to express thanks to God for His gifts. As such, it was similar to the previously considered claims of religiously motivated individuals to preach the gospel. It was a relatively low claim of conscience because it was based on a general duty which does not specify time, place, circumstances, or means, and allows the individual wide discretion in its implementation. Basically, the parents' claim in behalf of their children was like other claims to freedom of speech in the public school cafeteria. Like all such claims, it could run counter to the public interest in the order and discipline of the schools. The District Court, however, denied by implication that there had been any disruption as a result of the prayer chant in the instant case,[64] and the Circuit Court was silent on the point. Both courts were also silent on the divisive effect of the prayer chant, but this public interest in the moral goal of unity in common schools may have been an important factor in the Circuit Court's decision against the parents' claim. The Circuit Court held in effect that public school cafeterias (and classrooms) were not necessarily the proper place for public recitation of prayer, however voluntary, and that public authorities could reasonably conclude that such prayer would not be consistent with the overall objectives of common schools.

Controversies over the place of sectarian religious instruction in public school education have raised another set of conflicts between believers and nonbelievers. Although state-sponsored programs of sectarian religious instruction would violate the establishment clause of the First Amendment, what of programs which permit any and all religious sects to offer instruction within the framework of public education either on or off public school premises? The Supreme Court weighed this question in two important cases, *McCollum v. Board of Education* and *Zorach v. Clauson.*[65] In the first of these cases, the Champaign, Illinois, school board had permitted privately supported sectarian religious instruction in the local schools during school hours for children whose parents so requested. The mother of a pupil who did not attend these classes but was required to take a study period at the same time as the classes, during which he was often left to his own devices, objected to the program as an infringement of religious freedom and an establishment of religion. She carried her successful appeal to the United States Supreme Court, where the case was decided on the establishment issue. Since that issue is not directly within the focus of this work, only those portions of the decision which are relevant to Mrs. McCollum's claim of conscience will be treated here.

Speaking for the Court, Justice Black reaffirmed the absolute separation of church and state under the First Amendment and concluded that the Illinois program was inconsistent with such a standard. But Justice Frankfurter, in a concurring opinion which was joined by Justices Burton, Jackson, and Rutledge, touched directly on the social position of religiously unaffiliated children under a released-time program:

> The law of imitation operates, and nonconformity is not an outstanding characteristic of children. The result is an obvious pressure upon children to attend. . . . The children belonging to . . . nonparticipating sects will thus have inculcated into them a feeling of separatism. . . . As a result, . . . [released-time instruction] sharpens the consciousness of religious differences at least among some of the children committed to . . . [the public school's] care.[66]

All this, Frankfurter complained, militated against the very purpose of the public school, which is "at once a symbol of our democracy and the most pervasive means for promoting our common destiny." [67] Accordingly, he argued that in no activity of the state was it "more vital to keep out divisive forces than in its schools." [68] Justice Reed alone dissented, and his argument was concerned exclusively with the religious-establishment issue.[69]

In 1952, the Court modified the *McCollum* decision to the extent of permitting a New York City program of released time for religious instruction away from public school premises (*Zorach v. Clauson*).[70] The New York City Board of Education permitted pupils, on the written request of their parents, to leave public school buildings and grounds during school hours to attend classes at religious centers, while those not released remained in public school classrooms. The religious instructors made weekly reports on the children who were released from the public school but did not attend their classes. Justice Douglas, speaking for a majority of six justices, upheld the program. Although the decision rested principally on the right of a state to encourage religious instruction and cooperate with religious authorities "by adjusting the schedule of public events to sectarian needs," [71] Douglas also rejected as "obtuse reasoning" any claim that the nonbeliever was coerced into religious instruction by the program.[72]

Justices Black, Frankfurter, and Jackson dissented. They accused the majority of abandoning the standard of absolute separation of church and state and saw no significant difference between the Illinois program invalidated in *McCollum* and the New York program sustained in *Zorach*.[73] But Justices Frankfurter and Jackson were also concerned with the coercive effects of the New York released-time program on pupils, whether believers or not, who would not otherwise wish to attend. According to Jackson, the State first compelled each student "to yield a large part of his time for public secular education" and then released some of it to him "on condition that he devote it to sectarian religious purposes." [74] Moreover, Jackson charged that under the New York released-time program schooling was "more or less suspended" for those who chose, or whose parents chose for them, not to attend religious instruction.[75] Thus, the truant officer was said to dog the youngster who failed to attend his religious-instruction class, and the public school was said to serve as a "temporary jail for a pupil who will not go to church." [76]

There were two allegations of "coercion" in these cases. One, raised by Justice Jackson in his dissent in *Zorach*, contended that children who did not wish to attend religious instruction at the scheduled times, but whose parents did wish them to do so, would be coerced into attendance by truancy laws. This allegation would involve, basically, a conflict between the child and his parents about the right to specify the kind of education he should receive, and the only issue of law would be whether public authorities may act as surrogates of parents to enforce their children's attendance at religious instructions. In any event, no such claim was actually represented by either *McCollum* or *Zorach*. The other allegation, voiced in the Court by Justice Frankfurter in his concurrence in *McCollum,* was that children whose parents did not wish them to attend any religious instruction were coerced by psychological and social pressures under the program to do so.[77] As in the case of voluntary religious exercises, these dissenting parents claimed a right not to be pressured socially by the participation of others in the religious-instruction program, a right instrumental to their duty not to participate because of their beliefs. They thus advanced a moderate claim of conscience.

Although Justice Douglas denied that such pressure constituted any legally recognizable coercion, Frankfurter's contention deserves closer analysis. The main question to be asked is to what extent public authorization of the released-time programs at stake in these cases created psychological and social pressures on the children of nonbelievers or the religiously unaffiliated to participate. If public authorities fail to offer at least an equally attractive alternative to nonparticipation in the released-time program, they would be the responsible agents for engendering pressures on pupils to attend. But if public authorities make a genuine alternative available to nonparticipants, such psychological and social pressures which may come to bear on the children of nonbelievers would derive only from the consequences of parental or student choice, not from the state. The fact that children are young and impressionable may change the quantitative effect of the pressures, but it does not change its source. Indeed, public school authorities could not shelter their pupils from all incidents of religious diversity even if they would.

The nub of the coercion issue in released-time programs is whether public schools offer alternatives either acceptable to nonparticipants or capable of legal construction on their merits as genuine equivalents. The study periods offered as an alternative to nonparticipants in the released-time programs under attack in *McCollum* and *Zorach* may have been grossly deficient in this respect. According to the trial record, Terry McCollum was often left to his own devices, and Justice Jackson charged that scholastic activities were "more or less suspended" for nonparticipants at the time of the religious-instruction classes authorized under the New York City program.[78] Since study periods usually connote marking time, it is arguable that they are unacceptable under any conditions as an alternative to religious instruction.

Justice Frankfurter appeared to consider as critical the deficiencies of the study-period alternative in *McCollum* when he indicated by contrast his approval of a play period as an alternative for nonparticipants, at least if religious-instruction classes were conducted off public school premises. That arrangement, he thought, would "not cut into public school instruction or truly affect the activities or feelings of the children who did not attend the church schools." [79] Moreover, Justices Frankfurter and Jackson conceded in their *Zorach* dissents that public schools may close their doors early to allow students to go outside the schools for religious devotions or instructions, presumably without responsibility for any resulting psychological and social pressures on nonparticipants. Thus Justices Frankfurter and Jackson rejected the released-time programs in these cases, at least in part, because they objected to the suitability of a study period as the only alternative to religious instruction.

Since both the Illinois and the New York released-time programs provided only for a study period as an alternative to religious instruction, they would presumably have the same coercive effect on nonparticipants. If so, then from that perspective the *McCollum* and *Zorach* decisions are fundamentally inconsistent. Whatever the use of public school facilities for religious instruction may do to throw the weight of secular authority behind the dissemination of religious doctrines—an establishment issue—it would not seem to constitute coercion of nonparticipants when an equally attractive alternative is available to them. Of course, such use of public school facilities might add to the coercive effects of released-time programs on nonparticipants when no acceptable alternative is provided for them.

Fears of psychological and social pressures on nonbelievers from released-time programs of religious instruction may be exaggerated in any case. In the Champaign, Illinois, junior high school, for example, eighty per cent of the students did *not* attend religious instruction under the released-time program struck down in *McCollum*.[80] The situation was the reverse in the grade school attended by Terry McCollum,[81] and it may reflect in part the fact that children in lower grades are more amenable to parental wishes than teenagers. But whatever group pressures may have operated to induce conformity at the grade school level in Champaign, it is evident not only that they did not operate to that effect at the high school level, but that they may even have had exactly the opposite effect there. Thus, the mere existence of a released-time program does not necessarily lead to psychological and social pressures on nonbelievers—or believers—to participate.

What is the public interest asserted to be advanced by released-time programs of religious instruction? Critics contend that the programs are designed to foster religious belief, and thus violate the establishment clause. That was the view of the majority in *McCollum* and the dissent in *Zorach* with respect to the programs there involved. But that is not the only interpretation of the public interest at stake in released-time programs. Advocates contend in their turn that these programs implement the right of parents to give value-orientation to their children's education, of course within limits set by other public interests. Released-time programs are thus said by their advocates to be based on the democratic—and secular—principle that the child is not "the mere creature of the state," and that parents enjoy the primary right and duty to educate the child. Moreover, advocates would argue that released-time programs best serve the public—and secular—interest in developing the moral character of citizens. Against this public interest, however, the divisive effects of religious instruction in common schools would still have to be weighed, and Justice Frankfurter for one left no doubt about how important he considered these.

As in the case of complaints by patrons of church-related schools that the absence of public support impedes them from fulfilling their duty to give their children a religious education, so parents desirous of religious instruction for their children in public schools may raise a similar complaint against the absence of released-time programs. Since family and church can provide alternate means of implementing this duty, as in the former case, the claim of conscience represented by these parents is of a relatively low order. (One may sympathize with these parents, however; the complexity, mobility, and resulting dislocations in modern society may lessen the ability of family and church to transmit religious values within their own structures.) Moreover, the public interest against released-time programs might involve serious administrative difficulties in addition to the usual objections based on the establishment clause and the coercive effects on nonparticipants.

NOTES

1. Aristotle, *Nicomachean Ethics* ii. 1103B 3–5; the translation is that of Martin Ostwald, *Nichomachean Ethics* (Indianapolis: Bobbs–Merrill, 1962), p. 34.
2. See Chap. 5, pp. 127–131.
3. See Chap. 5, pp. 119–123.
4. Thomas F. O'Dea, *The Mormons* (Chicago: University of Chicago Press, 1957), p. 111.
5. *Reynolds v. U.S.*, 98 U.S. 145 (1878).
6. *Ibid.*, p. 161.
7. *Ibid.*, p. 163.
8. *Ibid.*, p. 164.
9. *Ibid.*
10. *Ibid.*
11. *Ibid.*
12. *Ibid.*, p. 165.
13. *Ibid.*, p. 166.
14. *Ibid.*, p. 167.
15. *Ibid.*, pp. 168–69, note.
16. *Davis v. Beason,* 133 U.S. 333 (1890).
17. *Ibid.*, p. 334.
18. *Ibid.*, p. 341.
19. *Ibid.*
20. *Ibid.*, p. 342.
21. *Ibid.*
22. *Ibid.*, p. 343.
23. O'Dea, *The Mormons*, p. 246.
24. *Ibid.*, pp. 246–47.
25. *Ibid.*

26. *Prince v. Massachusetts,* 321 U.S. 158 (1944).
27. *Ibid.,* pp. 160–61.
28. Is 11:6.
29. *Prince,* p. 168.
30. *Ibid.,* pp. 169–70.
31. *Ibid.,* p. 170.
32. *Ibid.,* p. 174.
33. See *Everson v. Board of Education,* 330 U.S. 1 (1947); *McCollum v. Board of Education,* 333 U.S. 203 (1948); *Zorach v. Clauson,* 343 U.S. 306 (1952); *McGowan v. Maryland,* 366 U.S. 420 (1961); *Engel v. Vitale,* 370 U.S. 421 (1962); *Abington v. Schempp,* 374 U.S. 203 (1963); *Board of Education v. Allen,* 392 U.S. 236 (1968); *Walz v. Tax Commission of City of New York,* 397 U.S. 664 (1970); *Lemon v. Kurtzman,* 403 U.S. 602 (1971); and *Tilton v. Richardson,* 403 U.S. 672 (1971).
34. *Pierce v. Society of Sisters of the Holy Names of Jesus and Mary,* 268 U.S. 510 (1925).
35. *Ibid.,* p. 535.
36. Cf. *Everson, Board of Education v. Allen, Lemon,* and *Tilton* (n. 33). The issue of tax-exemption of churches can also be analyzed from this perspective; cf. *Walz* (n. 33).
37. *Minersville v. Gobitis,* 310 U.S. 586 (1940).
38. *Ibid.,* p. 600.
39. *Ibid.,* p. 596.
40. *Ibid.,* p. 600.
41. *Ibid.,* p. 601.
42. *Ibid.,* p. 604.
43. *Ibid.,* p. 606.
44. *Ibid.*
45. *Jones v. Opelika,* 316 U.S. 584, 623–24 (1942).
46. *West Virginia v. Barnette,* 319 U.S. 624 (1943).
47. *Ibid.,* p. 623.
48. *Ibid.,* p. 642.
49. *Ibid.,* p. 638.
50. *Ibid.,* p. 644.
51. *Ibid.,* p. 646.
52. *Ibid.,* pp. 646–71.
53. *State v. Yoder,* 49 Wis.2d 430, 182 N.W.2d 539 (1971).
54. *Wisconsin v. Yoder,* 402 U.S. 994 (1971).
55. *Wisconsin v. Yoder* et al., 992 S.Ct. 1526 (1972).
56. *Ibid.,* p. 1530, n. 3.
57. *Ibid.,* p. 1544.
58. *Ibid.*
59. *Ibid.,* p. 1546.
60. *Ibid.,* p. 1544.
61. For *Engel* and *Abington,* see n. 33. In 1952, the United States Supreme Court refused to hear an appeal from a similar

practice of Bible reading and recitation of the Lord's Prayer in New Jersey public schools. *Doremus v. Board of Education,* 342 U.S. 429 (1952). A six-man majority dismissed the appeal on the jurisdictional ground that the objectors to the program had insufficient standing as citizens and taxpayers. Justices Burton, Douglas, and Reed, dissenting, thought that taxpayers had a sufficiently vital interest in the operation of the public schools to maintain standing. *Ibid.,* p. 435. The reasoning of this decision was undercut by *Flast v. Cohen,* 392 U.S. 83 (1968).

After *Abington,* the Court did not again grant full review to questions of religious exercises in public schools. The Court reversed a Florida ruling in favor of Bible reading and prayers, citing *Abington,* but dismissed the other issues presented. *Chamberlin v. Dade County Board of Public Instruction,* 377 U.S. 402 (1964). Justices Black and Douglas agreed with the decision on Bible reading and prayers and the dismissal of questions relating to baccalaureate services and a religious census of pupils but thought that a substantial federal question was presented by allegations of religious tests for the appointment of teachers. *Ibid.,* pp. 402–403. Justice Stewart would have set the case down for argument. *Ibid.,* p. 403. In the next term, the Court refused to review a complaint from New York against the inclusion of the words "under God" in the pledge of allegiance ceremonies of public school pupils. *Lewis v. Allen,* 379 U.S. 923 (1964).

62. *Stein v. Oshinsky,* 224 F.Supp. 757 (1963).

63. *Oshinsky v. Stein,* 348 F.2d 999 (1965); cert. denied, 382 U.S. 957 (1965).

64. *Stein,* p. 760.

65. See n. 33.

66. *McCollum,* pp. 227–28.

67. *Ibid.,* p. 231.

68. *Ibid.*

69. *Ibid.,* pp. 238–56.

70. See n. 33.

71. *Zorach,* p. 314.

72. *Ibid.,* p. 311.

73. *Ibid.,* pp. 315–25.

74. *Ibid.,* pp. 323–24.

75. *Ibid.,* p. 324.

76. *Ibid.*

77. See n. 66.

78. Transcript of the McCollum Trial Record, p. 255; *Zorach,* p. 324.

79. *McCollum,* p. 224.

80. Transcript, p. 177.

81. *Ibid.*

7

Conclusion

THE DECADE OF THE 'SIXTIES, in connection with the war in Vietnam and social inequities in the United States, witnessed a remarkable revival of "higher law" appeals to conscience as justification for immunity from public laws. These appeals have provoked the rejoinder that disobedience is violation of law, and that violation of law must be punished, whatever its purpose or motivation. If the issue is so stated, the claims of morality and legality are simply divorced from one another.

Such a dichotomy is doubly inadequate: it is inadequate from the viewpoint of morality because democratic societies express collective moral judgments in public laws as do the individuals who appeal to their dissenting private moral judgments as justification for immunity; and it is inadequate from the viewpoint of legality because the public law of democratic societies recognizes freedom of conscience and thus "implies respect for an innate conviction of paramount duty." [1] The issue in conflicts of conscience and law, then, is not simply one of morality versus legality, but, from the viewpoint of morality, one of competing moral judgments and, from the viewpoint of legality, one of conflicting legal claims.

Adjudication of the conflicting legal claims of private conscience and public law "presents, in part, a question of constitutional law and also, in part, a question of legislative policy in avoiding unnecessary clashes with the dictates of conscience." [2] Like all conflicts of legal claims, this adjudication requires a weighing of one claim against another, specifically, the claim of the conscientious objector against the claim of a public interest. Moreover, this adjudication involves a calculus of casuistry—a comparison of one case of conscientious objection with another.

A new approach to the calculus was suggested in Chapter 1.[3] Instead of weighing claims of conscience only on an *ad hoc* basis, a typology for the whole series of such claims was there suggested according to the degree of moral obligation perceived by individuals to be threatened by conformity to statutory law.

First, it was noted that individual consciences may forbid absolutely what public laws command under severe penalties, and these claims of conscience were rated high. Such claims were represented by conscientious objectors to military service like Seeger and Welsh,[4] by conscientious objectors to military service who, like Macintosh and Girouard, applied for naturalized citizenship,[5] by Jehovah's Witnesses like Gobitis and Barnette with conscientious objections to saluting the flag,[6] and by Sabbatarians like Sherbert who sought unemployment compensation while refusing to accept work on Saturdays.[7]

Second, it was noted that individuals may claim as rights instrumental to negative religious and moral duties what public laws forbid under severe penalties, and these claims were rated moderate. Such a claim was represented by Sabbatarian entrepreneurs like Braunfeld who sought to engage in business on Sundays.[8] Similarly, insofar as a claim of conscience was represented, Engel and Schempp objected to having their children pressured by publicly sponsored, though voluntary, religious exercises to participate in the exercises against their dissenting beliefs.[9]

Third, it was noted that individual consciences may command specifically what public laws forbid under threat of severe penalties, and these claims were also rated moderate. Such claims were represented by those who, like Harden, handled dangerous snakes to demonstrate their religious faith in response to what they interpreted as a scriptural commission,[10] and by Mormons like Reynolds and Davis who practiced polygamy in response to what they conceived as a divine mandate.[11]

Fourth, it was noted that individual consciences may claim as rights to implement general religious or moral duties what public laws forbid under threat of severe penalties, and these claims were rated low in relation to the other classes of conscientious claims. Such claims were represented by Jones and Murdock,[12] who peddled religious pamphlets from door to door, by Martin,[13] who distributed religious handbills by door-to-door canvassing, and by Prince,[14] who encouraged her young niece to offer religious pamphlets for sale on a street corner.

The claims of public laws against conscientious objectors were broadly classified according to the strength of countervailing public interests perceived by judges to be at stake. There were usually clear enough indications whether judges rated specific public interests high or low, and further precision in classifying their ratings may not be critical for an overall view of the conflictual situations.

The series of cases surveyed in Chapters 2 through 6 in terms of the conflicting claims of private conscience and public interest can now be studied more integrally. In the preceding chapters, some potential rather than actually litigated claims of conscience were considered. Moreover, in a few of the cases cited, claims of conscience, though actually litigated, never reached the Supreme Court in any form. Here the focus will be exclusively on those claims against the prescriptions or prohibitions of statutory law which were *ex professo* motivated by religious or moral considerations, and which reached the Supreme Court for adjudication at least on petition of certiorari.[15] Many of the claims to rights of religious or moral expression, of course, are indistinguishable from other claims to rights of free speech.

The most salient conclusion from the cases surveyed is that no claim of conscience, however high, prevailed against a public interest ranked high by a majority of justices. Although this conclusion is hardly surprising in terms of the central judicial function of maintaining the stability of the legal system within the larger political and social systems, it is for that very reason the most important to be drawn from the cases. Moreover, there are unities of subject matter with respect to the public interests represented by national and local governments and recognized by Court majorities as of high priority. Lastly, the margin of the majorities rarely fell below 7–2.

One unity of subject matter where Court majorities have recognized high public interests involves military service. The Court has refused to intervene in favor of (*Mora, Noyd*), or has ruled against (*Negre*), military personnel who conscientiously objected to service in Vietnam.[16] It has likewise refused to intervene in favor of (*Mitchell, Spiro*), or has ruled against (*Gillette, McFadden*), selective conscientious objectors to induction into the armed forces during the Vietnamese war.[17] (In one case, *Sisson,* the Court did rule in favor of a selective conscientious objector but on grounds unrelated to the selectivity of his conscientious objection.[18]) In the *Gillette* and *Negre* decisions, the Court majority rated high the dangers of administrative inequities and of selective disobedience to law which might result from legal recognition of the petitioners' claims of conscience. In the case of the military personnel involved, the

Court may have also considered the importance of military discipline to national security. In the *Berrigan* case, the Court declined without dissent to review the conviction of draft-card burners and thus apparently rated high the public interest in the orderly administration of the Selective Service System.[19] In the *Boardman* case, the Court declined without dissent to review the conviction of a conscientious objector who refused to accept alternate civilian service and thus apparently rated high the public interest in equitable administration of the Selective Service System.[20] Justice Douglas dissented from all these decisions except *Noyd*, *Berrigan*, and *Boardman*. Only Justice Stewart joined him in *Mitchell*, and only Justice Black joined him in *Spiro*.

Related to the public interest in actual military service by native-born citizens is that in potential military service by applicants for naturalized citizenship. In two cases, *Schwimmer* and *Macintosh*, Court majorities appeared to rate high the latter interest against the claims of conscientious objectors.[21] If so, these decisions would be consistent with the previously stated conclusion that high ratings of public interests by Court majorities prevailed against all counterclaims of conscience, however high. But the margin of the majorities in the two cases was narrow: 6–3 and 5–4, respectively. Moreover, the decisions were reversed a decade-and-a-half later (*Girouard*). It may be that the rhetoric of the earlier majorities was inflated, and that they did not rate the public interest at stake so high as their language would have seemed to indicate.

Another unity of subject matter on which Court majorities have recognized a high public interest against claimants of conscience is that of monogamous marriage. In the *Reynolds* and *Davis* cases, Court majorities unanimously upheld federal anti-polygamy legislation against Mormon claims of conscience to exemption. These decisions may have been culturally conditioned with respect both to the value of monogamous marriage and to sensitivity to dissenting conscience, but the results are unambiguous.

Still another unity of subject matter on which Court majorities have accepted a high public interest against claimants of conscience is that of protecting the life and welfare of third parties in blood-transfusion cases. In the cases of *Anderson* and *Jones*, Court majorities declined to review lower court orders of blood transfusions for women opposed to them on religious grounds, in order to protect the lives of unborn children and the welfare of children already born, respectively; in the case of *Labrenz* and *King Co. Hospital*, the Court refused to review, respectively, actual and potential court orders of blood transfusions for the children of parents opposed to them on religious grounds.[22] The decisions in the *Jones* and *Labrenz* cases were unanimous, although Mrs. Jones' petition was already moot concerning the transfusions by the time at which the Supreme Court was asked to hear it. In the *Anderson* case, only Justice Douglas would have granted review, and in the *King Co. Hospital* case, only Justices Douglas and Harlan would have granted review.

Whenever Court majorities rated even moderately high the public interests opposed to recognition of claims of conscience, national and local governments have also won the decisions. In several cases, the issues were assimilable to those of free speech, and moderate interests in public order prevailed by decisive margins. In *Cox*, a unanimous Court upheld a parade-license requirement.[23] In *Stein*, the Court without dissent declined to hear an appeal from a decision against the right of children to recite voluntary prayers in a public school cafeteria on their own or their parents' initiative.[24] In *Ballard*, eight members of the Court were unwilling to exempt assertedly religious solicitors of funds by mail from prosecution for fraud.[25] In *O'Brien*, a Court majority of seven upheld the prohibition of draft-card mutilation.[26] In *Watchtower*, a Court majority of seven declined to review the right of apartment-house owners to exclude uninvited religious canvassers from their premises.[27] And in *Poulos,* a Court majority of seven upheld a requirement of appeal by judicial process against an illegal denial of a speaking permit by a local administrator.[28] In three cases unrelated to any issue of free speech (*Clark* [8–1], *Ehlert* [6–3], *McGee* [8–1]), Court majorities upheld administrative regulations and procedures of the Selective Service System against claims of conscience.[29] In one other case unrelated to speech (*Stimpel*), a Court majority of eight declined to review the dismissal of a public construction worker who refused to accept work on Saturdays for religious reasons.[30]

A majority of six justices in *Zorach* thought that there was a moderate public interest in accommodating religious instruction within the framework of public education but outside public school buildings.[31] A minority of three justices, however, both challenged the legitimacy of such a public interest and stressed the socially coercive effects of the religious instruction on nonbelievers. In *Braunfeld,* a majority of six justices held the public interest in a common day of rest moderate enough to sustain the application of Sunday laws to Sabbatarian entrepreneurs, although three dissenters thought that interest not to be sufficiently "compelling." Only by the narrow margin of 5–4, however, did a Court majority uphold a child-labor law against a religious claim to exemption (*Prince*), and a vigorous minority challenged the majority's evaluation of the child-welfare interest at stake when the "work" involved was related to religious proselytism under the supervision of a guardian.

In *Gobitis,* a requirement compelling flag-salutes from public school children coerced Jehovah's Witness parents to act against their religious belief under the immediate threat of the financial costs of private schooling and the long-term threat of imprisonment if or when such costs could not be sustained by the parents. Over the dissent of only one justice, the Court upheld the compulsory flag-salute requirement as applied to the Witnesses, and the majority opinion rated low to moderate the public interest in fostering patriotism among children attending public schools. Three years later, after a storm of professional and popular criticism, a Court majority of six justices reversed the holding (*Barnette*), rating the public interest at stake in compulsory flag-salutes not only relatively low but even constitutionally null. Rather than create an exception for the Witnesses' claims of conscience, however, the new majority did not recognize the existence of a public interest in compelling any expression of beliefs or attitudes. Three justices dissented from the *Barnette* decision, holding to the view that there was a low to moderate public interest in exacting the flag-salutes, and that no exceptions should be made for the conscientious objectors.

The majority in *Gobitis* and the dissent in *Barnette* may have stressed the value of universal participation in the flag-salute ceremonies only as a matter of judicial tactics. Moreover, especially in view of their position on the issue of flat license taxes on the sale of religious literature by itinerant evangelists (*Jones*, *Murdock*), the *Barnette* dissenters were influenced by a judicial philosophy of wide deference to legislative judgment and an unwillingness to make exceptions for conscientious objectors to public laws. It is to be noted that Justice Jackson, who sided with the *Barnette* dissenters on the issue of the license taxes, wrote the Court opinion in favor of the conscientious objectors to the flag-salutes, and this may reflect his appreciation that the moral claims of Jehovah's Witnesses against flag-salutes were significantly higher than their claims against license taxes on the sales of their religious literature. It is also to be noted that in *Barnette* Justices Black, Douglas, and Murphy changed from their position of concurrence in *Gobitis*, and this may reflect not only a deeper insight into the moral plight of the conscientious objectors to flag-salutes but also a feedback phenomenon from public criticism of the *Gobitis* decision.[32]

At the other end of the spectrum from those public interests which justices rated high or moderately high are those which they rated unambiguously low. Here there has been an opposite pattern: when Court majorities have rated unambiguously low the public interests at stake against private claims of conscience, the latter, of whatever quality, have been regularly vindicated. (The exceptions from this generalization are the *Hamilton*, *Jones*, *Summers*, and possibly *Gobitis* decisions.[33]) In *Pierce*, a unanimous Court ranked low the public interest in compelling children to attend common schools and ruled in favor of parents' rights to send their offspring to religious schools.[34] And Court majorities were unanimous or almost unanimous in favor of claims of conscience when they recognized discrimination against particular religious groups (*Niemotko*, *Fowler*),[35] or discrimination against nonbelievers in eligibility for public office (*Torcaso*),[36] or discrimination against nonparticipants by religious programs in public schools (*McCollum* [8–1], *Engel* [8–1], *Abington*, and *Chamberlin* [8–1]).[37]

Unlike claims of religious discrimination, which can represent no constitutionally valid public interest by virtue of the establishment clause, religious claims fundamentally assimilable to freedom of speech can involve conflicts between individual rights and the requirements of public order. In three such cases, where Court majorities rated low the respective interests in public order (*Cantwell*, *Sellers*) and clean streets (*Jamison*), they ruled without dissent in favor of the religious claimants.[38] In *Kunz*, by a margin of 8–1, the Court rated low the interest in public order and ruled in favor of the religious claimant.[39] As has already been indicated, a majority of six justices in *Barnette* ruled in favor of religious dissenters from compulsory flag-salutes. In *Martin*, a majority of six justices rated low the public interest in securing the privacy of residents against itinerant evangelists by prohibiting uninvited door-to-door canvassing to distribute handbills. In two cases, *Marsh* and *Tucker*, Court majorities by a similar margin rated low the public interests in the protection of the "private" property of a company town and a federal housing project, respectively, and ruled in favor of the distributors of religious literature.[40]

But Court majorities did rule against claims of conscience on three occasions when they seemed to agree that the countervailing public interests at stake were of only low priority (*Hamilton, Jones, Summers*). In *Hamilton*, in an era when college education was regarded as a privilege rather than a right, a unanimous Court ruled against the claim of a conscientious objector to the military-training requirements of a state university. Although the Court did not indicate any perception of even a moderate public interest in the military-training program, it was evidently of the opinion that Hamilton's claim of conscience was not too pressing, and that the state had an otherwise valid interest in the program.

A similar issue of exemptions for conscientious objectors to otherwise valid public prescriptions of low priority was raised in *Jones*, namely, the applicability of flat license fees unrelated to sales or income to itinerant evangelists incidentally peddling religious literature. Two factors influenced the majority there against making an exemption for the evangelists: (1) a judicial philosophy of wide deference to legislative judgment in the wake of the New Deal confrontation with the Court; and (2) an unwillingness to recognize a claim of conscience against an otherwise admittedly valid tax. The Court was deeply divided on what the majority perceived as an issue of constitutionally requiring exemptions for conscientious objectors to otherwise valid laws. But one year later, another 5–4 decision (*Murdock*) reversed the *Jones* decision and recognized the claims of conscientious objectors to immunity from the license fees. The principle should logically apply to all basically non-commercial claims of free speech and press, but such applicability beyond the incidents of evangelism has never been legally tested before the Court.

The claims of conscience in the flat license cases, according to the typology suggested in Chapter 1, were of low priority in comparison with such claims of conscience as those against military service, and yet their claims were ultimately vindicated in *Murdock*. In 1944, one year after the *Murdock* decision, a Court majority extended exemption from the license taxes to an evangelist who maintained his home in the taxing municipality and earned his living by means of sales of religious literature (*Follett*).[41] Despite the fact that Follett's evangelical activities were more mixed with commercial rewards than were those involved in *Murdock*, the same personnel on the Court decided the case by a margin of 6–3. Justice Reed, who dissented in *Murdock*, voted with the majority in *Follett*, and this shift reflects the force of *stare decisis* in the American legal system.

Breaking the trend toward rulings in favor of claims of conscience when opposed to low public interests was the *Summers* decision of 1945. In that case, the Court by a 5–4 margin ruled against the claim of a conscientious objector to military service who had been denied admission to the state bar. This decision, however, is the last one in which low public interests were vindicated against claims of conscience. One year after *Summers*, the Court by a margin of 5–3 reversed the *Schwimmer* and *Macintosh* decisions (*Girouard*). The majority in that case, which was constituted by the addition of Justice Burton to replace Justice Roberts, reinterpreted congressional intent and admitted to citizenship an applicant conscientiously opposed to military service. Chief Justice Stone, who had dissented in *Macintosh*, also dissented in *Girouard* because he could not agree with the reinterpretation of Congressional intent. Both the majority and the minority rated low the public interest at stake against admitting conscientious objectors to citizenship, and their disagreement was roughly similar to that in the *Jones* and *Murdock* cases, although the dissenters' position was more nuanced because of Congress' undoubted power over the grant of citizenship. Thus, of the three decisions in which low public interests were preferred to claims of conscience, one (*Jones*) was reversed by *Murdock*, and the other two (*Hamilton*, *Summers*) are of doubtful constitutional validity as precedents after *Girouard*.

In 1950, by a margin of 6–3, a Court with three new members extended the *Girouard* ruling without opinion to cover a conscientious objector to noncombatant military service and even civilian work in war industries (*Cohnstaedt*).[42] In that case, the dissenters, newly appointed Chief Justice Vinson and Justice Clark, may have been influenced by the higher public interest against extending the exemption of conscientious objectors that far. Justice Frankfurter, however, abandoned the position he had taken in *Girouard* against the grant of citizenship to a conscientious objector asking for less exemption, presumably out of deference to the principle of *stare decisis*.

A related public interest is that in the military service of native-born citizens. In 1955, by a margin of 7–2, a Court majority extended the statutory exemption of conscientious objectors from military service to cover a Jehovah's Witness willing to fight in "theocratic" wars (*Sicurella*), and thus rated low the public interest opposed to such an extension.[43] In 1965, a unanimous Court extended the statutory exemption to include nontheistic conscientious objectors to war (*Seeger*) and again rated low the public interest opposed to the extension. In 1970, the Court by a margin of 5–3 extended the statutory exemption still further to include an avowedly nonreligious conscientious objector to war (*Welsh*). In 1971, the Court unanimously overturned Cassius Clay's conviction for draft evasion without ruling on the eligibility of Black Muslims as pacifists (*Clay*).[44] In 1968, the Court by a margin of 6–3 rejected the 1-A reclassification of a ministerial student for returning his draft card to protest the Vietnamese war and rated constitutionally null the public interest in thus procuring the student's military service (*Oestereich*).[45] And in 1969 eight members of the Court awarded a conscientious objector in military service the minor consolation of a temporary release from custody in order to preserve his claim before completion of sentence (*Levy*).[46]

In one other post-*Murdock* decision, in 1963, a Court majority rated low the public interest against unemployment-compensation eligibility of a Sabbatarian who refused to accept work on Saturdays, and ruled in her favor (*Sherbert*). The margin was 7–2, and the dissenters admitted the low priority of the public interest there involved against fraud. The majority insisted on a "compelling" (i.e., moderate to high) public interest in denying exemption to conscientious objectors from public laws. For their part, the dissenters echoed the views expressed by Court majorities in *Macintosh, Gobitis,* and *Jones,* and by dissenters in *Murdock* and *Barnette*; they were opposed to what they perceived as special treatment of conscientious objectors to otherwise valid public laws. In a subsequent case, *Jenison,* the Court without dissent extended the *Sherbert* ruling to cover a conscientious objector to jury service.[47] Unlike the status of conscientious objectors to military service, the Court in these two cases created exemptions for conscientious objectors without benefit of statute, and unlike *Murdock* and *Barnette,* the exemptions presumably could not be claimed by anyone other than the conscientious objectors.

Thus there have been relatively consistent results, depending on how Court majorities rated the public interests adverse to claims of conscience. When majorities have rated those public interests moderate or high, the decisions have uniformly favored the government; when majorities have rated those public interests low, the decisions have regularly but not uniformly favored the claims of conscience. After *Murdock*, with the exception of *Summers*, not only have the decisions consistently favored claims of conscience to exemption over public interests rated low, but they have done so by increasingly solid majorities. This indicates both that *Murdock* was a landmark decision insofar as it vindicated claims of conscience, although possibly not restricted to such, over admittedly low claims of public interests, and that the principle of *stare decisis* operates in this as in other areas of American law. The practical conclusion is that claimants of conscience who can convince judges of their sincerity and the low priority of countervailing public interests are very likely to win their cases, at least in the United States Supreme Court.

The Court divided most sharply on conflicts between private conscience and public law in the 'forties. Every 5–4 decision of the Court in this area of law, except for *Macintosh*, occurred in one three-year period (1942–1945): *Jones, Murdock, Prince,* and *Summers*. Moreover, after the advent of Justice Rutledge in 1942, the Court personnel remained the same during the period, and certain voting patterns are evident. In each of these cases, Justices Frankfurter, Jackson, Reed, and Roberts voted for the claims of public interest, while Justices Black, Douglas, and Murphy voted for the claims of private conscience. Both Chief Justice Stone and Justice Rutledge joined Black, Douglas, and Murphy in *Murdock*, and that shift, of course, determined the outcome in that case. (Rutledge was not on the Court at the time of the *Jones* decision.) But Rutledge joined the pro-public-law justices in *Prince*, and Stone joined them in *Summers*, to form the Court majorities in those cases.

Six-to-three decisions are not confined to any one decade or any one Court. But those decisions of the 'forties reflect variations of the bloc alignments evident in the 5–4 decisions of the period. Justices Black, Douglas, Murphy, and Rutledge were joined by Chief Justice Stone and Justice Frankfurter in *Martin*, by Stone and Justice Jackson in *Barnette*, and by Stone and Justice Reed in *Follett*. Moreover, in the 5–3 decisions during the absence of Jackson at Nuremberg, the pro-conscience bloc of justices was joined by Frankfurter in *Marsh* and *Tucker* and by Justice Burton (replacing Justice Roberts) in *Girouard*. Later 6–3 decisions are few and of less interest from the viewpoint of bloc analysis. It may be significant, however, to note that, in *Zorach*, Frankfurter and Jackson—but not Douglas—joined Black in a dissent on the side of objectors to a religious-instruction program for public school pupils off school premises. And in *Braunfeld*, Black—but not Douglas—supported the application of Sunday-law restrictions to Sabbatarian businessmen.

Seven-to-two and 8–1 decisions reveal little in terms of bloc analysis. But all such decisions against claims of conscience (*Watchtower, Poulos, Anderson, King Co. Hospital, Mitchell, Mora, Spiro, O'Brien, Clark, Stimpel, Gillette, Negre, McFadden*, and *McGee*), with the exception of *Gobitis*, were handed down after the deaths of Justices Murphy and Rutledge, and eight of the last nine cases arose in connection with the war in Vietnam. Moreover, Black joined Douglas in dissent in only two of these cases: *Poulos* and *Spiro*. Douglas, of course, stands out as the strongest champion of claims of conscience because he dissented in all but one (*Clark*) of these cases.

Claimants of conscience won twenty-five (63%) of the forty cases which resulted in real decisions on the merits by the Supreme Court since *Cantwell*.[48] Sixteen of the forty litigants representing claims of conscience (40%) were Jehovah's Witnesses, and these litigants were successful in eleven of the cases (69%).[49] Four of the litigants were from Jewish backgrounds, and these litigants won three of the four cases.[50] Two of the litigants were Seventh-Day Adventists, and both won.[51] But the three Catholic litigants, all Vietnamese-war dissenters, lost.[52] The American Civil Liberties Union and their counsel, Melvin Wulf, were active in most of these cases.

But the most interesting, if only suggestive, statistics relate to the decision-makers themselves. The following table ranks the Justices according to their percentage of votes in favor of claims of conscience.

Most of the individual results are not too surprising. On the one hand, Douglas, Rutledge, Murphy, and Black rank among the five most pro-conscience justices; on the other, Reed and Roberts rank among the four least pro-conscience justices. Some of the individual results are quite fragmentary. Eleven of the twenty-seven justices participated in seven or fewer decisions, and six justices in three or fewer. But the composite votes of the justices are more revealing.

Sixty per cent of the justices' votes favored claimants of conscience. The twenty-two Protestant justices cast 82% of the votes, and their percentage of pro-conscience votes (58%) approximates that of all the justices.[53] Among the Protestant justices, however, the score varies from 46% for Episcopalians to 75% for Presbyterians.[54] The percentage of pro-conscience votes by the three justices from a Jewish background (58%) also approximates that of all the justices,[55] but this largely represents a profile of Justice Frankfurter, who cast twenty-six out of these thirty-one votes. The two Catholic justices voted 73% of the time in favor of claimants of conscience.[56] Democratic justices (65%) were distinctly more favorable to claimants of conscience than Republican justices (49%).[57] Justices with

TABLE 2

JUSTICE	NO. OF CASES	NO. OF PRO-CONSCIENCE VOTES	PERCENTAGE
Goldberg	3	3	100
Douglas	40	34	85
Rutledge	12	10	83
Murphy	16	13	81
Black	40	31	75
Clark	14	10	71
Warren	12	8	67
Whittaker	3	2	67
Brennan	17	11	65
Burton	11	7	64
Stone	15	9	60
Vinson	7	4	57
Minton	7	4	57
Frankfurter	26	14	54
Jackson	17	9	53
Harlan	17	9	53
Marshall	6	3	50
Fortas	2	1	50
Stewart	17	8	47
White	14	5	36
Hughes	3	1	33
McReynolds	3	1	33
Burger	6	2	33
Reed	23	6	26
Blackmun	4	1	25
Roberts	11	2	18
Byrnes	1	0	0

prosecutor experience score relatively low in their voting for claimants of conscience (50%).[58] Justices with previous judicial experience score close to the overall percentage (62%).[59] But Justices with legislative experience score a relatively high 70%.[60] There are no appreciable differences —except for the West—in the voting patterns on the basis of the area from which the justices came to Washington (East 60%, South 60%, Midwest 63%, and West 50%).[61]

This, then, is the American settlement to date of conflicts between private conscience and public law. In the author's view, the settlement is a generous one, with the notable exceptions of the claims by Sabbatarian businessmen and by selective conscientious objectors to military service.

NOTES

1. *U.S. v. Macintosh,* 283 U.S. 605, 634 (1931), Chief Justice Hughes dissenting.
2. *Ibid.*
3. Chap. 1, pp. 10–14.
4. *U.S. v. Seeger,* 380 U.S. 163 (1965) and *Welsh v. U.S.,* 398 U.S. 333 (1970); see Chap. 2, pp. 26–29.
5. *U.S. v. Macintosh,* 283 U.S. 605 (1931) and *Girouard v. U.S.,* 328 U.S. 61 (1946); see Chap. 3, pp. 59–65.
6. *Minersville v. Gobitis,* 310 U.S. 586 (1940) and *West Virginia v. Barnette,* 319 U.S. 624 (1943); see Chap. 6, pp. 164–169.
7. *Sherbert v. Verner,* 374 U.S. 398 (1963); see Chap. 4, pp. 105–107.
8. *Braunfeld v. Brown,* 366 U.S. 599 (1961); see Chap. 5, pp. 136–141.
9. *Engel v. Vitale,* 370 U.S. 421 (1962) and *Abington v. Schempp,* 374 U.S. 203 (1963); see Chap. 6, p. 174.
10. *Harden v. State,* 188 Tenn. 17, 216 S.W.2d. 708 (1948); see Chap. 5, pp. 115–117.
11. *Reynolds v. U.S.,* 98 U.S. 145 (1878) and *Davis v. Beason,* 133 U.S. 333 (1890); see Chap. 6, pp. 150–154.
12. *Jones v. Opelika,* 316 U.S. 584 (1942) and *Murdock v. Pennsylvania,* 319 U.S. 105 (1943); see Chap. 4, pp. 108–109.
13. *Martin v. Struthers,* 319 U.S. 141 (1943); see Chap. 5, pp. 131–134.
14. *Prince v. Massachusetts,* 321 U.S. 158 (1944); see Chap. 6, pp. 156–159.
15. *Chaplinsky v. New Hampshire* (315 U.S. 296 [1940]) is not included here because Chaplinsky made no claim—quite understandably—that the vituperative language attributed to him was religiously or morally motivated. *Wisconsin v. Yoder* was not included because the case was not decided at the time of this writing (cert. granted, 402 U.S. 994 [1971]). Cases involving the tax-exemption of church property or financial aid to church-related institutions are not included because they were argued and decided exclusively on establishment issues unrelated to claims of coercion on conscience (see Chap. 6, n. 33, p. 183). Cases involv-

ing disputes over title to church property are not included here for the same reason (see Chap. 4, n. 87, p. 114).

16. *Mora v. McNamara,* 389 U.S. 934 (1967), *Noyd v. Bond,* 395 U.S. 683 (1969), and *Negre v. Larsen,* 401 U.S. 437 (1971); see Chap. 2, pp. 46–49.

17. *Mitchell v. U.S.,* 386 U.S. 972 (1967), *Spiro v. U.S.,* 390 U.S. 956 (1968), *Gillette v. U.S.,* 401 U.S. 437 (1971), and *U.S. v. McFadden,* 401 U.S. 1006 (1971); see Chap. 2, pp. 33–36, 40–43, and 54 n. 74.

18. *U.S. v. Sisson,* 399 U.S. 267 (1970); see Chap. 2, pp. 36–39.

19. *Berrigan v. U.S.,* 397 U.S. 909 (1970) and *Moylan v. U.S.,* 397 U.S. 910 (1970); see Chap. 3, p. 78 n. 47.

20. *Boardman v. U.S.,* 397 U.S. 991 (1970); see Chap. 2, pp. 31–32.

21. *U.S. v. Schwimmer,* 279 U.S. 644 (1929); see Chap. 3, pp. 57–59.

22. *Anderson v. Raleigh Fitkin–Paul Morgan Memorial Hospital,* 377 U.S. 985 (1964), *Jones v. President and Directors of Georgetown College, Inc.,* 377 U.S. 978 (1964), *Labrenz v. Ill.* ex rel. *Wallace,* 344 U.S. 824 (1952), and *Jehovah's Witnesses v. King Co. Hospital,* 390 U.S. 598 (1967); see Chap. 5, pp. 120–123.

23. *Cox v. New Hampshire,* 312 U.S. 569 (1941); see Chap. 4, pp. 93–94 and 107–108.

24. *Stein v. Oshinsky,* 382 U.S. 957 (1965); see Chap. 6, pp. 174–175.

25. *U.S. v. Ballard,* 322 U.S. 78 (1944); see Chap. 4, pp. 99–102.

26. *U.S. v. O'Brien,* 391 U.S. 367 (1968); see Chap. 3, pp. 69–71.

27. *Watchtower Bible and Tract Society v. Metropolitan Life Insurance Co.,* 334 U.S. 886 (1948); see Chap. 4, p. 98.

28. *Poulos v. New Hampshire,* 345 U.S. 395 (1953); see Chap. 4, pp. 95–96.

29. *Clark v. Gabriel,* 393 U.S. 256 (1968), *Ehlert v. U.S.,* 402 U.S. 99 (1971), and *McGee v. U.S.,* 402 U.S. 479 (1971); see Chap. 2, pp. 50–52.

30. *Stimpel v. State Personnel Board of California,* 400 U.S. 952 (1970); see Chap. 4, p. 107.

31. *Zorach v. Clauson,* 343 U.S. 306 (1952); see Chap. 6, pp. 177–178.

32. When asked by the author in the spring of 1969 about this change of opinion, Justice Douglas indicated the close social relations which existed among the three at the time. This fact, however, would seem to explain the cohesion of the three rather than the influences on them to change their opinion.

33. *Hamilton v. Regents of the University of California,* 293

U.S. 245 (1934) and In re *Summers,* 325 U.S. 561 (1945); see Chap. 3, pp. 73–77.

34. *Pierce v. Society of Sisters,* 268 U.S. 510 (1925); see Chap. 6, pp. 160–161.

35. *Niemotko v. Maryland,* 340 U.S. 268 (1951) and *Fowler v. Rhode Island,* 345 U.S. 67 (1953); see Chap. 4, pp. 94–95.

36. *Torcaso v. Watkins,* 367 U.S. 488 (1961); see Chap. 5, pp. 142–143.

37. *McCollum v. Board of Education,* 333 U.S. 203 (1948) and *Chamberlin v. Dade Co. Board of Public Instruction,* 377 U.S. 402 (1964); see Chap. 6, pp. 176–177 and 184 n. 61.

In *Doremus v. Board of Education* (342 U.S. 429 [1952]), a majority of six justices dismissed an appeal from the practice of Bible reading and recitation of the Lord's Prayer in New Jersey public schools on jurisdictional grounds. The Court dismissed other issues of discrimination raised in *Chamberlin,* although Justices Black and Douglas joined Justice Stewart in calling for argument on an allegation that religious tests were required of public school teachers. In *Lewis v. Allen* (373 U.S. 923 [1964]), the Court unanimously refused to review inclusion of the phrase "under God" in a public school pledge of allegiance to the flag. The Court thus held these allegations of discrimination either unsuitable for adjudication at the time or too nugatory to merit review. See Chap. 6, n. 61, p. 184.

38. *Cantwell v. Connecticut,* 310 U.S. 296 (1940), *Johnson v. Sellers,* 332 U.S. 851 (1948), and *Jamison v. Texas,* 318 U.S. 413 (1943); see Chap. 4, pp. 82–83, 85, 96, and 99.

39. *Kunz v. New York,* 340 U.S. 290 (1951); see Chap. 4, pp. 88–89.

40. *Marsh v. Alabama,* 326 U.S. 501 (1946) and *Tucker v. Texas,* 326 U.S. 517 (1946); see Chap. 4, pp. 96–97.

41. *Follett v. McCormick,* 321 U.S. 573 (1944); see Chap. 4, pp. 109–110.

42. *Cohnstaedt v. Immigration and Naturalization Service,* 339 U.S. 901 (1950); see Chap. 3, pp. 65–66.

43. *Sicurella v. U.S.* 348 U.S. 385 (1955); see Chap. 2, pp. 24–25.

44. *Clay v. U.S.,* 403 U.S. 698 (1971); see Chap. 2, p. 31.

45. *Oestereich v. Selective Service Board No. 11,* 393 U.S. 233 (1968); see Chap. 2, p. 50.

46. *Levy v. Parker,* 396 U.S. 804 (1969); see Chap. 2, p. 48.

47. In re *Jenison,* 375 U.S. 14 (1963); see Chap. 4, pp. 110–111.

48. *Cantwell,* Gobitis, Cox, Jones, Jamison,* Murdock,* Martin,* Barnette,* Prince, Follett,* Ballard, Summers, Marsh,* Tucker,* Girouard,* McCollum,* Cohnstaedt,* Niemotko,* Kunz,* Zorach, Fowler,* Poulos, Sicurella,* Braunfeld, Torcaso,**

Engel, Schempp,* Sherbert,* Jenison,* Seeger,* O'Brien, Oestereich,* Clark, Noyd, Levy,* Welsh,* Gillette-Negre, Ehlert, McGee,* and *Clay.** Asterisks indicate that the claimants of conscience won. Only substantive decisions are included here because of the ambiguity in denials of certiorari or appeal. *Doremus* and *Sisson* have been excluded because they were decided on technical grounds denying jurisdiction. Only the three *per curiam* decisions not identical with previous decisions (*Cohnstaedt, Jenison,* and *Clark*) have been included. See n. 15 for the exclusion of other cases.

49. *Cantwell,* Gobitis, Cox, Jones, Jamison,* Murdock,* Martin,* Barnette,* Prince, Follett,* Marsh,* Tucker,* Niemotko,* Fowler,* Poulos,* and *Sicurella.** Asterisks indicate that the Witnesses won.

50. *Zorach, Braunfeld, Engel,* and *Levy*. The Jewish claimant lost in *Braunfeld.*

51. *Girouard* and *Sherbert.*

52. *O'Brien, Negre,* and *McGee.*

53. Black, Blackmun, Burger, Burton, Byrnes, Clark, Douglas, Jackson, Harlan, Hughes, Marshall, McReynolds, Minton, Reed, Roberts, Rutledge, Stewart, Stone, Vinson, Warren, White, and Whittaker. These justices are here classified as Protestant only in the sense that they are neither Catholic nor Jewish.

54. Jackson, Marshall, Stewart, and White are Episcopalians; Douglas, Clark, and Harlan are Presbyterians (sources: *Who's Who in America* and *Who Was Who in America*).

55. Fortas, Frankfurter, and Goldberg.

56. Brennan and Murphy.

57. Black, Brennan, Byrnes, Clark, Douglas, Fortas, Frankfurter, Goldberg, Jackson, Marshall, McReynolds, Minton, Murphy, Reed, Rutledge, Vinson, and White are Democrats; Blackmun, Burger, Burton, Harlan, Hughes, Roberts, Stewart, Stone, Warren, and Whittaker are Republicans (sources: *Who's Who, Who Was Who*).

58. Burger, Clark, Jackson, Marshall, McReynolds Murphy, Reed, Roberts, Stone, Warren, and White had previous experience with government prosecution (sources: *Who's Who, Who Was Who*).

59. Black, Blackmun, Brennan, Burger, Harlan, Hughes, Marshall, Minton, Rutledge, Stewart, Vinson, and Whittaker had previous judicial experience. Black served eighteen months as a police court judge, and Chief Justice Hughes had been an associate justice fourteen years before his reappointment to the Court (sources: *Who's Who, Who Was Who*).

60. Black, Burton, Byrnes, Minton, and Vinson had previous legislative experience (sources: *Who's Who, Who Was Who*).

61. Brennan, Douglas, Fortas, Frankfurter, Harlan, Hughes,

Jackson, Marshall, Roberts, and Stone—East; Black, Byrnes, Clark, McReynolds, Reed, and Vinson—South; Blackmun, Burger, Burton, Goldberg, Minton, Murphy, Rutledge, Stewart, and Whittaker—Midwest; Warren and White—West (sources: *Who's Who, Who Was Who*).

APPENDIX

Western Traditions of Conscience

THE PURPOSE OF THIS APPENDIX is twofold: (1) to survey the history of the term "conscience" in Western thought; and (2) to indicate prominent theories on the rights and duties of conscience in relation to political authority.

No culture without some idea of moral conscience has yet been discovered. Primitive societies did not speak of "conscience," but they did appeal to the "heart" and "loins" as arbiters to distinguish morally good from morally bad behavior. From the perspective of Western civilization, the most important influence on the history of conscience was the Bible.

In the first book of the Old Testament, the Biblical writer described how "the man and his wife hid themselves from the presence of the Lord God among the trees of the garden" after eating the forbidden fruit.[1] Thus the writer of Genesis attributed to Adam and Eve a sense of moral guilt subsequent to their act of disobedience. Although worship of God and upright action were associated in the early history of the Jewish people more with the observance of ritual than with interior dispositions, a profound change was introduced into the religious and moral life of the Jewish people under the influence of the prophets. Jeremiah, for example, spoke of God as a searcher of mind and heart who judges men's actions as good or bad at the very moment of their performance.[2] The prophets did not challenge the claims of the Mosaic law but insisted rather on the primacy of interior disposition in its observance.

Yet the efforts of the prophets were not crowned with general success, and at the time of Jesus, the Jewish religion, at least as represented in the Gospels by the Pharisees and other leaders, was still absorbed more with the performance of external actions than with internal dispositions in the achievement of religious and moral virtue. In the Sermon on the Mount, Jesus echoed the prophets and called blessed the "pure in heart." [3] Jesus attacked the preoccupation of the Pharisees with ritual observance by arguing that it is not what goes into a man's mouth which defiles him but what comes out, since what comes out of the mouth proceeds from the heart.[4] Thus, like the prophets of the Old Testament, Jesus stressed the primacy of interior dispositions over external actions.

The word "conscience" (syneidesis) is used nowhere in the Gospels. Indeed, it appears only once in the Old Testament, where the Book of Wisdom, adapting Semitic thought to the Greek language and categories, declares that "wickedness is . . . condemned by its own testimony," and that "distressed by conscience, it has always exaggerated the difficulties." [5] Thus "conscience" was used by the writer of Wisdom in the sense of moral as distinguished from psychological consciousness, but only to describe a consciousness of guilt subsequent to a man's morally bad action.

Although the word "conscience" was not used frequently by Paul, it does appear twenty times in the letters attributed to him and ten times elsewhere in the New Testament. According to Paul, who probably took the term from contemporary Stoic philosophy, the purpose which the Mosaic law served for Jews was fulfilled by conscience in pagans since "what the law requires is written on their hearts, while their conscience also bears witness, and their conflicting thoughts accuse or perhaps excuse them on that day when . . . God judges the secrets of men by Christ Jesus." [6] But conscience pertains to Christians too: "The aim of our charge is love that issues from a pure heart and a good conscience and sincere faith." [7] Indeed, Paul urged Christians to obey secular governing authorities "not only to avoid God's wrath but also for the sake of conscience," that is, as a matter of moral principle.[8] Paul appealed to his own good conscience in preaching the gospel: "I am speaking the truth in Christ, I am not lying; my conscience bears me witness in the Holy Spirit. . . ." [9] For his past preaching, Paul also claimed a good conscience: "I have lived before God in all good conscience up to this day," [10] and "our boast is this, the testimony of our conscience that we have behaved in the world and still more toward you with holiness and godly sincerity." [11]

Of the twenty references to conscience in the letters attributed to Paul, eight appear in the First Letter to the Corinthians in connection with the controversy over eating meat used in pagan sacrifices. There and in Romans Paul indicated clearly his view that even an incorrect conscience is morally binding for the individual. Although he considered it no sin for Christians to eat meat which had been offered to idols, he recognized the moral obligation of scrupulous members of the Roman and Corinthian communities with an opposite view not to do so: "I know and am fully persuaded that nothing is unclean in itself, but it is unclean for anyone who thinks it unclean." [12] He therefore cautioned other members of these communities to respect the consciences of their scrupulous brothers to the extent of not eating such meat themselves: "If anyone sees you . . . at table in an idol's temple, might not he be encouraged, if his conscience is weak, to eat meat offered to idols? . . . Thus, sinning against your brethren and wounding their consciences when they are weak, you sin against Christ." [13]

Although many of Paul's uses of the word "conscience" seem to have been linked to negative, legal, and rule-oriented contexts ("thou shalt not"), his central theme of the supremacy of a living faith over external works indicates that his moral doctrine was broader than those citations of conscience.[14] There are in the New Testament, as in the Old, two strands in the Biblical traditions of morality: one negative, legal, and rule-oriented; the other positive, prophetic, and oriented toward the realization of ideals of justice and love. At any rate, Paul's writings were probably more influential than any other source in the popularization of the concept of conscience in the Western world.

In the context of the Israelite theocracy, there was no doubt about the general religious duty of citizens to obey God's anointed. Even in the case of the kings of the northern kingdom, all of whom the writers of Scripture condemned for refusing to accept David's descendants, subjects were not encouraged to claim a general right or duty to disobey their rulers. Moreover, although the prophets indicted kings both of the North and of the South for their infidelities to Yahweh, they threatened the kings with retribution by Him rather than revolution by their subjects. But Israelites were held to obey Yahweh's commands when they conflicted with those of their kings, absolutely in the case of the prohibition against the worship of idols, and as circumstances permitted in the case of the positive prescriptions of the Mosaic law.

The Israelites, of course, never fully accepted the legitimacy of foreign rulers or the corresponding obedience to them, whatever accommodations they had to accept in those circumstances. Because the religious aspirations of the New Testament were ethnically and territorially universal, however, Jesus urged obedience to Caesar—except for "the things that are God's." [15] The spread of Christianity, the hierarchical structure of the Church, and the power of the papacy were to make that exception almost a rule.

In the Greek world, Democritus of Abdera used the term "conscience" (*syneidesis*) in the sense of moral as distinguished from psychological consciousness.[16] Later, when Greek ethical thought probed the relation of nature (*physis*) to law (*nomos*), Socrates appealed to a divine monitor (*daimonion*) to justify his actions: "I am subject to a divine or supernatural experience [*theion kai daimonion*], . . . a sort of voice which comes to me." [17] Moreover, "when it comes, it always dissuades me from what I am proposing to do and never urges me on." [18] But elsewhere Socrates refers to a positive moral mandate communicated to him in a recurring "dream": "In the course of my life, I have often had the same dream, appearing in different forms at different times but always saying the same thing: 'Socrates, practice and cultivate the arts.' " [19] Without appeal to mythical language or mystical experience, Aristotle stated summarily the Socratic position on the centrality of reason in moral action thus: "Practical wisdom [*phronesis*] issues commands; its end is to tell us what we ought to do and what we ought not to do." [20]

While Socrates was convinced of the wrongfulness of the Athenian law court's sentence of death against him for following his "voice," he refused to escape the penalty. In an ingenious dialogue with "the laws" before his death, Socrates argued that a refusal to accept the penalty of the court would undermine the principle of law and the state itself, that legal regulation of marriage and education conferred the benefits of life and human fulfillment on citizens and made them contractually responsible to obey "the laws" even when disagreeable, that Socrates himself had ratified the contract by choosing to live in Athens when he was free to leave, and that the wrong done to Socrates was committed by his fellow men, not by "the laws." [21] Socrates' arguments were historically conditioned by the identification of society with the city-state in the Greek *polis* and the city-state with its laws, but they are echoed today in the controversies surrounding civil disobedience in this country. Martin Luther King, for example, proclaimed his willingness to accept the penalty for his disobedience of law, but his opponents rejoined that civil disobedience itself, in pursuit of whatever ideals, is simply a violation of law and threatens the foundations of organized society.

Neither Plato nor Aristotle used the term "conscience," but philosophers influenced by Stoicism did. Cicero, for example, wrote that "the moral consciousness [*conscientia*] of living well and the record of many deeds done well is most pleasing," [22] and Seneca expressed the idea of conscience as "a sacred spirit in man" which is "an observer and guardian of good and evil in us." [23]

But the Roman interpretations of Stoic philosophy modified the Greek idea of moral judgment in one important respect: more legally oriented than the Greeks, the Romans identified reason with (natural) law and moral consciousness with legal obligation. This concept of conscience as law was adopted by medieval theologians in the theocentric context of a divine legislator.

One of the most developed theories on conscience is that of Thomas Aquinas. In the first part of the *Summa*, in the treatise on man and the section on man's intellectual powers, Aquinas spoke of "synderesis" and "conscience." [24] He claimed that synderesis is not a special power but rather a *habitus* (disposition) of the soul:

> Man's act of reasoning . . . proceeds from the understanding of certain things . . . as from an immovable principle; it also terminates in the understanding, inasmuch as, by means of those naturally known principles, we judge of those things which we have discovered by reasoning.[25]

From this analysis, Aquinas declared that the function of synderesis is to "incline to good and murmur at evil."[26]

In the article following that on synderesis, Aquinas argued that conscience is not a power but rather an act, a judgment of practical reason, with respect to a particular action.[27] He appealed to the common usage of the term "conscience" as referring knowledge to something else (*cum alio scientia*) and indicated that "the application of knowledge to something else is done by some act."[28] According to Aquinas, this application of knowledge to action occurs in three ways: (1) insofar as we recognize that we have or have not done something, and conscience is accordingly said to witness; (2) insofar as we judge through conscience that something should or should not be done, and conscience is accordingly said to judge; and (3) insofar as we acknowledge in conscience that something has been done well or ill, and conscience is accordingly said to approve or accuse. Since *habitus* is the principle of act, however, Aquinas admitted that the term "conscience" is sometimes applied to the *habitus* of first practical principles, synderesis, rather than to the act of judgment itself.

The application of knowledge to action in the first way described by Aquinas would seem to have identified conscience with psychological consciousness, reflecting the root meaning of the Latin term *con-scientia* (and the Greek equivalent, *syn-eidesis*). The second way, though called judicial by Aquinas, perhaps better deserves to be called legislative since Aquinas regarded this function of conscience as morally authoritative for the individual and legally binding on him. The third way, where knowledge is applied to past action, perhaps better deserves to be called judicial. In any case, it is the second way with which Aquinas was principally concerned in his treatment of conscience.

When Aquinas dealt with the qualities of specifically human acts in the *Prima secundae,* he asked whether the will is evil when it acts at variance with an objectively erroneous judgment of conscience, and he concluded that "absolutely speaking, every will at variance with reason, whether right or erring, is always evil." [29]

In the next article, Aquinas asked whether the will is good when it abides by erring reason.[30] The answer, according to Aquinas, depends on the voluntariness of the ignorance involved: "When ignorance causes an act to be involuntary, it takes away the character of moral good and evil," but when ignorance is willed in any way, directly or indirectly (through negligence), it does not cause the act to be involuntary.[31] Although Aquinas broadly concedes the contingency of knowledge of secondary precepts of the natural law in his treatise on law,[32] he took a "hard line" on ignorance of law in his treatment of conscience. Thus he excused errors of fact but not an "ignorance of the divine law" which the individual is "bound to know." [33]

From the foregoing sketch of Aquinas' doctrine on conscience, several points are evident: first, moral judgment, in his view, is founded on a pre- or para-rational disposition of the soul toward moral goodness and away from moral evil; second, conscience in the strict sense is a judgment of reason that a contemplated action should or should not be done; third, conscience should be followed even when erroneous; fourth, Aquinas conceived conscience in a theocentric and legal context of human responsibility to divine and natural law; fifth, Aquinas' treatment of conscience emphasized the observance of negative rules rather than positive actions in the fulfillment of prophetic witness to the ideals of justice and love.

Aquinas held that the conscience of the individual is bound to obey political authority because that authority is derived from God, the author of the human nature which requires it. But when political authority is defective in title or excessive in exercise, there is no obligation of conscience to obey. Thus neither a usurper nor a legitimate ruler abusing his authority by unjust commands can bind the consciences of citizens to obey him. Indeed, if the ruler contravenes the very purpose of his authority by commanding a sinful action, the subject is under an obligation not to obey him. In the case of a usurper, Aquinas allowed active resistance when no other recourse is open to the citizen, but in the case of an abuse of authority, he endorses nothing more than passive resistance.[34]

Luther and other Protestant reformers appealed prominently to conscience to justify their break with Rome.[35] Although they accepted the authority of Scripture as normative, they stressed the necessity of private interpretation. Their appeals to conscience were to prophetic witness rather than to legal rules and to experience rather than to reason. Reacting to the reformers' rejection of the Church's authority, post-Tridentine Catholic theologians not only stressed the objective, rational, and legal bases of conscience but also, unlike Aquinas, attempted to codify rules of conscience by means of comprehensive legal casuistry.

The political consequences of the Reformation's appeals to private judgment were enormous. Within the context of the then-existing sacral societies, fragmentation of religious unity meant a fragmentation of political unity. To confront this challenge, two radically different approaches were open: (1) to secularize religion; or (2) to secularize government. The first approach would require subordination of religion to the state and the restriction of religious freedom (*cujus regio, ejus religio*); the second, a regime of religious toleration. Hobbes and Locke, respectively, were articulate philosophical spokesmen for these two approaches.

To meet the political disunity consequent upon the religious dissidence of the Reformation, Hobbes was consciously concerned to elaborate a political theory which would allow no claim of private judgment or religious belief against the command of the sovereign. In the state of nature, where every man wars against every other man, nothing can be called just or unjust. But "reason suggests convenient articles of peace, upon which men may be drawn to agreement," and these articles are "laws of nature." [36] Hobbes' "laws of nature" are thus dictates of a calculating, self-interested reason; they are the conditions for the rational pursuit of self-preservation and the rules which a calculating human being would observe in pursuing his own advantage if he were conscious of man's predicament in a universe ruled by passion. These laws are not given by God or ordered to a natural whole, except in the sense that God is sovereign of the universe, and that man is endowed with a calculating reason. Indeed, they oblige only "*in foro interno,* that is to say, they bind to a desire that they should take place, but *in foro externo,* that is, to the putting them into act, not always." [37]

The science of the "laws of nature" is "the true and only moral philosophy." [38] For moral philosophy studies what is good and evil, "names that signify our appetites and aversions." [39] Men differ in their judgment not only of what is pleasant or unpleasant but even of what is conformable or disagreeable to reason. "Nay, the same man, in diverse times, differs from himself" on what is good or evil.[40] Hence there arise "disputes, controversies, and at last war." [41] So long as men are in the condition of nature alone, which is a condition of war, "private appetite is the measure of good and evil." [42] The "laws of nature," therefore, are only improperly called laws, "for they are but conclusions or theorems concerning what conduces to the conservation and defense of [individuals] themselves, whereas law properly is the word of him that by right has command over others." [43]

Hobbes' theory on the relation of conscience to the law of the commonwealth is quite different from his theory of the individual's obligations to the "laws of nature." By the covenants of every man with every man, the multitude is united in one person, "that great Leviathan or . . . mortal God." [44] And "he that carries this person is called sovereign and said to have sovereign power." [45] Among the prerogatives of the sovereign, for all practical purposes unlimited, Hobbes enumerated that of judging what doctrines are fit to be taught: "It belongs . . . to him that has sovereign power to be judge or constitute all judges of opinions and doctrines, as a thing necessary to peace [and] thereby to prevent discord and civil war." [46] This broad prerogative of the sovereign, of course, is as much a limitation on thought and speech generally as on religious expression specifically.

When Hobbes discussed those things which weaken the commonwealth, he clearly indicated what doctrines he considered most dangerous to the peace of the commonwealth. First, he condemned as seditious the doctrine that "every private man is judge of good and evil actions." [47] Although "this is true . . . where there are no civil laws, and also under civil government in such cases as are not determined by the law," it is otherwise manifest that "from this false doctrine men are disposed to debate with themselves and dispute the commands of the commonwealth and afterwards to obey or disobey them as in their private judgments they shall think fit," and thereby "the commonwealth is distracted and weakened." [48] Hobbes then related the latter position to appeals to conscience: "Another doctrine repugnant to civil society is that whatsoever a man does against his conscience is sin, and it depends on the presumption of making himself judge of good and evil." [49] Indeed, "the law is the public conscience by which he has already undertaken to be guided." [50] Otherwise, "the commonwealth must needs be distracted, and no man dare to obey the sovereign power farther than it shall seem good in his own eyes." [51]

Hobbes' severe strictures against private judgment and responsibility to individual conscience reflect in part the political consequences of religious dissension in seventeenth-century England. But they are also consequences of his philosophical views of "nature" and "reason." For Hobbes, "nature" is simply the sum total of material elements and their motion, and "reason" is simply that faculty of men which calculates what is to their self-interest or loss. There is in this theory no finality in nature and no faculty of reason to take its measure. Hence, since nature and reason are so conceived, Hobbes logically concluded that individual judgment and conscience are not only irrelevant but even harmful in society.

According to Hobbes, sin is "nothing but the transgression of the [civil] law." [52] When spiritual authorities claim the right to declare what is sin, they "challenge by consequence to declare what is law." [53] As in his discussion of the diseases of the commonwealth, Hobbes argued that "if men were at liberty to take for God's commandments their own dreams and fancies, . . . scarce two men would agree upon what is God's commandment, and . . . every man would despise the commandments of the commonwealth." [54] He concluded, therefore, "that in all things not contrary to the moral law (that is to say, to the law of nature), all subjects are bound to obey that for divine law which is declared to be so by the laws of the commonwealth." [55]

Hobbes did admit that it is "equity . . . that every man equally enjoy his liberty" in anything not regulated by the commonwealth.[56] This concept of religious freedom accords perfectly with his general concept of the liberty of subjects, which lies "only in those things . . . the sovereign has praetermitted."[57] Hobbes gave no examples of the religious freedom which he thinks the sovereign should "praetermit," but one area may be inferred from his general definition of liberty of private religious opinion. Indeed, in another place he said expressly that no sovereign can command or forbid belief in Christ because "belief and unbelief never follow men's commands."[58]

Locke drew heavily on Hobbes' theory of the construction of civil society, and he, like Hobbes, started with the idea of a prepolitical state of nature. This state is one of perfect freedom for men "to order their actions and dispose of their possessions and persons as they think fit, within the bounds of the law of nature, without asking leave or depending upon the will of any other man."[59] The state of nature is also one of equality, which is "the foundation of that obligation to mutual love among men on which . . . the duties we owe to one another and . . . the great maxims of justice and charity" are derived.[60] Although the state of nature is a state of liberty, it is not a state of license: "The state of nature has a law of nature to govern it which obliges everyone, and reason, which is that law, teaches all mankind who will but consult it that, being all equal and independent, no one ought to harm another in his life, health, or possessions."[61] All men have the right in the state of nature to restrain another from invading their rights but "only to retribute to him, as far as calm reason and conscience dictate, what is proportionate to his transgression."[62] Locke also remarked that "truth and keeping of faith belongs to men as men and not as members of society."[63]

Natural law, therefore, seems to have meant something quite different for Locke than it did for Hobbes. To Hobbes, it meant a rule of reason calculated to help to preserve man's life and insure his security; to Locke, it meant a moral law promulgated by human reason and obligatory on all men as they reflect on their fundamental equality. But Locke's treatment of the construction of political or civil society indicates that the state of nature giving rise to society is in fact a state of war quite similar to Hobbes' model. Civil society is instituted "to avoid and remedy these inconveniences of the state of nature which necessarily follow from every man being judge in his own case." [64] In the state of nature, man's enjoyment of his freedom is "constantly exposed to the invasions of others." [65] Indeed, "were it not for the corruption and viciousness of degenerate man," there would be no need of civil society.[66] It is a state of war which makes men "willing to quit a condition which, however free, is full of fears and continual dangers." [67]

But Locke differed from Hobbes on the function of government in his construction of political society, a difference which is of central importance for the question of the relation of government to religious freedom and the dictates of conscience. Where Hobbes' construction of political society resulted in a Leviathan or "mortal God" characterized by absolute power and constituting the font of all morality, Locke's construction of political society resulted in a government limited to securing the physical integrity of person and property from violence. From this framework of *gendarme* government, Locke declared in his *Letter Concerning Tolerance* that he esteemed it "above all things necessary to distinguish exactly the business of civil government from that of religion and to settle the just bounds that lie between the one and the other." [68]

The commonwealth, said Locke, is a "society of men constituted only for the procuring, preserving, and advancing their own civil interests," which he enumerated as "life, liberty, . . . indolency of body, and the possession of outward things." [69] "All civil power, right, and dominion is bounded and confined to the only care of promoting these things," and "it neither can nor ought in any manner to be extended to the salvation of souls." [70] Among other reasons, Locke argued that "the care of souls cannot belong to the civil magistrate because his power consists only in outward force," while "true and saving religion consists in the inward persuasion of the mind." [71] Thus Locke concluded that "all power of civil government relates only to men's civil interests, is confined to the care of the things of this world, and has nothing to do with the world to come." [72]

Again unlike Hobbes, Locke clearly affirmed the role of conscience in moral decisions: "No way whatsoever that I shall walk in against the dictates of my conscience will ever bring me to the mansions of the blessed." [73] Citing approvingly Dr. Sharp, an archbishop of York, and echoing Aquinas, he expanded on the duty to follow conscience in his *Third Letter for Toleration*:

> Where a man is mistaken in his judgment, even in that case it is always a sin to act against it. Though we should take for a duty that which is really a sin, yet so long as we are thus persuaded, it will be highly criminal in us to act in contradiction to this persuasion; and the reason for this is evident, because by so doing we willfully act against the best light which at present we have for direction of our actions.[74]

But Locke was aware of the possibility of conflicts between dictates of conscience and commands of government:

> A good life, in which consists not the least part of religion and true piety, concerns also the civil government; and in it lies the safety both of men's souls and of the commonwealth. Moral actions belong, therefore, to the jurisdiction both of the outward and inward court, both of the civil and domestic governor, I mean, both of the magistrate and conscience.[75]

Locke asked what the result should be if the magistrate enjoins something which the conscience of an individual judges to be "unlawful." Although he deemed the case unlikely if government were faithfully administered, he allowed that in such a case "a private person is to abstain from the actions that he judges unlawful"; he is, however, "to undergo the punishment, which is not unlawful for him to bear, for the private judgment of any person concerning a law enacted in political matters for the public good does not take away the obligation of that law nor deserve a dispensation." [76]

Locke was thus circumspect on the rights of conscientious objectors to the commands of governments. In his view, an individual who judges a command of government to be against the dictate of his conscience is apparently morally justified, even obliged, to refuse to perform the command, but he is, likewise, apparently morally obliged to submit to punishment for his disobedience. He may, of course, be physically obliged to submit to such punishment, but why should he consider himself *morally* obliged to undergo punishment for following the dictates of his conscience? Perhaps Locke thought submission to punishment necessary to distinguish the morally motivated opposition to government policy from the politically motivated. Or perhaps Locke thought that conscientious objectors owed submission to punishment simply out of a general duty to the organized society in which they live. In any case, he did not elaborate his reasons. From the perspective of the dissenting individual, Locke's admission of a right of conscientious objection to a command of government may seem severely joined to a prescription of moral duty with respect to punishment for such refusal to obey, but his position has both ancient models (e.g., Socrates) and modern disciples (e.g., Martin Luther King).

Locke's dictum on conscientious objection invites a comparison with the contemporary American phenomenon of civil disobedience. Although there is agreement between Locke and many current civil disobedients on the duty to submit to punishment, there is one important difference: Locke allowed disobedience only to a specific command of government, the performance of which is enjoined by the dictate of an individual's conscience; many current civil disobedients, however, claim a right to disobey laws more broadly in order to protest specific laws and policies they consider unjust or immoral, a claim which Locke would have regarded as quasi-revolutionary in nature.

But whatever the complexity of potential conflicts between the commands of civil governments and the dictates of individual consciences in "political" matters, Locke declared clearly his view that civil governments have no competence to legislate purely religious matters, such as "that the people or any party amongst them should be compelled to embrace a strange religion and join in the worship and ceremonies of another church." [77] In such cases, men are not "obliged by that law against their consciences, for the political society is instituted for no other end but only to secure every man's possession of the things of this life." [78] Thus legislation of purely religious matters concerns "things that lie not within the verge of the magistrate's authority." [79]

Locke's views rather than Hobbes' prevailed in most of the Western world and are reflected in the First Amendment of the United States Constitution. Locke was able to envision a harmonious world of religious tolerance largely because he limited the functions of both government and religion. According to Locke, government exists to secure the physical well-being of person and property, while religion is a matter of internal, psychological conviction; government is concerned about this world and religion about the next. He agreed with Aquinas that conscience is a judgment of reason and should be followed even when erroneous, and he conceived conscience in a theocratic and legal context of human responsibility to divine and natural law, although these laws, in the last analysis, were only matters of opinion morally binding on the individual. Locke accordingly disagreed with Aquinas about the accessibility of these laws to human intelligence. Like Aquinas', Locke's treatment of conscience emphasized the observance of negative rules rather than of any positive function of religious prophecy. He thus restricted the operation of conscience, at least for the most part, to negative judgments of reason from religious premises which were only opinions. In this respect, he was a forerunner not only of the modern Western constitutional settlement in favor of religious tolerance but of modern subjectivist interpretations of conscience as well.

Conscience played no role in the moral philosophy of the empiricist Hume. In fact he claimed that "reason is, and ought only to be, the slave of the passions and can never pretend to any other office than to serve and obey them." [80] This strong, anti-rationalist proposition, of course, must be understood within the framework of Hume's general philosophical system. Hume used "passion" to signify not unregulated or violent emotion but emotion or affection in general, and argued that "reason" could pave the way for the operation of the moral sense of approbation or disapprobation by showing the utility or futility of particular modes of human behavior. But Hume allowed reason only two functions: "the comparing of ideas and the inferring of matters of fact." [81] Moral distinctions were said not to be derived from reason as concerned with logical relations because they are not capable of mathematical demonstration, and they were said not to be derived from reason as concerned with matters of fact because values are not objective facts governed by the psychological association of ideas. Thus Hume concluded that morality "is a matter of fact, but it is the object of feeling, not of reason." [82]

Hume's moral philosophy, lacking the classical and

medieval conception of practical, moral reason and its mode of operation, rested ultimately on feeling, and this emphasis is reflected today in the emotive ethical theories of modern empiricists. The function which Hume assigned to a calculating reason—namely, to determine the utility of particular behavior for self or others—was later developed by Bentham and the two Mills. Contemporary empiricists and utilitarians follow Hume's narrower conception of human reason, and it is no accident that the idea of conscience does not feature in their respective theories.

Rousseau also stressed the primacy of feeling in his moral philosophy, and his Savoyard vicar tells Émile that:

> To exist is to feel; our feeling is undoubtedly earlier than our intelligence, and we had feelings before we had ideas. . . . To know good is not to love it; this knowledge is not innate in man. But as soon as his reason leads him to perceive it, his conscience impels him to love it. It is this feeling which is innate.[83]

Although reason and reflection play a part in the development of morality, ultimately "what I feel to be right is right, what I feel to be wrong is wrong." [84] "Feeling" may have signified for Rousseau immediate apprehension or intuition rather than emotion, but its subjective emphasis is clear enough.

In the *Social Contract,* Rousseau claims that man passes at once from an amoral to a moral state through the institution of political society: "The passage from the state of nature to the civil state produces a very remarkable change in man, by substituting justice for instinct in his conduct and giving his actions the morality which they had formerly lacked." [85] Indeed, "the mere impulse to appetite is slavery, while obedience to a law which we prescribe to ourselves is liberty." [86] Nature herself has directed man's will to the good, but individuals, even when gathered in assembly, may form erroneous ideas of it. Only the "general will" is always right, and it is the business of the legislator to interpret this will and bring the laws into conformity with it. There are undeniably incompatible elements in Rousseau's theory of the nature and source of the moral order. On the one hand, the moral law is written in men's hearts and individual conscience, and the collective legislative voice may fail to express the general will. On the other, individuals should conform to the will of the sovereign people and, if necessary, even be forced to be free. Rousseau's problem in this respect was not his alone—Plato faced a similar dilemma—but the Enlightenment's tendency to make an artificial construct of human society radically complicated it.

Although Kant is celebrated for the rational and formal character of his moral philosophy, certain subjective emphases of his system are particularly relevant to modern concepts of conscience. Kant acknowledged morality as an imperative instinct, and he made subjective intention the absolute moral good: "Nothing can possibly be conceived in the world, or even out of it, which can be called good without qualification except a good will." [87] Moreover, Kant divorced this absolute moral good from any consideration of products or purposes: "A good will is not good because of what it performs or effects, not by its aptness for attaining some proposed end, but simply by virtue of the volition." [88] Even the formal *a priori* principle of morality, the categorical imperative, contains the idea of a radically autonomous will: "*Act as if the maxim of your action were to become by your will a general law of nature.*" [89] Man is subject "*only to his own general laws,*" [90] and this autonomy of the will, "the supreme moral principle," [91] is opposed to all "false principles of morality" [92] which are not the result of the individual will's own legislation. In this sense, Kant rejected both the Biblical moral norm of the will of God and the classical moral norm of an order of nature.

Where eighteenth-century philosophers were individually and a-historically oriented in their treatment of conscience, many nineteenth-century philosophers responded to the burgeoning development of modern science by a concentration on the social and historical bases of conscience. In the wake of the Darwinian evolutionary hypothesis and the data of comparative religion, Spencer and Durkheim stressed the social conditioning of conscience by particular cultures.[93] Marx, too, made conscience socially conditioned by economic factors—by class-consciousness, for example.[94] Moreover, expanding on the Hegelian dialectic of history, he made conscience or class-consciousness not only a product of history but also a determining factor in its evolution.[95] Nietzsche distinguished two primary types of morality, the master or superman morality, which creates its own values out of life-forces, and the slave or herd morality, which, out of resentment, imposes a uniform system to the benefit of the weak and the powerless; in Nietzsche's view, the first type is the morality of modern man, and the second, the morality of classical philosophy and Christian theology.[96] Thus both Marx and Nietzsche made conscience a function of class, although Marx emphasized purely economic factors in the context of an historical dialectic in favor of what Nietzsche would call slave morality. Freud, in his turn, made conscience socially conditioned in terms of the suppression of primitive libido by a family-conditioned superego.[97]

On the other side of the spectrum, many nineteenth-century philosophers and theologians stressed the autonomous value of conscience. Fichte, following Kant, tells us to "act according to . . . conscience," i.e. according to the "immediate conscience of . . . determinate duty."[98] Thus conscience was a feeling, although the immediate feeling in question expressed agreement or harmony between "our empirical ego and the pure ego." [99] From the Christian perspective, the existentialist Kierkegaard, Cardinal Newman, and the liberal historian Acton all insisted on the authenticity and primacy of conscience.[100]

Twentieth-century philosophy reflects the nineteenth-century division between "scientific" and "instinctive" interpretations of conscience: speaking "scientifically," logical positivists will point out that moral propositions are not verifiable, and early spokesmen of linguistic analysis called them "emotive" [101] (later linguistic analysts accept the givenness of moral language and seek the utilitarian grounds for it in various forms of self-interest[102]); but existentialists, phenomenologists, and value philosophers "instinctively" stress the centrality of moral commitment.

Like Luther, religious dissenters in America appealed prominently to the role of conscience in the moral life of the individual. Like Locke, they demanded regimes of religious toleration, and their demands were ultimately met. But the most unique American contribution to Western traditions of conscience was made by Henry David Thoreau. Convinced that he should not cooperate with the government's waging of the Mexican War, or with its tolerance and acceptance of slavery, Thoreau refused to pay his taxes. He wrote of conscientious objection committed to social change, and, faced with war and slavery, he thought that a man of moral principle should do more than stand aside. Thoreau meant to affect his society by breaking its laws, and he was willing to go to prison: "Under a government which imprisons any unjustly, the true place for a just man is also in prison." [103] At the end of his life, Thoreau defended John Brown's raid on Harper's Ferry and accepted the principle of violence: "I do not wish to kill or to be killed, but I can foresee circumstances in which these things would be by me unavoidable." [104] Against the evil of four million Negroes in slavery, "the Sharps rifles and the revolvers were employed in a righteous cause."[105] Thoreau linked individual conscience to social revolution, and it is understandable why he is accordingly the philosophical exemplar of many contemporary civil disobedients.

There were two strands in the Biblical traditions of morality; one positively oriented toward religious witness and action according to ideals of justice and love, and the other negatively oriented toward the observance of rules and obedience to divine law. The Platonic and Aristotelian view of morality was concerned with contemplative reason rather than prophetic action, with self-mastery and perfection rather than social reform, and with habitual behavior rather than particular acts. The Stoics modified the classical Greek view of morality to the extent of identifying reason with natural law and moral consciousness with legal obligation. Accordingly, the Stoic model of conscience was more rule-oriented than the Platonic and Aristotelian model of practical reason. Aquinas adopted features of the Biblical, classical, and Stoic views of morality. He founded moral judgment on a pre- or para-rational disposition of the soul toward moral good, but he considered conscience itself a judgment of reason with respect to a prospective particular action. He conceived the operation of conscience in a theocratic context of natural and divine law and directed toward the observance of negative rules more than the fulfillment of prophetic witness.

Like the prophets, Luther's appeals to conscience were to witness rather than to rules and to experience rather than to reason, but he isolated private from community judgment more than they. Modern philosophers emphasized the subjective bases of conscience. Although both Hobbes and Locke viewed individual conscience largely as a religious product, Hobbes condemned it as a threat, and Locke allowed it a private normative value for the individual. With the exception of theologians like Kirkegaard and Newman, most other modern spokesmen secularized conscience. Hume founded his moral philosophy on a moral sense or feeling of approbation, but he also accorded utilitarian considerations or enlightened self-interests an ancillary role. Rousseau and Fichte identified conscience with feeling, and Kant, too, autonomized conscience, although in the context of a rational, categorical imperative. Spencer, Durkheim, Marx, Nietzsche, and Freud conditioned conscience on social, economic, historical, or psychological factors. On the American scene, Thoreau stands in the tradition of Biblical prophecy, although his role was more socially and politically oriented than most religious prophets of pre-modern times.

There are many points of comparison between Western traditions of conscience and contemporary appeals to conscience as justification for exemption from, or disobedience of, public law. Many such disobedients are not religiously motivated in any traditional sense, but most are prophetically oriented toward witness and action to promote ideals of peace and justice. In this respect, even those who profess no religious motivation have more in common with the tradition of Biblical prophecy than they may expressly acknowledge. Most contemporary morally motivated disobedients, whether of religious or secular stamp, have an individualistic and subjective conception of conscience like such moderns as Luther, Locke, Rousseau, Kant, Fichte, and contemporary existentialists. Like Rousseau, they exalt feeling rather than reason; like Kant, they exalt the autonomy of conscience; like contemporary existentialists, they exalt commitment rather than passivity; like Thoreau, they are politically conscious social reformers.

But contemporary disobedients also argue forcefully that moral conscience is not merely a subjective or socially conditioned phenomenon. They reject deterministic theories of conscience like those of Spencer, Durkheim, Marx, and Freud. They reject positivistic attempts to reduce conscience to emotion and utilitarian attempts to reduce conscience to self-interest. Their zeal even when excessive indicates that they do not consider the ideals of peace and justice merely private opinions. Indeed, every appeal to conscience, whether as a norm worthy of respect by others or as a force moving to social action, presupposes a moral order of reality which transcends the individual. The Biblical view of morality, both prophetic and legal, centered that order in the word of God; the classical view centered the moral order in a cosmos; and modern man centers it in the dignity of the person. In any case, to insist that another respect one's conscience or that one has a duty to act in furtherance of social ideals is to presuppose the reality and relevance of a moral order in human life.

NOTES

1. Gen 3:8. This and other scriptural citations are from the Revised Standard Version.
2. Jer 11:20.
3. Mt 5:8.
4. Mt 15:18.
5. Wis 17:11.
6. Rom 2:15–16.
7. I Tim 1:5.
8. Rom 13:5.
9. Rom 9:1.
10. Acts 23:1.
11. 2 Cor 1:12.
12. Rom 14:14.
13. 1 Cor 8:10,12.
14. E.g., Rom 4.
15. Mt 22:21; cf. Rom 13:1–7.
16. Hermann Diels, *Die Fragmente der Vorsokratiker,* ed. Walther Kranz (10th ed.; Berlin: Weidmann, 1960), 2:206–07.
17. Plato, *Apology* 31C,D.
18. *Ibid.*
19. Plato, *Phaedo* 60E.
20. Aristotle, *Nicomachean Ethics* 1143A.
21. Plato, *Crito* 50A–54B.
22. Cicero, *De senectute* 3:9.
23. Seneca, *Epistulae* 41,1.

24. Thomas Aquinas, *Summa theologica,* I, q. 79, aa. 12 and 13, respectively.
25. The translation is from *Basic Writings of St. Thomas Aquinas,* ed. Anton C. Pegis (New York: Random House, 1945), I, 765.
26. *Ibid.*, p. 766.
27. *Summa theologica,* I, q. 79, a. 13.
28. *Basic Writings,* I, 767.
29. *Summa theologica,* I–IIae, q. 19, a. 5; *Basic Writings,* II, 340.
30. *Summa theologica,* I–IIae, q. 19, a. 6.
31. *Basic Writings,* II, 342.
32. *Summa theologica,* I–IIae, q. 94, a. 2.
33. *Basic Writings,* II, 342.
34. Thomas Aquinas, II *Sent.*, dist. 44, q. 2, a. 2.
35. E.g., Martin Luther, *The Freedom of a Christian* in *Selected Writings of Martin Luther,* ed. Theodore G. Tappest (Philadelphia; Fortress, 1967), II, 19–53.
36. Thomas Hobbes, *Leviathan* (New York: Dutton, 1950), chap. XIII, p. 105.
37. *Ibid.*, chap. XV, p. 131.
38. *Ibid.*, p. 132.
39. *Ibid.*
40. *Ibid.*
41. *Ibid.*
42. *Ibid.*
43. *Ibid.*, p. 133.
44. *Ibid.*, chap. XVII, p. 143.
45. *Ibid.*, p. 144.
46. *Ibid.*, chap. XVIII, p. 148.
47. *Ibid.*, chap. XXIX, p. 277.
48. *Ibid.*, pp. 277–78.
49. *Ibid.*, p. 278.
50. *Ibid.*
51. *Ibid.*
52. *Ibid.*, p. 283.
53. *Ibid.*, pp. 282–83.
54. *Ibid.*, chap. XXVI, p. 246.
55. *Ibid.*, pp. 246–47.
56. *Ibid.*, p. 247.
57. *Ibid.*, chap. XXI, p. 180.
58. *Ibid.*, chap. XLII, p. 435.
59. John Locke, *The Second Treatise of Government,* ed. Thomas P. Peardon (New York: Liberal Arts Press, 1952), chap. II, p. 4.
60. *Ibid.*, pp. 4–5.
61. *Ibid.*, p. 5.
62. *Ibid.*, p. 6.

63. *Ibid.*, p. 10.
64. *Ibid.*, chap. VII, p. 50.
65. *Ibid.*, chap. IX, p. 70.
66. *Ibid.*, p. 72.
67. *Ibid.*, p. 70.
68. John Locke, *A Letter Concerning Toleration* in *The Works of John Locke* (12th ed.; London: Rivington, 1824), v, 9.
69. *Ibid.*, p. 10.
70. *Ibid.*
71. *Ibid.*, p. 11.
72. *Ibid.*, p. 13.
73. *Ibid.*, p. 28.
74. John Locke, *A Third Letter for Toleration* in *The Works of John Locke,* v, 146–47.
75. Locke, *A Letter Concerning Toleration,* p. 41.
76. *Ibid.*, p. 43.
77. *Ibid.*
78. *Ibid.*
79. *Ibid.*
80. David Hume, *A Treatise of Human Nature,* ed. L. A. Selby-Bigge (Oxford: Clarendon, 1951), bk. II, part III, sect. iii, p. 415.
81. *Ibid.*, bk. III, part I, sect. i, p. 469.
82. *Ibid.*, p. 463.
83. Jean Jacques Rousseau, *Emile,* ed. Barbara Foxley (London: Dent, 1911), p. 253.
84. *Ibid.*, p. 249.
85. Jean Jacques Rousseau, *Social Contract and Discourses,* ed. G. D. H. Cole (London: Dent, 1913), p. 18.
86. *Ibid.*, p. 19.
87. Immanuel Kant, *Metaphysical Foundations of Morals* in *The Philosophy of Kant,* ed. and trans. Carl J. Friedrich (New York: Random House, 1949), p. 140.
88. *Ibid.*, p. 141.
89. *Ibid.*, p. 170; italics in original.
90. *Ibid.*, p. 181; italics in original.
91. *Ibid.*, p. 187.
92. *Ibid.*, p. 188.
93. E.g., Herbert Spencer, *The Principles of Ethics* (New York: Appleton, 1892), especially part IV, and Emile Durkheim, *Moral Education,* trans. Herman Schnauer (New York: Free Press, 1961).
94. E.g., Karl Marx, *A Contribution to the Critique of Political Economy,* trans. N. I. Stone (Chicago: Kerr, 1911), pp. 11–12.
95. E.g., Karl Marx, *Theses on Feuerbach* in *Karl Marx and Friedrich Engels on Religion* (Moscow: Foreign Language Publishing House, 1957), p. 72.
96. Friedrich Nietzsche, *Beyond Good and Evil* in *The Com-*

plete Works of Friedrich Nietzsche, trans. Helen Zimmern (New York: Russell and Russell, 1964), XII, 227.

97. E.g., Sigmund Freud, *Taboo and the Ambivalence of Emotions* in *The Basic Writings of Sigmund Freud,* ed. A. A. Brill (New York: Random House, 1938), pp. 821–864.

98. Johann Gottlieb Fichte, *Sämmtliche Werke,* ed. I. H. Fichte (Berlin: Veit, 1845), IV, 173–74.

99. *Ibid.*, IV, 169.

100. E.g., Søren Kierkegaard, *Purity of Heart,* trans. Douglas V. Steere (New York: Harper, 1948); John Henry Cardinal Newman, *A Letter to His Grace, the Duke of Norfolk* (London: Pickering, 1875); John Emerich Lord Acton, *Essays on Church and State,* ed. Douglas Woodruff (London: Hollis and Carter, 1952).

101. E.g., Alfred J. Ayer, *Language, Truth, and Logic* (2d ed.; New York: Dover, 1946), pp. 107ff.

102. E.g., P. H. Nowell–Smith, *Ethics* (Oxford: Blackwell, 1957).

103. Henry David Thoreau, *Essay on Civil Disobedience* in *Walden and Other Essays,* ed. Brooks Atkinson (New York: Random House, 1950), p. 646.

104. Henry David Thoreau, *A Plea for Captain John Brown* in *Thoreau: People, Principles, and Politics,* ed. Milton Meltzer (New York: Hill and Wang, 1963), p. 187.

105. *Ibid.*

Index

TABLE OF CASES*

Abington v. Schempp, 374 U.S. 203 (1963)
174
Abrams v. U.S., 250 U.S. 616 (1919)
68–69
Anderson v. Raleigh Fitkin–Paul Morgan Memorial Hospital 42 N.J. 421, 201 A.2d 537 (1964); cert. denied, 377 U.S. 985 (1964)
122–123
Barron v. Baltimore, 32 U.S. 243 (1833)
111*n*1
Berrigan v. U.S., 417 F.2d 1009 (1969); cert. denied, 397 U.S. 909 (1970)
78*n*47
Boardman v. U.S., 419 F.2d 110 (1969); cert. denied, 397 U.S. 991 (1970)
31–32
Board of Education v. Allen, 392 U.S. 236 (1968)
163–164
Braunfeld v. Brown, 184 F.Supp. 352 (1960), 366 U.S. 599 (1961)
136–141
Breard v. Alexandria, 341 U.S. 622 (1951)
134–135
Breen v. Selective Service Board No. 16, 396 U.S. 460 (1970)
55*n*109
Brooks' Estate, In re, 32 Ill.2d 316, 205 N.E.2d 435 (1965)
119–120
Brown v. Board of Education, 347 U.S. 483 (1954)
75
Buck v. Bell, 274 U.S. 200 (1927)
125–126

* Cases adjudicated by the U.S. Supreme Court are listed by their title before that tribunal.

Burns v. Wilson, 346 U.S. 137 (1953)
54–55*n*77
Cantwell v. Connecticut, 310 U.S. 296 (1940)
82–83, 99
Chamberlin v. Dade Co. Board of Public Instruction, 377 U.S. 402 (1964)
184*n*61
Chaplinsky v. New Hampshire, 315 U.S. 568 (1942)
83–85
Clark v. Gabriel, 287 F.Supp. 369 (1968), 393 U.S. 256 (1968)
50–51
Clay v. U.S., 403 U.S. 698 (1971)
31
Cohnstaedt v. Immigration and Naturalization Service, 167 Kan. 456, 207 P.2d 425 (1949); 339 U.S. 901 (1950)
65–66
Commonwealth of Massachusetts v. Laird, 400 U.S. 886 (1970)
52
Cox v. New Hampshire, 312 U.S. 569 (1941)
93–94, 107–108
Crown Kosher Super Market v. Gallagher, 176 F.Supp. 466 (1959), 366 U.S. 617 (1961)
136–141
Davis v. Beason, 133 U.S. 333 (1890)
153–154
Dewey v. Reynolds Metal Co., 300 F.Supp. 709 (1969); cert. granted, 400 U.S. 1008 (1971)
113*n*71
Doremus v. Board of Education, 342 U.S. 429 (1952)
183–184*n*61
Ehlert v. U.S., 422 F.2d 332 (1970), 402 U.S. 99 (1971)
51–52
Engel v. Vitale, 370 U.S. 421 (1962)
174
Erickson v. Dilgard, 44 Misc.2d 27, 252 N.Y.S.2d 705 (1962)
120
Everson v. Board of Education, 330 U.S. 1 (1947)
163
Feiner v. New York, 340 U.S. 315 (1951)
86–88
Flast v. Cohen, 392 U.S. 83 (1968)
184*n*61

Follett v. McCormick, 321 U.S. 573 (1944)
109–110
Fowler v. Rhode Island, 345 U.S. 67 (1953)
95
Friedman v. New York, 341 U.S. 907 (1951)
135
Gillette v. U.S., 420 F.2d 298 (1970), 401 U.S. 437 (1971)
40–43
Girouard v. U.S., 149 F.2d 760 (1945), 328 U.S. 61 (1946)
63–65
Gitlow v. U.S., 268 U.S. 652 (1925)
111*n*2
Gonzalez v. The Roman Catholic Archbishop of Manila, 280 U.S. 1 (1929)
114*n*87
Gutknecht v. U.S., 396 U.S. 295 (1970)
55*n*109
Hamilton v. Regents of the University of California, 293 U.S. 245 (1934)
73–75
Hardin v. State, 188 Tenn. 17, 216 S.W.2d 708 (1948)
115–117
Hart v. U.S., 382 F.2d 1020 (1967), 391 U.S. 956 (1968)
53*n*42
Holmes v. U.S., 387 F.2d 781 (1967), 391 U.S. 936 (1968)
53–54*n*42
Jacobson v. Massachusetts, 197 U.S. 11 (1905)
117–119
Jamison v. Texas, 318 U.S. 413 (1943)
96
Jehovah's Witnesses v. King Co. Hospital, 278 F.Supp. 488 (1967); cert. denied, 390 U.S. 598 (1968)
123
Jenison, In re, 265 Minn. 96, 120 N.W.2d 515 (1963); 375 U.S. 14 (1963)
110–111
Johnson v. Sellers, 69 F.Supp. 778 (1946), 163 F.2d 877 (1947); cert. denied, 332 U.S. 851 (1948)
85
Jones v. Opelika, 316 U.S. 584 (1942)
108
Jones v. President and Directors of Georgetown College, Inc., 331

F.2d 1000, 1010 (1963); cert. denied, 377 U.S. 978 (1964)
121–122

Kedroff v. St. Nicholas Cathedral, 344 U.S. 94 (1952)
114*n*87

Kreshik v. St. Nicholas Cathedral, 363 U.S. 190 (1960)
114*n*87

Kunz v. New York, 340 U.S. 290 (1951)
88–89

Labrenz v. Illinois ex rel. *Wallace,* 411 Ill. 618, 104 N.E.2d 769 (1952); cert. denied 344 U.S. 824 (1952)
120

Leary v. U.S., 383 F.2d 851 (1967), 395 U.S. 6 (1969)
128–130

Lemon v. Kurtzman, 403 U.S. 602 (1971)
183*n*33

Levy v. Corcoran, 387 U.S. 915 (1967)
47

Levy v. Corcoran, 389 F.2d 929 (1967); cert. denied, 389 U.S. 960 (1967)
47

Levy v. Parker, 396 U.S. 804 and 1204 (1969)
48

Levy v. Resor, 384 F.2d 869 (1967); cert. denied, 389 U.S. 1049 (1968)
47

Lewis v. Allen, 14 N.Y.2d 867, 200 N.E.2d 767 (1964); cert. denied, 379 U.S. 923 (1964)
184*n*61

Luftig v. McNamara, 252 F.Supp. 819 (1966), 373 F.2d 664 (1967); cert. denied, 387 U.S. 945 (1967)
45–46

Marsh v. Alabama, 326 U.S. 501 (1946)
96–97

Martin v. Struthers, 319 U.S. 141 (1943)
131–134

Maryland and Virginia Eldership of the Churches of God v. The Church of God at Sharpsburg, Inc., 396 U.S. 367 (1970)
114*n*87

McCollum v. Board of Education, 333 U.S. 203 (1948)
176–177

McGee v. U.S., 426 F.2d 691 (1970), 402 U.S. 479 (1971)
51

McGowan v. Maryland, 220 Md. 117, 151 A.2d 156 (1958); 366 U.S. 420 (1961)
135–136
Minersville v. Gobitis, 310 U.S. 586 (1940)
164–166
Mitchell v. U.S., 369 F.2d 323 (1966); cert. denied, 386 U.S. 972 (1967)
33–35
Mora et al. *v. McNamara*, 387 F. 862 (1967); cert. denied, 389 U.S. 934 (1967)
46–47
Moylan v. U.S., 417 F.2d 1002 (1969); cert. denied, 397 U.S. 910 (1970)
78*n*47
Murdock v. Pennsylvania, 319 U.S. 105 (1943)
109
Negre v. Larsen, 418 F.2d 908 (1969), 401 U.S. 437 (1971)
48–49
Niemotko v. Maryland, 340 U.S. 268 (1951)
94–95
Noyd v. Bond, 285 F.Supp. 785 (1968), 89 S.Ct. 478 (1968), 402 F.2d 441 (1969), 395 U.S. 683 (1969)
48
Noyd v. McNamara, 267 F.Supp. 701 (1967), 378 F.2d 538 (1967); cert. denied, 389 U.S. 1022 (1967)
48
Oestereich v. Selective Service Board No. 11, 280 F.Supp. 78 (1968), 390 F.2d 100 (1968), 393 U.S. 233 (1968)
50
Parker v. Commissioner of Internal Revenue, 365 F.2d 792 (1966)
102–103
People v. Woody, 40 Cal. Rptr. 69, 394 P.2d 813 (1964)
127–128
Peter v. U.S., 324 F.2d 173 (1963), 380 U.S. 163 (1965)
26–27
Pierce v. Society of Sisters, 268 U.S. 510 (1925)
160–161
Poulos v. New Hampshire, 345 U.S. 395 (1953)
95–96
Presbyterian Church in the U.S. v. Mary Elizabeth Blue Hull Memorial Presbyterian Church, 393 U.S. 440 (1969)
114*n*87

Prince v. Massachusetts, 321 U.S. 158 (1944)
156–159
Reynolds v. U.S., 98 U.S. 145 (1878)
150–153
Schenck v. U.S., 249 U.S. 47 (1919)
67–68
Selective Service Cases, 245 U.S. 366 (1918)
22–23, 50
Sherbert v. Verner, 374 U.S. 398 (1963)
105–107, 141–142
Sicurella v. U.S., 213 F.2d 911 (1954), 348 U.S. 385 (1955)
24–25
Spiro v. U.S., 384 F.2d 159 (1967); cert. denied, 390 U.S. 956 (1968)
35–36
Spock v. U.S., 416 F.2d 165 (1969)
71
Stein v. Oshinsky, 224 F.Supp. 757 (1963), 348 F.2d 999 (1965); cert. denied, 382 U.S. 957 (1965)
174–175
Stimpel v. State Personnel Board of California, 6 Cal. App.3d 206, 85 Cal. Rptr. 797 (1970); cert. denied, 400 U.S. 952 (1970)
107
Summers, In re, 325 U.S. 561 (1945)
75–77
Supple's Estate, In re, 55 Cal. Rptr. 542 (1966)
102
Terminiello v. Chicago, 337 U.S. 1 (1949)
86
Tilton v. Richardson, 403 U.S. 672 (1971)
183*n*33
Torcaso v. Watkins, 367 U.S. 488 (1961)
142–143
Tucker v. Texas, 326 U.S. 517 (1946)
96–97
Two Guys From Harrison v. McGinley, 179 F.Supp. 944 (1959), 366 U.S. 582 (1961)
146*n*45
U.S. v. Ballard, 35 F.Supp. 105 (1940), 138 F.2d 540 (1943), 322 U.S. 78 (1944)
99–102

U.S. v. Berman, 156 F.2d 377 (1946)
53*n*19
U.S. v. George, 239 F.Supp. 752 (1965)
120–121
U.S. v. Jakobson, 325 F.2d 409 (1963), 380 U.S. 163 (1965)
26–27
U.S. v. Kauten, 133 F.2d 703 (1943)
53*n*20
U.S. v. Macintosh, 42 F.2d 845 (1930), 283 U.S. 605 (1931)
59–63
U.S. v. McFadden, 309 F.Supp. 502 (1970), 401 U.S. 1006 (1971)
54*n*75
U.S. v. O'Brien, 376 F.2d 538 (1967), 391 U.S. 367 (1968)
69–71
U.S. v. Schwimmer, 27 F.2d 742 (1928), 279 U.S. 644 (1929)
57–59
U.S. v. Seeger, 216 F.Supp. 516 (1963), 326 F.2d 846 (1964), 380 U.S. 163 (1965)
26–27
U.S. v. Sisson, 294 F.Supp. 511 (1968), 297 F.Supp. 902 (1969), 399 U.S. 267 (1970)
36–39
Valentine v. Christensen, 316 U.S. 52 (1942)
96
Walz v. Tax Commission of City of New York, 397 U.S. 664 (1970)
183*n*33
Watchtower Bible and Tract Society v. Metropolitan Life Insurance Co., cert. denied, 334 U.S. 886 (1948)
98
Watson v. Jones, 80 U.S. 697 (1872)
114*n*87
Welsh v. U.S., 404 F.2d 1078 (1968), 398 U.S. 333 (1970)
27–29
West Virginia v. Barnette, 319 U.S. 624 (1943)
166–169
Wisconsin v. Yoder et al., 49 Wis.2d. 430, 182 N.W.2d 539 (1971), 92 S.Ct. 1526 (1972)
170–172
Zorach v. Clauson, 343 U.S. 306 (1952)
177–178

GENERAL INDEX

Acton, John E. E. Dalberg, Lord, 228
American Civil Liberties Union, 200
Amish, 170–172
Aristotle, 7, 149, 211, 212, 229

Bentham, Jeremy, 225
Birth control, 127
Black, Hugo, 27, 28, 36, 42, 43, 51, 65, 66, 76, 87, 88, 96, 97, 108, 109, 132–135, 142, 143, 166, 168, 176, 177, 184*n*61, 189, 192, 198–201
Blackmun, Harry, 27, 37, 201
Black Muslims, 31
Brandeis, Louis, 59, 61, 68, 72, 74, 78*n*11
Brennan, William, 27, 43, 50, 51, 106, 138, 140–142, 170, 171, 201
Brethren, 21
Brewer, David, 118
Brown, John, 228
Burger, Warren, 29, 37, 70, 71, 201
Burton, Harold, 65, 66, 98, 134, 176, 184*n*61, 195, 199, 201
Butler, Pierce, 58, 60, 62, 73, 74, 145*n*20
Byrnes, James, 108, 109, 166, 201

Cardozo, Benjamin, 74, 75
Catholics, 35, 36, 125, 126, 160, 161, 200
Child welfare, 156–159
Christian Scientists, 124, 125
Church property, conflicts of title to, 111
Cicero, 212
Civil disobedience, 16, 17, 69–73, 90–93
Civil Rights Act of 1964, 91
Clark, Tom, 25, 46, 66, 134, 196, 201
Conscience,
  and conflicts with public law, 10–19
  definition of, 1
  profile of claimants of, 199, 200
  sincerity of, 5–7
  see also Moral obligation
Conscientious objection (pacifist),
  and conscription, 21–33
  and naturalization, 57–66
  and the states, 73–77
  in the armed services, 44
Conscientious objection (selective),
  and conscription, 33–44
  and war protests, 67–73
  in the armed services, 44–52

Conscription, *see* Conscientious objection *and* Draft laws

Darwin, Charles, 227
Democrats, 201
Democritus, 211
Divinity students, draft exemption of, 50
Douglas, William, 27, 34, 37, 40, 42, 43, 46–53*nn*40 & 42, 54*n*75, 55*n*96, 63, 64, 66, 71, 76, 86, 87, 95–98, 100, 107–109, 123, 132–135, 137, 138, 140, 166, 171, 177, 178, 184*n*61, 189, 190, 192, 198–201
Draft laws,
  Federal Conscription Act (1863), 22
  Federal Conscription Act (1864), 22
  Selective Service Act (1917), 22, 23, 77
  Selective Service Act (1940), 23, 24, 64, 77
  Universal Military Training and Service Act (1948), 25–30, 69
  Military Selective Service Act (1967), 36–43
Drugs, 127–131
Durkheim, Émile, 227, 230

Episcopalians, 200
Espionage Act of 1917, 67, 68
Espionage Act of 1918, 68, 69
Existentialists, 228

Fichte, Johann, 227, 228, 230
Field, Stephen, 153, 154
Flag-salutes, *see* Public schools
Frankfurter, Felix, 65, 66, 76, 77, 95, 97, 98, 100, 108, 109, 132–134, 164, 165, 168, 169, 176–180, 196, 198–201
Fraud, 99–107
Freud, Sigmund, 227, 230

Goldberg, Arthur, 201

Harlan, John Marshall (elder), 118
Harlan, John Marshall (younger), 28, 50, 52, 53*n*40, 71, 106, 123, 142, 190, 201
Hegel, G. F. W., 227
Hobbes, Thomas, 7, 9, 10, 18, 216–221, 223, 229
Holiness Church, 115–117
Holmes, Oliver Wendell, 59, 61, 68, 69, 72, 78*n*11, 125, 126
Hughes, Charles Evans, 61, 62, 64, 166, 201
Hume, David, 224, 225, 230

Jackson, Robert, 65, 66, 76, 77, 89, 98, 101–103, 105, 108, 109, 132, 134, 166–169, 176–180, 192, 198, 199, 201
Jehovah's Witnesses, 2, 3, 6, 13, 23–25, 82–85, 93–99, 107–110, 119–123, 131–134, 156–159, 164–169, 200
Jefferson, Thomas, 151
Jeremiah, 208
Jesus, 208, 211
Jews, 2, 200
Jury service, 110, 111
Justices,
  bloc analysis of, 198–200
  voting profile of, 200, 201

Kant, Immanuel, 226, 227, 230
Kellems, Vivian, 143–145
Kierkegaard, Søren, 228, 229
King, Martin Luther, 212, 222

Life, protection of, 115–125
Locke, John, 8, 143, 216, 219–224, 228, 229, 230
Luther, Martin, 215, 228–230

Marriage, *see* Polygamy
Marshall, Thurgood, 27, 40–43, 46–48, 51, 55*n*96, 201
Marx, Karl, 227, 230
McReynolds, James, 58, 60, 160, 201
Mennonites, 21, 23, 24
Mill, James *and* John Stuart, 225
Minton, Sherman, 25, 66, 134
Molokans, 23
Moral obligation,
  degrees of, 1–5
  degrees of, in relation to conflicting laws, 10–14, 185–187
  see also Conscience
Morality,
  as public interest, 7, 8
  norm of, 5
  relation to public law of, 8–10
Mormons, 2, 12, 150–156
Murphy, Frank, 65, 76, 84, 97, 98, 108, 109, 132–134, 158, 166, 168, 192, 201

Native American Church, 127, 128
Naturalization, *see* Conscientious objection (pacifist)
Naturalization Act of 1906, 57–63
Naturalization Act of 1940, 65
Newman, John Henry Cardinal, 228, 229
New Testament,
  and moral judgment, 208–210
  and political authority, 211
Nietzsche, Friedrich, 227, 230
Nuremberg trials, 35

Old Testament,
  and moral judgment, 207, 208
  and political authority, 210, 211

Pacifism, *see* Conscientious objection (pacifist)
Parochial schools, 14, 160–164
Paul, 208–210
Peace, breach of, 82–90
Peckham, Rufus, 118
Penalties, 11, 13, 15, 17
Phenomenologists, 228
Plato, 7, 212, 229
Polygamy, 2, 12, 150–156
Positivism,
  legal, 9, 10
  logical, 228
Powell, Lewis, 171
Presbyterians, 200
Privacy, 131–135
Protestants, 200
Public facilities, use of, 93–99
Public interests, 7–9, 15–19
Public office, atheist's right to, 142, 143
Public schools,
  and the Amish, 169–172
  and flag-salutes, 1, 2, 6, 13, 14, 164–169

and religious exercises or instruction, 11, 14, 172–182

Quakers, 6, 21, 23, 24, 32

Reed, Stanley, 25, 65, 66, 76, 77, 96, 98, 108, 109, 132, 134, 177, 184*n*61, 195, 198–201
Reformation, 7, 8, 215, 216
Rehnquist, William, 171
Republicans, 201
Roberts, Owen, 60, 65, 76, 77, 83, 99, 100, 108, 109, 132, 134, 195, 201
Roman Catholic Church, 7, 102, 211, 215
Rousseau, Jean Jacques, 225, 226, 230
Rutledge, Wiley, 65, 76, 97, 109, 132–134, 157, 158, 166, 176, 198–201

Sabbatarians, 11, 105–107, 135–142
Sanford, Edward, 59, 77*n*11
Second War Powers Act (1942), 64, 65
Seneca, 212
Seventh-Day Adventists, 23, 105–107, 200
Socrates, 7, 211, 212, 222
Spencer, Herbert, 227, 230
State universities and military training, 73–76
Sterilization, 125–127
Stewart, Potter, 29, 46, 47, 50–54*n*42, 106, 138, 140–142, 170, 171, 174, 184*n*61, 201
Stoics, 209, 212, 229
Stone, Harlan Fiske, 58, 59, 61, 65, 74, 76, 98, 100, 101, 108, 109, 132–134, 165, 166, 195, 198, 199, 201
Sunday laws, 11, 14, 135–141
Sutherland, George, 58, 60, 62, 63

Taft, William Howard, 58
Tarr, Curtis, 30
Taxes, 6, 107–110
Thomas Aquinas, 7, 212–215, 229
Thoreau, Henry David, 30, 228–230
Tonkin Bay Resolution, 47
Treaty of London, 34, 35

Value philosophers, 228
Van Devanter, Willis, 58, 60
Vietnamese war, 1, 2, 4, 11, 33–52, 185
Vinson, Fred, 66, 87–89, 94, 95, 135, 196, 201
Virginia Statute of Religious Freedom, 151

Waite, Morrison, 150–152
Warren, Earl, 70, 71, 136, 137, 139, 141, 142, 201
White, Byron, 29, 37, 48, 50, 106, 171, 201
Wulf, Melvin, 200
Wyzanski, Charles, 8, 37–39